About the Author

Magnus Walker grew up in Sheffield and first fell in love with cars as a ten-year-old after a trip to the 1977 London Motor Show. He moved to Los Angeles as a teenager and established Serious Clothing, outfitters to Madonna, Alice Cooper, Mötley Crüe and a host of rock stars, before developing properties in Downtown LA and expanding into the film-location business. Today he is one of the world's most prominent collectors and modifiers of Porsche 911s.

www.penguin.co.uk

About the Author

Martina Walker grew up in ... she too ... falling in love with ...
... ... the 1977 ... ...
... ...
... California, ...
... ...
... ...
... ... Pegasus ...

URBAN OUTLAW

Dirt Don't Slow You Down

MAGNUS WALKER

With MARTIN ROACH

CORGI BOOKS

TRANSWORLD PUBLISHERS
61–63 Uxbridge Road, London W5 5SA
www.penguin.co.uk

Transworld is part of the Penguin Random House group of companies
whose addresses can be found at global.penguinrandomhouse.com

First published in Great Britain in 2017 by Bantam Press
an imprint of Transworld Publishers
Corgi edition published 2018

A CIP catalogue record for this book
is available from the British Library.

ISBN
9780552173391

Typeset in Sabon by Falcon Oast Graphic Art Ltd.
Printed and bound by Clays Ltd, Elcograf S.p.A.

Penguin Random House is committed to a sustainable
future for our business, our readers and our planet. This book
is made from Forest Stewardship Council® certified paper.

MIX
Paper from
responsible sources
FSC® C018179

3 5 7 9 10 8 6 4 2

This book is dedicated to
the loving memory of
Karen Ann Caid Walker

Contents

Foreword   ix

1 A Story Unfolding   1

2 Down to Earth and Difficult to Cure   17

3 Welcome to the Jungle   27

4 Dreams, Jeans and a Hatful of Opportunity   47

5 My First Porsche and a Lil' Georgia Peach   63

6 Serious Gets Serious   77

7 A Diamond in the Rough   91

8 Wheels of Steel   119

9 277   137

10 *Urban Outlaw*   145

11 How Bad Can It Be, Right?   159

12 A Hobby That Got Out of Control   183

13 Karen   211

14 A Steel Town and the City of Angels   223

15 Go With Your Gut Feeling   231

Acknowledgements   247

Index   248

Foreword

I like to get in a car and drive. That's my meditation, my exercise; I've said it's my drug, my religion – because nothing beats it when you are behind the wheel. It is from the gritty streets of Downtown LA that I have set out on some of my most memorable adventures – which I will tell you about in this book – but it is also from my warehouse there that I take out one of my Porsches for a drive.

Every journey begins by walking through a big rusty gate into the compound, then into the warehouse and through a second big black gate into my garage. Inside this former machine shop, you will find my Porsches parked up, some super-rare, some less so, but they all mean something special to me. Some people call that garage a little slice of heaven. It's one of my favourite places in the world.

Each of those cars gives me a very different experience, just like in my life I have been lucky enough to enjoy so many great and varied adventures. Any journey I take begins by deciding on the destination and how I want to get there. If I want to step back fifty years and feel what it was like driving in the sixties for a laid-back Sunday outing, then maybe I'll choose the Irish Green '66. If it's more of an adrenaline fix, a pedal-to-the-metal, spirited run, then maybe I'll take my most famous car, 277, or perhaps the '78 SC. I don't always know what I'm going to choose until I get to the garage, just as I haven't always known where my life would take me next over all these years. I'm not precious about them, either; these cars are there to be driven. They are not all examples of concours perfection. They've lived a life. They have rough edges. Like me. I'm not polished, let's put it that way.

Today I'm going to take 277, so jump in.

Driving one of these early 911s covers all the senses. As I am walking over to the car, the sensory journey has already started. They might be forty and in some cases fifty years old, but they can still fire up the heart-rate instantly. Each car is visually stimulating and really exciting in its own way; even just walking up to them pulls you in. 277 has the red, white and blue of so many of my childhood influences and also of so much Americana, and as you get close you can see the paint chips and scuffs that signify a hard life of being raced and enjoyed.

You walk over to the driver's side door, feel the door handle – the cars are never locked, so you know there's no fumbling around with keys, they're always in the cars ready to go, because I don't want anything to delay the adventure. Sure, the cars are exciting to look at standing still, but the real adventure starts the minute you get in. Slide into the seat and pull the door shut with that reassuring Porsche clunk. You breathe; you're relaxed. Hopefully the car starts, because sometimes it may not have been driven for a couple of weeks, but even that creates a sense of anticipation, excitement. You know within the first twist of the key and two or three pumps of the accelerator pedal if that day's adventure will begin – clutch in, gear into neutral, pump the accelerator, prime the fuel pump, wait for the car to fire. Then you hear a buzzing and *that smell* of the oil that's just spewed out from the exhaust because it's drained down while the car's been sitting there, waiting for you. Smoke flickers up in the rear-view mirror as the engine springs to life, so now you can smell the car, hear the car and feel its power.

Let the car idle for a minute, pull it outside and then close the garage gate, then open the front gate on to the street, engage first gear, let the clutch bite and roll out on to Willow, turn right at the corner, take a right turn on the bridge, drive a mile out to the freeway, getting on through the gears.

By now, the car is getting up to operating temperature, so I give it a little blast on the ramp, then through second, third gear, merge into traffic, get over as quickly as possible to the left lane – the fast lane.

The adventure is under way.

The destination is often either Angeles Crest Highway or the Santa Monica Mountains. Out there, it's almost eight thousand feet above sea level, even though that's less than sixty miles from where I'm sat writing these words in my warehouse in Downtown LA. One of the greatest features of southern California is the accessibility and diversity of spectacular world-class roads that begin within thirty minutes or so of my 1902 two-storey brick warehouse hidden away down one of Downtown's many side streets. Just eight miles in and you begin to see the mountain range up ahead of you. It's a sweeping freeway that gains altitude pretty quick, so the excitement level increases, you feel the senses fire up even more, your whole body is starting to merge with the car. This is where I believe man and machine become at one with the open road. You get into the pace and the rhythm, inseparable from the car. At this point, nothing else matters. There is no cell-phone reception, I don't have radios in the car, it's a little ideal slice of paradise. Ultimately, it's all about freedom up there.

You need context too: 120mph in a forty-year-old 911 feels pretty fast; 150 in a modern 911 feels like you are probably doing 80. Newer cars can make the driver feel isolated from the experience. You don't really smell them; you don't really necessarily even hear them. 277 is loud, it's moving all over the place, the sound insulation is not great. With a car like 277 you smell the gas, you smell the oil, you just smell every-thing, you can almost taste the engine, you hear the wind, you know the seals don't work good, so it's ssssshhhhhhh, there's all this road noise because there's not much insulation, it's the mechanical-ness, the creaky-ness, the throttle response, the squeaky brakes, the smell of the rubber, the oil, the smell of the brake pads when they get hot, it's all of that stuff . . . to me it's an emotional high. Like I say, driving one of these machines uses all of your senses.

Now it's just me and the car, working the throttle, match-ing the revs. Ultimately, you are engaged in trying to get the smoothest transfer of engagement of clutch, throttle and brake along with steering input, all together, seamless. I set little challenges: get on the gas earlier, get on the brakes later, execute the perfect heel-and-toe gear change, getting the balance more slick each time I go out. Fast and smooth, as I always say.

No two vintage Porsches ever drive the same; in fact, no two drives are ever really the same, even in the identical car. You have to be able to adapt to changing circumstances, knowing that there are no constants. I'm pretty familiar with these routes, but the terrain is always changing. You don't know what you are going to encounter on the road – there is always someone you want to pass or maybe some motorbike that's hounding you. You might turn a corner and suddenly see a cyclist or a slow-moving tourist, or maybe a coyote that you have to swerve around. Fuck, I've even come across a mountain bear on the road once. You are always thinking ahead, decisions become second nature, you anticipate and learn to expect a surprise around the corner. You adapt. It's all part of the adventure.

You don't necessarily have to be going fast to experience this sensory overload. However, whatever speed you are driving at, you have to be focused. There is a vast amount of movement in these cars. The 911's motor is in the rear, there's no weight over those front wheels, so straight away the nose of the car is constantly moving around. You have to work with this and find the groove in the road; you feel every imperfection in the road surface in your fingertips through a steering wheel that's seen so many years and has been used by so many different hands. You need a light grip though – too tense and you will lose feel, lose control. That steering wheel is constantly moving, those two front wheels are constantly fighting for grip or tram-lining a crack in the road or hopping over a bump. The car is alive. It's physical; you have to be completely focused – a spirited drive is always an acute adrenaline rush. What I love about these early cars is they are all manual, so essentially it's your brain, your two hands and your two feet controlling the car down the road. Some people like to go to the gym and work out. I go for a drive. There's no power steering; your arms, wrists, sides are all being worked out. You need stamina in your muscles, but you also need a fast response, quick reflexes. Sharp eyes, too.

Most of my drives are done solo; I don't tend to go on these big group runs. I like to do things at my own pace and be on my own. I am a little bit of a lone wolf. Maybe that's me attempting to control my own destiny to a certain degree, like I have tried to do all these years. Maybe that instinct goes back to my time as a young cross-country runner, trying to find a release from challenges at school and home, the loneliness of a long-distance athlete. Running to the hills in southern California is not so very different to when I was just a kid from Sheffield doing cross-country all those years ago; back then I was getting some release, feeling motivated, expressing myself. The only difference now, thirty-five years later, is that I've stopped running and instead got behind the wheel of a car.

The exhilaration of driving these vintage Porsches never ends for me. It's the thrill of the chase and the smell and that 'seat-of-your-pants' feel and the excitement and the adrenaline and the pulse and the sweat and the energy. It's a release, it's exciting, it's an adventure, it's rewarding, it's challenging, it's unforgettable. You are not thinking about anything else. Nothing else matters when you are up there.

Life is a journey on the open road, not knowing what's around the corner. Certainly in my life, for the past thirty years or so I've had to react to the unknown; I've been continually seeking what's around the next corner in my journey, not overthinking, not overanalysing too much, just being in the moment, acting on instinct, following my gut. Whatever your aim in life, however you want to make that journey and regardless of the adventures you will experience along the way, always trust your instinct.

Now, let's put the pedal to the metal and get out and drive.

Magnus Walker, Downtown LA, February 2017

Chapter 1

A Story Unfolding

Truth be told, you didn't see many Porsches in Sheffield in the seventies. My hometown was a working-class city, suffering at the time with industrial disputes, unemployment lines and crammed with ordinary people just struggling to get by. The average person in Sheffield often didn't have enough money to get through each week, never mind enough spare to buy exotic cars. So, no, there weren't many Porsches in Sheffield. There weren't exactly hundreds of them in England, either. Back then, you were looking at three years' average wages to buy a 911. For all but a tiny majority then, that ain't gonna happen.

That rarity just fuelled the attraction. Add to that the fact that the Turbo was launched just as the oil crisis gripped and petrol prices were rocketing, which meant that you had a really rare and exotic beast. Porsches were objects of fantasy. Any kid growing up pretty much anywhere in the world in the seventies . . . well, chances are you had one of three posters on your bedroom wall: a Porsche Turbo, the Lamborghini Countach or the Ferrari 512 Berlinetta Boxer. Those were *the* supercars of the decade, the top three. I had the poster of the 911-930 Turbo where the car was dissected into its component pieces. I had a die-cast toy model, too. We all played a card game called Top Trumps, where you had a shoot-out between all these supercars – who had the most BHP, the fastest acceleration, all that. In the deck of cards, you'd get all these wacky creations like the Vectors and the Lancia Stratos, all those kinda crazy cars, but the cream of the crop was the Porsche 911 Turbo. That car was how you won. You put that down on the table, it was unbeatable. For me, the 911 Turbo remains the iconic Porsche. Even back then it was the Daddy.

Crucially to this story, one day in 1977 the 911 Turbo created a pivotal episode in my young life, a moment when that car meant more than just a poster Sellotaped on my bedroom wall or a guaranteed win at Top Trumps.

It's funny how certain memories stick in your mind. Or more specifically certain parts of certain stories. In various interviews I've done over the years, I've talked a lot about the 'Porsche slippery slope', when I first started buying and then modifying them, but looking back it all started in 1977. I was ten years old when I went with my dad down to the Earls Court Motor Show in London, the first such event I'd ever gone to. In fact, I'm pretty sure it was the first time I'd even been to London. We didn't travel much as a family, so this trip to the bright lights was quite an expedition. This was the year of punk rock and the Queen's Silver Jubilee, so

London was a very vibrant and incredibly busy place to visit.

I remember leaving Sheffield and taking a coach to London, and then I guess we took a bus or a train somehow across the capital to Earls Court. I'm not sure of the details. I don't really remember much about the hall itself. I've since Googled the motor show that year and the photos are filled with all sorts of bright seventies colours, blue carpets, red drapes, not really the glitz and glamour of the big motor shows that we have today; it was a much smaller industry back then. I've actually got an old dog-eared magazine that reviewed the show and it lists the Ferrari 308 GTB on sale at the time as being £1,500 cheaper than the £12,750 Porsche Turbo.

We spent the entire day there, you know, grabbing brochures, looking at cars, just wandering around. Again, I don't really remember much detail. However, what I can remember *very clearly* is the white Martini Turbo on the Porsche stand with its iconic red, white and blue livery, the stripes, those wide rear arches and, of course, the whale tail. I only vaguely recall the stand itself; I've since found out that Porsche were also exhibiting a 924 and an SC, so it was actually quite a small display, but to my ten-year-old eyes this Turbo stood out more than anything else – more than the Lamborghinis, the Ferraris, more than anything.

I remember my dad trying to explain about a limited slip diff, but I didn't quite understand the logic of how that worked. Yes, I had that exploded poster, but I didn't really know much about the car in detail, it wasn't like I had all this technical knowledge on how a turbo spools up. I certainly wasn't one of those kids that would take something apart, maybe strip a lawnmower into pieces then put it back together again for fun. I just liked the look of the Turbo, simple as that. There was something about that red, white and blue livery, the spoiler was pretty much at my ten-year-old eye-level and I noticed the little plaque that said 'Turbo'. At that age, you don't really know why you like a car, it's a pretty instinctive reaction. I just saw that car and reacted. Of course, as a kid, you are not aware of the significance of events like this.

It was a life-changing moment.

I came away from the show with a Porsche brochure, this little fold-out marketing pamphlet, maybe six pages. We went back up to Sheffield and a couple of weeks after the show I decided to write a letter to Porsche in Stuttgart, telling them that when I was older I was going to design cars for them. Amazingly, they wrote back – true story – and said words to the effect of, 'Call us when you're older . . .' Regretfully, I no longer have that letter. You know, things get lost in the shuffle.

However, the passion for Porsche was never lost. Little did I know that the cars with which I am now most associated were going to be just one small part of a complex and exhilarating adventure that lay ahead of me, a life that would take in the Steel Town of Sheffield, the urban jungle of Los Angeles, eighties rock 'n' roll, the intense world of fashion, the chaotic face of Hollywood, some admittedly 'spirited' driving and a million crazy moments along the way.

Long story short, I never gave up on that childhood dream of owning a Porsche, however far-fetched it seemed to me at that young age.

I just had no idea of the journey I would take along the way . . .

Let me keep this simple and start at the beginning of the beginning of the beginning. My childhood seemed like a normal upbringing to me; it wasn't really anything super-different to other people's. There wasn't a lot of money around, truth be told. As a kid, there were things that everyone else seemed to have but I didn't, like a bike or a skateboard. However, don't feel sorry for me; it's not like I look back and think I was underprivileged or anything. It was just a pretty ordinary Sheffield childhood in the seventies.

My dad was born in 1940, my mum in '44, so they were part of that beatnik generation of parents growing up through the fifties and sixties. I remember them telling me stories of seeing the Beatles and the Kinks, but in fact their musical taste went back further than that, because they'd have been leaving school in the mid to late fifties when the concept of the modern 'teenager' first arrived. They were into Lonnie Donegan and Buddy Holly, Bill Haley and His Comets, very early rock 'n' roll. Like millions of kids of that era, my dad was suitably inspired to join a skiffle band.

My mum, Linda Bennett, was sixteen when she started dating Dad. My dad's name was Miguel Walker, so unusual names run in the family. People used to call him Mig Walker. I guess that Dad's side of the family was a little eccentric. His dad was a mechanic in the air force and this skill passed on to Dad, who picked up an understanding of machinery and was actually pretty good at fiddling with cars (years later, of course, that would become something I'd find myself involved

5

with). After the war, Grandpa Walker went into car sales and later antiques dealing. He lived on the other side of town and he was a typical old-school brigadier kinda guy, stiff upper lip. Truth be told, as a young kid I didn't really take to him – he wasn't that friendly, wasn't a lot of fun. I do remember, though, that for a time Grandpa Walker was a sales rep for the Moskvitch motor company, the Russian car firm. So he'd go and do car shows and trade fairs, and my grandma would be there with him handing out brochures. Again, decades later this is something I would find myself doing with my beautiful wife Karen; funny how when you sit back years later to write these events down, there are so many moments that perhaps influenced you in ways that you weren't aware of at the time.

There were some real characters on Mum's side, too – the Edwards and the Bennetts, who were market traders. My grandad Joe and his wife Bib were in pottery, and during the fifties and sixties they had stalls in the now-defunct Sheaf market in Sheffield. They were successful enough selling this pottery that they eventually travelled to all these trade fairs across Europe.

They were always looking for new opportunities, too. At one time, they added 'miracle' cleaning products to their roster of goods, as well as decorating accessories like paint rollers. There was a whole generation of working-class people in Britain during that era who made a living selling these types of products. Looking back now, in many ways they were the forerunner of the home-shopping channels on TV. These real old-school characters standing behind stalls and tables at trade shows or markets, you know, 'Step right up, don't be shy, buy one, get one free,' a very old-fashioned approach to selling, face-to-face. Hard work, too.

They lived literally four hundred yards away from where we did, so we saw a lot of them; Grandma Bib would come up all the time for tea. Occasionally, I'd go with them out and about selling. I remember once driving with my grandad Joe across the Pennines to Manchester because he had to sell this miracle cleaning product called Tex Clean. He used to do these brilliant demonstrations at fairs where he'd dress up in this typical English country gentleman gear – top hat and a three-piece suit with a waistcoat. I used to love watching him. He'd put a little stain on a shirt collar and then he'd do the pitch, 'Watch this stain here, ladies and gentlemen, do you know what that is, ladies? That's iodine . . .' and then he'd get out the Tex Clean powder, mix it up in water and put a little dab right there and – of course – it miraculously disappeared! Even up until five years before my grandad died, he was still wheeling and dealing in Bakewell in the Peak District. At weekends, he'd go and set up a little stand selling these jars of toffee for a few quid.

None of them ever had retail stores, just stalls in markets. I think for the large part that's something of a bygone era. You still see demonstrations, of course, but maybe I'm being sentimental in saying that the old-school characters were just amazing. These were real personalities, these market grafters; they'd been doing that for ever. So you can see that selling was in the family's blood, and I think this is where the seed was sown for me becoming a bit of a salesman myself, which you will see later in the story.

The first place I remember living in was actually quite a big house in Wigfull Road, a really nice Victorian home that my parents bought for £3,150. That house was in an area near Sheffield University, so they used to rent rooms out to students. I vaguely remember one of the students was an Indian guy who was studying to be a dentist, because Sheffield is quite a big medical university town. That's how I got into Indian food. My dad liked to cook, and this guy showed him how to make a proper curry.

My mum and dad were fairly typical working class; my dad was a salesman who went through various jobs but never really stuck at one place too long. At one point, he worked for British Telecommunications in phone sales, then he had an opportunity to invest in a company that he passed on, thinking he could do it himself, but he tried and failed, which must have been a knock to his confidence. Then he went to work for a relative selling air-conditioning supplies. Dad was pretty creative but didn't really ever pursue that part of his personality, he didn't seem to take the risk, although maybe his circumstances prevented that, you know . . . three kids, bills to pay. That said, he did try with a passion project once. He'd always been fascinated by precision clocks and watches, so he actually went to Wythenshawe College and studied for an horological degree specializing in clocks and watches, which must have been a financial strain on the family. Once he'd qualified, he then set up his own watch and clock repair business above my grandpa Walker's antique shop. Unfortunately, it didn't really take off, and looking back now I realize that must have been quite difficult for him and, indeed, my mum. So then he had to go and get a job, this time working for a company called Motor Link that essentially sold nuts and bolts and stuff like Snap-on tools. He would drive around to all these independent shops with boxes full of nuts and bolts and shit, selling them out of the back of his van.

Dad never quite seemed to achieve what he wanted. He was an intelligent man, and in fact we always used to laugh that he knew all this useless information that he could just recall so easily. He was very knowledgeable, but he never applied it in an area that really worked for him. To make matters more frustrating for him, a lot of the friends and family around him had become successful, but my dad was never really a self-starter . . . I don't know why that was, but there must have been frustration there.

Like I said, money was pretty short at times when I was a kid. For example, the seventies was a decade when British families started to take holidays further afield, so you'd get people going to France or Majorca, and it became quite a big thing. Well, we never did that. Mostly my parents would take me places I didn't want to go. With my dad's dad being into antiques, a day trip for us would be some form of cultural visit, say to Chatsworth House. Well, as a teenager you've got no interest in that whatsoever. The only times we ever went anywhere further afield were to Scarborough, Skegness or Bridlington, all these old-school British seaside towns. We did one of those British holiday camps the one year. It certainly wasn't the glamour of the south of France, more kiss-me-quick hats, a stick of rock and you were lucky if you even saw the sun.

To be fair, we went to Switzerland a few times, which sounds very far-flung (relatively), but there was a family connection. I vividly remember one particular trip in 1977 because we took a coach; we couldn't afford to fly, so all five of us sat on this coach for what seemed like days. That was a pretty miserable journey for three young kids and, to be fair, probably also for Mum and Dad.

Believe it or not, once we arrived in Switzerland we were staying at a castle! My aunt had married a Swiss guy during the 'Swinging Sixties' and ended up moving to Switzerland because he was the curator at the Château de Grandson Museum. The castle's owner was an Italian industrialist who had bought this medieval estate in a small town. He'd also had a race team called Scuderia Filipinetti and actually raced Ferraris at Le Mans. When he passed away, he'd left his car collection to be turned into a museum, and my aunt's husband's job was to oversee the maintenance of this museum and collection, so his family lived on the private floors of the castle. In the museum, there was one of these racing Ferraris and, if I recall correctly, Greta Garbo's Rolls-Royce, plus a very early steam car. Shit like that. They had a kid called Oliver, my cousin, who was the same age as me, and usually they'd drive over to Sheffield at Christmas every year in a Daimler. There'd be me, Oliver and my brother hanging out at Christmas, playing together. Well, in 1977 we visited them in Switzerland, which was a considerable improvement on our previous British seaside holidays. So that was pretty cool, hanging with my cousin, playing toy soldiers, roaming around the museum looking at all these cool cars. I have very vivid memories of that year's holiday, because that was the year that Elvis died.

Car-wise, my family didn't have anything worth talking

about. Although Dad had a passion for motorsports, he only ever owned company cars such as an Austin 7 or a Ford Cortina. So we didn't grow up with any sports cars in the garage and certainly no Porsches. I remember we went to a dentist locally who had a Porsche, although that might have been a 924. That was still a really rare sight. However, looking back now as I research this book, there were actually some pretty exotic cars around in the extended family, and that makes an impression on you when you're so young.

One of my mum's three sisters, Susan, married a guy called David who was a graphic designer and had a pretty successful business. Well, Uncle David had some amazing cars! The most memorable was a Ferrari Dino. This was around 1974, so that was a pretty rare and spectacular sight in a city filled with fumes from the steel mills and a long, long way from the Italian glamour of Modena. Sometimes I used to go round his house just to look at the Dino. Then he traded that in for a 308 GTB, which in retrospect might not seem like the best investment choice, but hey, that's not a bad problem to have – which Ferrari do you choose next? After that, he had a Lotus Type 47, which to this day is a pretty low-slung and extreme-looking car. He bought that in kit form direct from the manufacturer. The problem was that he didn't really have the engineering knowledge to put it together, so my dad helped him out. That kinda makes me realize my dad must've been pretty useful on the tools.

Another uncle on my mum's side, Mick, was a market trader, and he had an E-Type Jag. We only used to see that part of the family once a year, but it was a real thrill because of this Jag. So, to be fair, although my dad's cars were very ordinary, I was exposed to more flamboyant vehicles. It's fair to say that at the time you don't overthink it, but I guess being around cars like that must have made some impression on my young mind, at least in terms of being interested in cars as more than just something that got you from A to B.

Looking back, I can see that Dad did influence me in many ways. As I mentioned, he was really into his motorsport, and after I grew old enough to share this passion with him in the mid seventies, it would play a part in my lifelong fascination with cars, too. Dad certainly didn't have the money to buy fast cars, but he enjoyed driving around the beautiful Yorkshire and Derbyshire roads. We also watched a lot of motorsport together, Formula 1, the lower formulas too, and not just on telly. I remember going to race days at Oulton Park, Donington, Mallory Park and Cadwell Park. This was an era when motor racing was hugely popular, always exciting and very often extremely dangerous. James Hunt won the Formula 1 title in 1976 and Barry Sheene was a double motorbike world champion, so it was a golden period for British motorsport. I was also into the rallying – people such as Roger Clark and Stig Blomqvist. We would go to watch all sorts of race cars, soaking in the smell of rubber, the fumes, the sounds and the danger. I really enjoyed that whole period. There was a TV programme called *World of Sport* on at weekends, presented by this guy called Dickie Davies who had a thick mop of hair with a white stripe at the front. It was a weekly round-up of all sorts of sports, motor racing, rallying, wrestling, horse racing, skiing, even ten-pin bowling and go-karting. It ran for nearly twenty years until the mid eighties, and *everyone* watched that programme. Every Saturday I would be glued to the show, keeping up with all the motorsport news.

By contrast, school wasn't exactly a passion for me. Growing up in a working-class city such as Sheffield with a name like Magnus will leave you open to getting picked on. At school, there were a lot of Andrews, Davids, Stephens and Pauls, so when the register was called out in assembly there was only one Magnus. I don't actually know where my parents got the name from, maybe the beatnik generation vibe, I'm not sure. Similarly, my elder brother is named St. John, while my sister is in more conventional territory with Naomi Isabel Bennett Walker. Let's be honest here, Magnus was bad enough, so I never bothered telling anyone at school that my middle names were Lucian Titus Bennett. I mean, fuck, you think you get picked on because you're called Magnus ... throw in Lucian Titus and then see what happens! 'Magnus' has its roots in Latin, and means 'great', which is kinda cool, although that's not much consolation when you are at primary school and kids are being cruel. Truth be told, I hated my name as a kid, because I just got picked on about it. There was some verbal bullying, but nothing ever really physical. Once I had a fight with the 'tough kid' by the local pub, but I actually beat him, so there was no physical trouble after that. Plenty of verbal abuse, though; that was pretty constant. At the time, I didn't think about shit like this, but forty years later I have realized that the name I hated as a kid sort of helped me develop a thick skin, it built my character up early on. To make matters more tricky, for a while I suffered with a stutter. I did get over that in time, but it really didn't help me at school. Like I said, kids of that age can be cruel.

13

Perhaps inevitably, being picked on made me something of a loner. I wasn't the cool kid in the cool crowd. I was more of an outsider. I was never in the sports teams with all the popular lads, I didn't play football, cricket, all that, I just wasn't a team-sports player. Instead, around the age of nine, I gravitated towards long-distance running. That was my escape. No one picked on me, no one called me names, I didn't need to be part of the popular crowd, I could just go out and do my running alone. I actually don't quite recall how I got into cross-country running in the very first place, but somehow those two ideas are linked. The loner and the runner.

Incredibly, at that point England was pretty much the centre of the middle-distance running world – this was the era of Seb Coe versus Steve Ovett, two famous runners whose battles on the track became the stuff of legend. They'd actually first raced against each other in a schools cross-country race back in 1972 (which neither won), but by the tail end of that decade they were the kings of the track and every second of every race was played out in full view of the watching world. There were also other world-class runners such as Brendan Foster and, later, Steve Cram. Like a generation of sports fans, I watched as they swapped world records and Olympic medals. To a kid struggling at school who found solace in the solitary life of a long-distance runner, these individuals were an inspiration.

Turns out I had a talent for running, and once I discovered this I was so motivated. For the next four years or so, running was my life, it became all-consuming. I used to train twice a day, five or six days per week around the streets and hills where I lived. Quite quickly, I won a few races and got to take home some trophies and was really loving it. Then I stepped up a level and joined the Hallamshire Harriers, the local athletics club. This was a very well-respected running club based at Hillsborough Park, just near to the Sheffield Wednesday football team's stadium. At one time, Seb Coe had actually run at my club, so he was a particular inspiration. One of my proudest mementoes then – and still to this day, to be fair – is a certificate for a race I entered that was signed by Seb Coe.

At that point, Dad was very supportive. After school, I'd take the bus to Hillsborough to go running and he'd meet me there after work, when he'd regularly follow along in the car, pacing me as I ran. He was very proud. I religiously kept running journals, this little 'Runner's Almanac' which I still have, in which I wrote about how far I had run each day, how I felt, what speed, ways to improve, the weather; I was so precise and dedicated. At the peak of my obsession, I was averaging thirty-five to fifty miles a week. The training paid off when I won quite a few races locally, culminating in victory at the Sheffield Schoolboys Championship. Eventually, I started competing across the UK and I was even entered into events across Europe. I remember one particular race in Germany where the course was very tough and the standard incredibly high. So I was running at a pretty good level.

Cross-country was just me on my own, never giving up, always keeping going, staying motivated, being relentless and determined to achieve my goal – that whole attitude really appealed to me. Aside from enjoying some decent success, I certainly think running gave me a sense of self-reliance and also an early taste of independence, let's put it that way. Running really helped shape my character. There's a lot to be said for the loneliness of the long-distance runner.

URBAN
OUTLAW

Chapter 2

Down to Earth and Difficult to Cure

For all that Dad and I watched motorsport together and he supported my running, as I grew through my teens we started to clash. Long story short, at times during my teenage years my dad struggled, both in terms of his own life and also later because of the way my interests changed. After work, he used to go down the pub quite a bit, like most working-class men of that period in Britain. My dad was also a heavy smoker, Senior Service or John Player Special unfiltered. Back in the seventies, that was very common; as a kid you just took it for granted that everyone smoked and that every five years you'd have to paint the woodchip wallpaper because the magnolia paint had been stained nicotine-brown. Dad was probably miserable doing a job he didn't like and frustrated by the struggles he'd had. I think he became disillusioned because he wasn't quite as successful as some of

17

his peers, even though he was probably smarter than them.

His fortunes at work were reflected in where we lived. After the big Victorian house in Wigfull Road, we had to move to a smaller house in Penrhyn Road, so I guess there were some issues with the family's finances. As the years went by, there were periods when my dad just wasn't around for me. Through our previously shared interest in motorsport and running, you can argue that he was a big influence on me, especially when you consider what I have gone on to do in later life. However, when I discovered rock music, then girls and later alcohol, our relationship started to change. I said I didn't have a skateboard earlier – well, what actually happened was that one time I bought a skateboard but my dad wouldn't let me use it. That was how he could be at times. He could be super-controlling, which to a teenager growing up into a young man could be an issue.

By the age of fourteen, I was really starting to get into rock music. Although Dad had been in a skiffle band when he was younger, there was just an average amount of music around in our house. There was an eight-track cassette player on which they played the *Best of Bread* and albums by the Carpenters, but music was never really on that much. Dad kind of taught me how to play guitar and at one point he actually bought a Gibson SG, but he wouldn't really let me touch it. One time when for some reason my brother and I were fighting over the guitar, we dropped it and, of course, the fucking neck broke. You can imagine two teenage lads watching this guitar fall in slow motion and then seeing the neck break. *Shit!* The guitar went away to be repaired and never came back.

Like I say, around fourteen, I grew my hair long and within a couple of years I'd also discovered girls and alcohol. All of a sudden I'm not really into running any more, because you could get in to the pub at fifteen and start drinking and having girlfriends. Neither of these new 'interests' particularly suited being a finely tuned long-distance runner, so my training mileage started to drop pretty dramatically and I stopped keeping the training diaries as the running started to fade away. That was the beginning of the end of the cross-country.

Instead, in came albums by the likes of Motörhead, Status Quo, UFO, Saxon, Rainbow and the whole new wave of the British heavy-metal scene. Motörhead's 'Ace of Spades' came out in 1980 and I was certainly fully into that; I remember seeing them at the university. I never became a punk. For some reason, Motörhead seemed to appeal to punks and rockers. You'd go see them play and be standing next to someone with an Exploited jacket on with a Mohawk and a UK Subs T-shirt. In the early eighties, the Sheffield band Def Leppard was just starting to conquer the world, so they were the local heroes and, for a time, the biggest band on the planet. I also loved Saxon, who were from nearby Barnsley. I was lucky that pretty much all these bands came through the City Hall, so I got to go to gigs by all the big acts. I'd wait for *Top of the Pops* on a Thursday night to see Motörhead or Saxon or Thin Lizzy; I loved it.

Sheffield is a great musical town. The nightclub owner Peter Stringfellow had a club there in the sixties, and Joe Cocker was the big local export of that era. As well as all the rock bands I've mentioned, by the early eighties Sheffield also had a thriving electronic music scene, courtesy of bands such as the Human League, Heaven 17, ABC and Cabaret Voltaire. The Human League's lead singer Phil Oakey lived down the road in a big Victorian house, and we'd occasionally see him in the fish and chip shop, even after they'd had their massive Number 1 hit 'Don't You Want Me'. Even so, Sheffield always got overshadowed by Liverpool and Manchester with bands like Echo & the Bunnymen, Joy Division and New Order. For me, however, it was always about rock music. I was never drawn to electronic music, even though I was around it locally.

I started to meet a few mates who were also into the same music. We would get to see all these big bands for £2.50, maybe £3. I'd buy the ticket a month in advance and couldn't wait for the date. I would get *NME*, *Sounds* and *Kerrang!* every week, religiously, and I began going to the rock clubs around Sheffield pretty regularly. Rebels was a full-on heavy-metal club, so we used to go there on a Monday when it was free to get in before 10 p.m. and beer was 50p a pint. The student crowd tended to go to the Leadmill, to see bands such as the Cure and Bauhaus, but if your poison was rock, you went to places like Rebels.

I'd be out at clubs and gigs three or four nights a week. The first Monsters of Rock Festival I went to was in 1982 with a buddy from school who had a driver's licence. The journey from Sheffield to Donington was kind of a big deal and, of course, it rained. We didn't get back till midnight, to find my mum waiting up for me, worried sick.

As well as the long hair, I was wearing denim and leather, dirty ripped-up jeans, combat boots and, like a lot of rockers,

I started putting embroidery on my jacket. That idea of patches goes way back to the forties and even earlier in biker culture; it's all about personalization but also wanting to be a part of something. I'd buy denim jackets and cut the arms off then bleach them up. My mum could sew and would often make her own dresses and clothes for my sister with a Singer sewing machine that she had. She always supported me in whatever I wanted to do, so when I started to show an interest in customizing my denims, Mum showed me how to stitch old Levi's so they'd be real tight and also how to sew all these band patches on to my jackets. I embroidered a Saxon logo on the back of my denim jacket and painted 'MSG' for Michael Schenker Group on there, too. I also stitched a Rainbow patch on it, as well as a Black Sabbath one. Little did Mum or I know how important those sewing lessons would later become.

At school, I was struggling. Thanks to my mum (who kept everything from when I was a kid) I've still got all my old school reports and they make fascinating reading, although perhaps not for the right reasons! The Silverdale School report card from 1981 has some memorable quotes. How about: 'The overall message of this report seems to be that Magnus is not using his abilities to the full. He cannot hope to improve his standards until he makes the necessary effort.' Or what about: 'Magnus has worked poorly throughout the year . . . Magnus is not finding this particularly easy . . . Magnus is not a linguist . . . a disappointing end result . . .' My personal favourite was a biology teacher whose response to my mark of 51 per cent was summed up in just two words: 'Totally unsatisfactory'. Well, looking back as an adult, I accept that maybe I could have made more effort in some classes, but equally he could have made more effort with his fucking report, right?

I got a girlfriend when I was fourteen and along with the rock music that sort of took over. No extra revision classes for me; we'd go home at lunchtime and make out. Even though I had intelligence, you only have to read those school reports to realize I didn't put the effort in. At that point, I had decided school wasn't for me, so I kind of flunked out at the end of the final year. I just sort of gave up; I didn't really care. I wasn't ditching class altogether and bunking off, but I wasn't putting the work in when I was there. Some of the kids in my year were doing ten subjects. I only took four. I ended up with two O levels in the final exams, a C in English language and a B in geography. Failed maths, failed physics. At the time, there was a lot of unemployment both in Sheffield and nationally, so leaving school with just two O levels wasn't exactly a guarantee of a bright future.

I had no grand plan or vision for what I wanted to do or where I wanted to go; I was just a kid enjoying music and going out. The focus I had shown with the running didn't really translate to rock music, although like a lot of fans I had vague ideas of being in a band myself. I spent that summer going to all of these rock concerts and I still have all the programmes, which bring back fantastic memories. But in other ways this wasn't a great point in my life. I was living at home, on the dole and clashing with my dad quite a bit. Growing my hair long really aggravated my dad. I'd get the old, 'You're not living under my roof with long hair, cut your hair and get a proper job', all that. This coincided with him

22

losing his job, so he went on the dole, started complaining about bad back problems and he would be in bed till noon, then get up in the afternoon and go to the pub at seven and stay there till eleven. So my mum became the breadwinner.

Looking back, I realize now that my dad was probably depressed, but people didn't talk about stuff like that back then. So truth be told it became a bit of a toxic environment. My mum was always supportive; she didn't really care about me having long hair, but it was like a red rag to a bull for my dad. There was a lot of conflict, so in the end I'd try to avoid him. I'd go out if I knew he was gonna be around; I'd just try and not run into him. My mum was much more the stable influence. She kept the same job at Broomhill Infants School (which I went to) for over twenty years. So she provided real stability and kind of kept the family together. My mum's fantastic. I have such a strong relationship with her and I feel very lucky that she has always been there for me. She is remarkable, strong, intelligent, motivated and she was always so kind to me. Gotta love your mum, right?

Despite what might seem on the surface to be a teenage kid just listening to music, drinking and making out, it wasn't quite that simple. When I did find something to focus on, I really applied myself. For example, one of my dad's friends gave me a cash-in-hand job on a construction site, basically doing all the shit jobs like cleaning mortar off bricks, mixing plaster, all that sort of manual labour, for £10 a day. That guy Martin always said I was the best labourer he'd ever had. I really got quite motivated about the job, even though it was just labouring. I wasn't sat around feeling bored on the site; the days went by pretty quick for me, as everything sort of became a challenge: fill the skip as quickly as I could, make the bucket of plaster before the plasterer had actually finished with the previous one so I was one step ahead of him. I was always motivated in whatever I did; I wasn't one of those guys that was waiting for the tea break. It wasn't so I could be better than the other guys on the site; it was just to motivate myself. Cross-country running had given me that edge at an early age, but I have always been more competitive with myself than with my peer group.

When I was seventeen, I got a new girlfriend and moved in with her for six months. She was an air stewardess working for Monarch Airlines and was based out of Milton Keynes, so I'd take a coach and go down south for the weekend. Then she relocated to Sheffield and got her own flat, so I temporarily moved in with her. By this stage, I'd sort of gone from the long rocker's hair into more of the bleached-out Hanoi Rocks/ Vince Neil/spiky peroxide-blond look, crimping it, back-combing it, make-up, mascara, more of the glam-rock vibe.

At this point, I still wasn't really sure what I wanted to do. I'd had enough of bumming around the construction site, and I was disillusioned by going to the dole office where career advisers would put me forward for these completely random jobs that had nothing to do with my interests or abilities. Sheffield is known as 'Steel City' and has a history stretching back centuries in that industry. In fact, the stainless steel that we all use on our car parts was invented in Sheffield. However, by the seventies and eighties, there was fierce competition from overseas steel manufacturers; the industry around which Sheffield had boomed then started to dwindle and within a relatively short period of time was

24

pretty much decimated. This coincided roughly with the collapse of the mining industry – which was a central part of much of northern England's communities and way of life – meaning that this was not a great time to be growing up and looking for opportunities across many cities in the north. Strikes, protests, clashes with police, unemployment was rife, families were queueing for the food-bank handouts – this was a bleak period in the history of the north of England. So there were a fair few people around at the time who were pretty politicized, but to be perfectly honest, that wasn't me. I wasn't anti-Thatcher, anti-Scargill, ranting and raving. When I was younger I didn't even know who Margaret Thatcher was, truth be told. Kids of a young age are obviously not into politics. Having said that, the consequences of those more political times were plain to see, especially as I grew older – even to a kid like me who was not really involved on a daily basis. For me as a teenage kid in a northern town which had been devastated by unemployment and the decline of industry, there were pretty slim pickings.

So I thought I should try going back into education and see what happened. At one point, I enrolled on a graphic design course, but that didn't really fit and I stopped quite quickly. Next up, I went to Stannington College to study for a City & Guilds qualification in Sports Management, Leisure and Recreation. Obviously, I'd been into running and I quite liked swimming too, so it seemed like a reasonable idea at the time. I wasn't sure what else to try, and it's not like there were hundreds of options for a lad of seventeen with just two O levels. The course was actually kinda cool, I learnt a little bit about sports studies and marketing, and they taught you how to become a coach, too. I did my Bronze Medallion life-guard certification and learnt first aid and CPR, so there was some useful stuff involved. It was just a one-year course, but the pivotal point about that period in my life had nothing to do with my course or the actual work I was doing in class, it was when someone at college told me about an experience called Camp America, which was to completely and utterly alter the course of my entire life.

Chapter 3

Welcome to the Jungle

Before I knew it, I'd been out of school for three years, been on the dole for a year, doing odd jobs, so I was like, *What am I going to do? I can't keep bumming around with no future, no hope.* As I've said, growing up as a kid in Sheffield we never really travelled. Apart from the trips to Switzerland to see my cousin, we didn't go very far afield. So when one of the lecturers at my college mentioned that some students were applying for this summer job called Camp America, it was about as far removed from my world as possible. Basically, Camp America organized summer camps for kids from underprivileged areas and they recruited overseas students to supervise and help the kids out. Some of the lecturers at college had already been and said it was a great experience. For me, it was like, *Fuck, how bad can this be?* I just felt like it was *an opportunity*, and something in me said to just go, to grab the moment. I saw a spark of something and leapt at it. At home, there was still conflict with my dad, so I think there was also an element of me thinking, *Fuck you, I am going to America to do my own thing.*

America itself was a big part of the attraction. As a kid growing up in the seventies and eighties, I watched a lot of American TV and movies, much of which was car related, *Starsky & Hutch, Dukes of Hazzard, CHiPs, Smokey and the Bandit, Bullitt.* I loved all that stuff. Of course, it's not just all the car-related stuff; it's *Kojak, The Streets of San Francisco*, it's *The Rockford Files*, Paul Newman, Robert Redford and Steve McQueen, you know. Even though we might only have had three TV channels, everybody watched those iconic shows and movies. And, like millions of kids, I had one of those Evel Knievel motorbike toys and a rocket car as well. Americana was a pretty key feature of my childhood years, as it was for a lot of my mates.

By this time, my musical taste had expanded so that as well as all the British rock bands, I was also listening to American groups such as Guns N' Roses and Mötley Crüe, as glam rock morphed with punk rock. Guns N' Roses was about to become the biggest band in the world. I was aware of the Sunset Strip and the rock 'n' roll lifestyle out in LA. Even further back than that, I'd heard about LA and the Doors, all that; you just pick bits up.

So that's why when this Camp America opportunity came up, my gut instinct told me something that has been absolutely central to my entire life and pretty much everything I have done – *How bad can this be?* Going to America wasn't a life-long dream, I hadn't even really thought about the idea, but now that the opportunity had presented itself I thought, *They speak English, it's a free flight, I'm fascinated by the culture, and the idea of breaking out on my own appeals, too.* For me, going to America just seemed cooler and easier than staying in Sheffield, struggling to get by. *Give it a go.* So I applied to join, and for some reason they accepted me. Once I got my letter of acceptance, I literally packed a big duffel bag and off I went. In hindsight, thirty years later, that was the best thing I ever did.

Pretty soon after being accepted, I was on a train down to London, en route to Heathrow Airport for my flight on 14 June 1986. Looking back, that really was a leap of faith, quite literally taking me completely out of my world and into a totally alien environment. There were probably about five hundred people meeting up at the airport, all going to America but not knowing exactly where we were ultimately going to be stationed. You just got on a plane and off you went to New York for a one-night stopover, after which you were given your eventual destination.

I vaguely remember going out in New York with a bunch of complete strangers on that first night and that was a big culture shock. Remember, at this point I'd been to Switzerland with my family, competed in cross-country in Germany, been on holiday to Morocco with the air stewardess I told you about (because she got free flights) and down to London a few times, but I was hardly a globetrotter.

I was only in the Big Apple for twelve hours before I was given my final destination, which was at a camp in Michigan. The next leg of this journey was a big turning point for me, getting on a Trailways bus from Penn Station to Detroit, which is a *long* way. That was the start of what I would call my American road trip. I don't even remember how many hours that journey was – it might have been a ten-hour drive – then we were picked up somewhere in Detroit and had another hour's drive to this camp north of Detroit near Lake Michigan, in the middle of nowhere.

There were two types of summer camps – one for rich kids and one for underprivileged kids. Mine was not for the rich kids. By this point, I'm actually a little bit fucking worried and scared. Detroit is a real urban city. I'm almost the token white kid on the camp. It's all inner-city kids. *No one* is into rock 'n' roll. They're all into Run DMC, LL Cool J and carrying these big ghetto-blaster boom-boxes. Remember, back then I've got spiky peroxide platinum hair, I'm tall, skinny and white. I'm looking like I should be in Mötley Crüe. They don't know if I'm a chick or a guy. To make matters worse, everyone seems to know everyone else, there's cousins, nephews, siblings – everyone seemed friends with each other already . . . all except this lanky white kid from Sheffield, England. Whatever their ethnic background, they were all pretty hard inner-city kids. Like I say, this was not a camp for rich kids, this was a 'we can't keep control of these kids so let's ship them off for a few months of the year' camp. I was completely out of my element. Let me tell you, it was a *severe* culture shock. I was like, *Fuck! What have I got myself into?*

These were kids from broken homes – you know, dad's in jail, mum's on welfare or the kids are living with their aunts because their mum's working and can't afford to keep them. They were only supposed to be there for two weeks, but a lot of them just kept getting dumped back there time after time.

As a so-called 'camp counsellor', I had to get them out of bed at 7 a.m., get them to breakfast at 7.30 a.m. and at 8 they started doing art studies or swimming or going for a walk or playing basketball or some other camp activity. However, these kids didn't want to listen to anybody, especially not some skinny white guy with peroxide hair and tight trousers; they just wanted to goof off and go run around. So I've got to somehow try and control them. Easier said than done. Almost immediately I was not really liking being in a log cabin with twelve kids aged from eight to fifteen where I'm supposed to be in charge even though I'm not that much older. I was essentially a babysitter, but I spent half of the time trying to make sure they were not drowning each other in the lake. Try telling them to clean their dorms or write a letter home or wash up . . . And lights out at 9.30 . . . yeah? Not gonna happen. It was kind of miserable, truth be told. I remember being pretty lonely, because that was not exactly a super-uplifting environment. It's not like I could go out for a beer to relax – I was too young to buy a beer and too skint to afford one.

Big moments change your life. Looking back, that's where I learnt to become what I like to call an 'adaptive swimmer'. Dropped into this completely unfamiliar environment, not knowing anybody and, like it or not, it's sink or swim. The instinct to survive was just naturally there; maybe it came from the cross-country running, you know, keep on pushing and don't give up. I definitely got some of that from my parents, too, who worked very hard.

The kids would come for ten days and then there'd be two days off before the next lot arrived, and during those breaks you'd spend time with the other counsellors. As part of the deal, we were all given $100 pocket money for the summer, so you had to be careful how you spent that. There weren't many English students doing this, so I ended up making friends with some guy that lived in a suburb of Detroit. One night we went into Detroit and that was a big eye-opener because that was a real inner-city town, you know, 'Motor City' and all that. At the time, Detroit was even worse than Sheffield. Sure, it was the home of the auto industry, but by the mid eighties that legacy was starting to crumble as quickly as the disused car factories. People had started leaving Detroit in the sixties and seventies, so by the time I visited, certain areas were just a ghost town. Like Sheffield, a lot of the steel plants and factories were closing down, there was a lot of unemployment and people were having a real hard time. That was unsettling to see, because even just from a rock fan's perspective I knew that Detroit was a city with so much culture – the MC5, the Stooges, Alice Cooper, the proto-punk scene in the late sixties – but when I first experienced it in 1986, people were struggling.

I ended up finding this little area in Detroit called Royal Oak, which was a suburb where there were a couple of cool stores and something of a thriving punk rock scene. There was also a little area called Greektown and Trappers Alley that was in Downtown that was kind of cool. I remember going across the border into Canada and you can look back over the lake – Detroit looks great from Windsor. Despite everything I've said about people struggling and the city having a tough time, I felt a connection. Maybe it was the defunct manufacturing, maybe it was the history and the cars, I'm not sure, but there was something fascinating about that place. Standing there looking at Motor City as a nineteen-year-old kid, little did I know that ten years later the same punk rock stores would be selling my clothing range and thirty years after that I'd eventually make a video called *Motor City Outlaw*, driving one of my outlaw Porsches through Detroit.

But I'm getting ahead of myself. Back in 1986, my life was very different. I met a local girl in one of the gritty clubs in town and she started coming to visit me in the camp, which brightened my days. Eventually, *finally*, the camp ended in late August. My cousin Oliver had arranged to fly over from Switzerland so we could go off on some travels around the States, my first American road trip. We bought ourselves a Trailways ticket each and caught the bus from Detroit to LA. For me it was always going to be LA, because Los Angeles is more of a music town than New York. At the time, I didn't think much about the film business, but I had watched all those TV shows I mentioned and I clicked with that idea. As a heavy-metal fan, LA obviously also had the Sunset Strip/ rock 'n' roll/heavy-metal culture, too. So off we went on this bus from Michigan, LA bound.

Now, check out a map of that journey and you will see that it is a pretty massive trek. Well, what they didn't tell us was that they went via Memphis and Tennessee! The buses were the cheapest way for people to travel, so there were all sorts of 'interesting' characters on board. The trip was endless and made worse by the fact we had to stop every four hours or so at these pretty grimy truck stops in the middle of nowhere. Remember, I'm still looking all glammed out and punk rock

33

at this point, so I was sticking out like a sore thumb. There was a bathroom on the bus, but it was kind of stinky. That was some journey. It wasn't like we got off and went to Graceland and did the tourist stuff; we were just sitting or sleeping on this bus for what felt like an eternity. One particularly vivid memory is of my Sony Walkman running out of batteries so that the tape and the tunes were getting all wobbly.

Eventually, we arrived at Union Station in Los Angeles, less than a mile from where I sit writing this book right now. The bus must have come in at like 4 a.m. in the morning. I was so excited, I was thinking, *Wow! We're in LA. It's going to be full of all the beautiful people, the movie stars, the rock stars,* Baywatch . . . *where's Pamela Anderson?*

Pamela never showed.

We fell asleep on a bench.

As Axl Rose once said in a song, 'Welcome to the Jungle' . . .

I vividly remember getting woken up by a security guard at six in the morning, 'Hey, you can't sleep here . . .' I told him we were going to Venice Beach or maybe to Hollywood to stay at a youth hostel, but he wasn't interested and made us move along. Truth be told, we hadn't got a clue what was going on, and we'd had two hours' sleep at the end of a bus journey that seemed to take years. All we had was an idiot's guide to LA, and of course there were no mobile phones or internet back then.

We just wandered around fairly aimlessly before finally getting a bus that took for ever to get to Hollywood, where we bunked up in the YMCA (and were sharp enough to pay for our own room, rather than one of the shared dorms). The reality had hit home pretty immediately that what I had seen on TV was not everyday life on the real streets of America. But hey, as a teenager, you don't know that. Besides, once we'd dumped our bags, we went straight out exploring. Despite all the tiredness, the aches and pains and the lack of food, we were just excited to be in Hollywood and eager to look around. After a while wandering about, we found Hollywood Boulevard.

This is 1986. Back then, Hollywood Boulevard was just great because it was like Soho in New York meets the Kings Road or West End in London, but on steroids. It was a massive culture clash of sights, smells, people, music, tattoo parlours, crazy shops and all these peculiar but fascinating characters wandering around. It had everything: the sleaze, the pimps, the runaway kids, the people hawking change, the Chinese Theatre, the cheap, seedy rock 'n' roll stores, the stripper chick stores. Everybody looked cool to me. Even though some cultural naysayers were shouting that it was the decline of Western civilization, to this kid from Sheffield, it was just mesmerizing.

Like I said, at this point I'm looking pretty glam – tight pants, spiky peroxide hair, all that – so I kinda fitted in. I was walking by this cheap clothing store and in the window they had these black PVC alligator pants for $9.99, so I bought a pair and took them back to the YMCA. They didn't fit good, they weren't skin-tight, just cut like a 501 or similar. So I bought a basic sewing kit and altered them, changed the seams so that they were real tight. I wore those customized trousers with a Meatloaf-style white ruffled shirt and a black jacket with my hair all teased up – it was kind of like 'Robert Smith from the Cure meets Mike Monroe from Hanoi Rocks meets Ian Astbury from the Cult'. Oliver and I were a bit of an oddball couple. I was rocking the Hanoi Rocks look, but he was the total opposite. Olly was a Mod; he was into scooters and Lambrettas and dressing in Ben Sherman and Fred Perry; he had a parka and Sta-Prest trousers with his Jam shoes; he was listening to the Who, the Specials, the Selecter and all the Two Tone scene. So, yeah, we looked like a strange combination walking around LA.

A few days later, we headed back to Hollywood Boulevard, and I asked someone where all the cool clothing shops were. They told me Melrose, so we got a bus there, but of course we got off at the wrong end of what is a very long street. So it's ninety degrees, I'm sweating buckets because I'm wearing PVC pants, that ruffled shirt and all that hair, and we have to walk over a mile along Melrose to get to the cool shops.

Eventually, we made it down to the interesting end, and one of these cool stores was called Retail Slut (there was another similar one called Let It Rock). I'd visited London a few times previously, so I was familiar with places like Malcolm McLaren's Sex shop on the Kings Road, and these seemed to me to be the LA equivalent. Retail Slut was the coolest, so we went in there. It was a heavy-metal store stocking Dr. Martens, Lip Service, Let It Rock shoes, all this rock 'n' roll gear, and there was this guy working behind the counter with spiky hair, looked a bit like me, similar vibe. Turned out it was Taime Downe of the band Faster Pussycat. To this day, it's a pretty common story for LA musicians to work in retail because the stores don't open till midday, so these kids can be out till two in the morning rehearsing or gigging, then turn up for work the next day still hungover but it's okay.

So this guy Taime goes, 'Hey, man, cool pants,' just like that. 'Where you from?'

I tell him England and then he goes, 'Where'd you get the pants from?'

Now, for some reason that I don't really know, gut instinct I guess, I literally just said, 'London. Why? You want to buy some?'

'Yeah, sure, how much are they?'

Again, instinct . . . I just threw out a price for these $9.99 pants that I'd customized with a cheap sewing kit in a youth hostel round the corner.

'Twenty-five bucks a pair. How many do you want?'

'I'll take eight pairs.'

Again, without overthinking it, just going with the flow, I said, 'Okay, no problem, I'll be back within the hour.'

We realized we didn't have time to walk back to the cheap store where I'd bought these $9.99 pants, so we got a cab there, bought twelve pairs, took them back to Taime and he was good for his word and paid us $25 for each pair out of the till. Just sold them as is, didn't even make them tight, didn't take the seams in. Now I may not have excelled at maths in school, but I knew that twelve pairs at $10 was $120, and this guy had just paid us $200 for only eight of them. So I was $80 up and still had pants left to sell. That had made me more profit in one sale than I was earning in a week on a building site in the UK. This cheap store where I'd bought these PVC pants for $9.99 was literally only a mile away from Retail Slut on Melrose, but nobody went to Hollywood Boulevard because it wasn't considered a cool place to shop.

None of this was planned. It was an opportunity that just evolved. The adaptive swimmer again, the ability to just go with the flow, make a decision when presented with what could be an opportunity, reacting quickly to a moment. This is an approach to life that has served me well and is an idea I will come back to. I didn't buy the pants because I figured I could go and sell them on Melrose. It happened purely organically, by chance, but that sort of moment has happened to me half a dozen times over the years. Those organic happenings, opportunities, unexpected openings or whatever you want to call them are crucial. When they happen, I always try to say yes rather than no.

Well, later in my story I would come to start my own fashion label and you would be forgiven for thinking this was how it all began. Well, not really, no. After selling those pants to Retail Slut, I basically spent the next three or four months couch-surfing in LA. I sank myself into the club scene around Hollywood Boulevard, which at the time was fantastic. This is pre-internet, so everyone's promoting their clubs or bands or venues on little flyers printed on neon paper, all these little dayglo scraps of ambition littered across the sidewalks. I'd go to these clubs and watch the bands, and pretty quickly I made some cool friends and found myself part of that scene. Olly had to fly back to Switzerland, but I stayed on and had a great time sofa-surfing and making new mates. I even spent a few weeks in San Francisco at a youth hostel near Fisherman's Wharf with a girl I'd met at a club.

Like I said, this was pre-internet, no mobile phones, so staying in touch with my parents was pretty slow. I used to write to my mum quite a lot, and she has kept all those post-cards. Those Hollywood streets, let's be honest, were not exactly brimming with law-abiding citizens. Plenty of good people, of course, but also a fair share of shady characters. There was a scam going on where people were getting hold of stolen phone calling cards, so you'd see a guy hanging outside of the post office around the phone box and you'd go buy these 'magic numbers' – essentially it was a calling-card number. They'd only be good for say a day or two before they were stopped, but that's how a lot of people were calling home. I couldn't afford to be making four- or five-dollar phone calls to my mum, so once a week I'd call her on one of these phone cards. Sometimes you'd be mid-conversation and it would just be cut off, but it was always great to speak to Mum.

I had a great time, but there was no real progress in terms of making money or getting a job. When my temporary visa ran out I didn't even have enough money to get a ticket home. I was totally skint, I'd grown tired of couch-surfing and, to be fair, my friends' patience was understandably wearing thin. I had no choice: I had to fly home and head back to Sheffield. I even had to rely on a girlfriend to give me the $150 to buy a one-way flight back to Gatwick. It had been fun while it lasted, but it looked like my American dream was over.

It's funny, isn't it, how music can sometimes make you feel like you are somewhere else in the world. When I was still in Sheffield, I would listen to some of the hair-metal bands from LA and I could almost feel like I was in Hollywood. Yes, it was six thousand miles away from the north of England, but those bands could make that distance seem irrelevant. Well, let me tell you, travelling back to Sheffield that winter with my tail between my legs having run out of money and ideas in LA, it felt like a fucking long way home. To make matters worse, there were no seats at all on the train back up north, so I had to stand for hours. Bear in mind I'm still all glammed up, my grubby washing stuffed into my bag, a skint, washed-up, exhausted and depressed alien who'd just landed from the west coast of the USA, heading back to the harsh reality of Steel City. Don't get me wrong, I love Sheffield, it's a great place, but at that point in my life, the idea of going back to face a few cynical local people who would have a wry smile on their faces as the local boy slunk back home from his American travels was not one that filled me with joy. When I got accepted into Camp America, that was the first big achievement I'd enjoyed. Sure, I'd had some minor success with running, but at school I'd obviously not done so well, which wasn't something that I was proud of. Going to America was a big deal for me, it meant I had succeeded at something . . . you know, I told a few of my buddies, 'Yeah, I'm going to America, I might never be back . . .' Now I was back. I was really pleased to see Mum, always, although relations with Dad were still somewhat strained. I moved back in with them in Bents Green, straight back on the dole.

Fuck.

I'd had this taste of freedom, of this lifestyle in America, but nothing had changed at home. Obviously, it was great to see my family, but apart from that it was just like, *What the fuck am I going to do?* It was not a good time. Immediately,

I got back into the old habit of going down to Rebels and the other rock clubs and pubs around Sheffield. However, this time it was different, because now I was *restless*.

Dejected, I reapplied for Camp America in the May of 1987, but they declined my application. Door shut. *Shit*.

Then, a few weeks later, I suddenly got a letter one Tuesday from Camp America saying there was a place after all, but I had to fly out that Saturday.

American Dream Part II.

I left England on four days' notice. This second time I flew out for Camp America, they stationed me in New Jersey. It was essentially the same type of set-up as Detroit – inner-city, underprivileged kids, more of the same rap, LL Cool J, Run DMC and me still cast as the outsider. However, this camp was a little better because it wasn't as hectic or as big. I was actually somehow appointed swimming instructor and life-guard, so that was a little bit easier, too. Best of all, crucially, this camp was only a forty-five-minute train ride from New York.

A few of us from camp used to go into New York for one or two days every fortnight, and it was a great time to be around the Big Apple. We would go to the usual rock 'n' roll haunts such as CBGB, and there was a club we found called L'Amour in Brooklyn. New York was very cool, it was the epicentre, gritty; I really liked it. I was a year older and wiser, the camp was easier, New York was nearby, everything felt pretty good. Then, around the last week of August, I got a job as a lifeguard over Labour Day weekend on the housing estate next to the camp, and that paid pretty well. The camp paid better this time, too, so by the end of the summer I had about a thousand bucks in my pocket. And there was only ever going to be one place I went to with that . . . back to LA.

I'd kept in contact with all the people in bands and from the club scene that I'd met on my first trip, so when I went back to LA second time around I was a little bit more hooked up. Initially, I ended up staying with a pen pal, another girl I'd met. One of her friends was dating a guy who was in the Cars, and through her we ended up getting invited to an MTV awards party one night at Universal Studios. It felt crazy, such a swift change from standing on that train back to Sheffield only a few months earlier, depressed and skint, to suddenly being at a glitzy music-biz party in LA. I was like, *Fuck! How did I get here?*

That night I met a musician called Johnny who was in a band named Johnny Outrageous. He thought I'd be great in his band, but although I wasn't quite talented enough to do that (I never really learnt more than three chords on the guitar), I started hanging out with him anyway, and I ended up staying in his little spare bedroom for about nine months. He was very good about it, you know, 'You can stay with me for a little bit,' and even though a few weeks became a few months, he stayed pretty chilled.

Within a few weeks of landing back in LA, I had met quite a lot of people who were in up-and-coming bands on the LA scene, and I quickly fell in with the crowd of 'cool' people. That was kind of the beginning of the great times for me in LA over the next two years. The bands that I knew weren't at the level of Guns N' Roses, of course, who were top of the tree by then, but my friends were all having a go at breaking their bands, working in the day at telemarketing companies or in retail stores, then gigging at night, playing the Sunset Strip. I'm not trying to make out I was some kind of big name in these clubs; I was sort of low level. I wasn't in the VIP room with Axl Rose; I'm more milling around on the dance floor, watching the bands. One of the bands that I became friendly with was called the Zeros; they were kind of a New York Dolls type of band, with a Hanoi Rocks vibe. They were hard-working guys, gigging all the time and on the verge of getting a record deal, but unfortunately they never quite made it really big. So I'd hand out flyers for those guys, help roadie for them occasionally, too, just setting the gear up. I got to know a lot of bartenders and they kinda liked the English vibe, so I wasn't buying many drinks or paying to get into clubs or gigs. I was getting really immersed in that whole scene, going to clubs such as Scream, Power Tools, Cat House, hanging out with people like Johnny and of course Taime (whom I'd sold the PVC pants to the year before; by now his band Faster Pussycat had become relatively big news). They were great days.

During the daytime, these guys were either working or if they were not on a shift we would hang out around Hollywood. I was doing odd jobs maybe one or two days a week, decorating, that sort of shit, getting fifty bucks a day, so I was living meagrely, essentially hand to mouth, but that was okay, I was only twenty, I could handle it. I actually really enjoyed it for a while.

I would get up around eleven, go down Melrose, walk the street, go to the stores, hang out, shoot the shit, 'What's going on tonight? Where are you guys going?' Probably wait for whoever I'm staying with to come home at five to let me in. Hang out with them, maybe go eat, you know something cheap and cheery at a hot dog stand or El Coyote where you could eat for like two or three bucks, then probably head to a club. The goal was always to get there early, because then you get in free or, failing that, be on someone's guest list. Then hang out at the clubs till two in the morning. Each night there was always a lottery of how you could find a way to crash with someone. Aside from when I was living with Johnny, I didn't always have a place to sleep, so sometimes it'd be, 'Where you going later, Magnus?', 'Well, I've actually got nowhere to stay, can I sleep on your couch?' So there was a little bit of that for two or three nights here, three or four nights there. I never actually roughed it on the street, but there was a long period where I wasn't sure which sofa I would be sleeping on each night. Someone said to me that essentially that qualified me as homeless, and to a degree that's true. I guess I could have always gone back home, although for much of that period I simply didn't have the money to buy a plane ticket.

Don't get me wrong, I wasn't sitting there feeling sorry for myself. It was a pretty wild and carefree time. Yes, it was hedonistic in a way; this period is what I would call my sex and rock 'n' roll time. That wasn't necessarily the big motivation, though; that was just a part of it. There was a lot of drinking. There were drugs on the scene, too, of course. Myself? I never did drugs, but people around me were doing blow and heroin and stuff like that. I spent a lot of my days just bumming around on Hollywood Boulevard trying to kill time, trying to stretch the day out, living on fifty-cent frozen burritos. Cash did go a certain way but it didn't go that far. I do remember stealing people's quarters out of a change jar and a few scrapes like that. I also remember occasionally asking for pocket change because everyone seemed to be doing that on Hollywood Boulevard. At times, it was literally hand to mouth . . . but I was loving life. You have to make the best of what is given to you, simple as that. It's all about survival tactics. Besides, I loved the people I was meeting. Happy times.

There was no goal there, no grand masterplan. It was just a case of, *This is great. I'm getting by, the sun is shining, people are super-friendly, I'm getting into gigs and clubs and partying, hanging out with cool people who are into the same music as me. I'm having a great time.* It was still an era when being English in America was a little bit of a novelty in a sense, so people were super-nice to me. I was only twenty, I looked cool and I was just having a good time. I was with a bunch of rebellious teenager vagabonds that were one step away from being runaways, and we had all come to LA from somewhere else . . . to find something else.

Chapter 4

Dreams, Jeans and a Hatful of Opportunity

Let me tell you the story about how I went from getting a $10-a-day job on Venice Beach to having my own fashion company and putting clothes on rock stars for the front of *Rolling Stone* magazine. How bad can it be, right?

You know now about my Hollywood years, the rock 'n' roll lifestyle, the bands, the gigs, all that. Well, when I think about that phase for a minute, as much fun as those times were, a lot of that was kind of dependent on other people's generosity. I was living off the goodwill and kind-heartedness of friends. I hadn't actually achieved anything personal to me, made my own mark or actually become able to stand on my own two feet. I was relying on other people's help, other people's sofas, other people giving me lifts. After a while, that became a little awkward. I was overstaying my welcome on this guy's floor and goodwill only goes so far before even the most patient of friends start getting a bit resentful.

Equally, the novelty was starting to wear thin for me, too. It was the same story over and over: go out at night, hit the rock 'n' roll joints and hook up with girls, then hang out in the day, always pretty skint . . . yes, have a good time, all well and good, but then that kind of got a little bit tiring, a little bit burnt out, a little bit like, *Fuck, what am I doing?* I was running out of money, I didn't actually have a proper job, I was even starting to think, *Am I going to have to go back to England again?*

So, eventually, I changed scene and moved in with a friend in Century City, outside of Hollywood. He worked nights, so we'd hang out together in the day. During this time, I met this chick in Venice called Linda, and I started hanging out with her. She was kind of a little bit in the hippy scene, a bit spiritual, a bit Zen, and we got on well. Venice was a lot more bohemian back then; although it's a bit more commercialized today, Venice's history is full of beatniks and hippies and counterculture, it has been genuinely hip since the fifties and sixties. So I immediately felt right at home there with the hippy/Grateful Dead/gypsy/vagabond vibe. At the boardwalk down by the beach, on the one side it was all artists selling whatever they'd personally made – paintings, ceramics, whatever – and on the other side it was basically cheap T-shirts and sunglasses, socks, baseball caps and a little bit of clothing. A very similar vibe to London's Camden Market. Venice Beach was also the second-biggest tourist destination in LA behind Disneyland, so there were always plenty of tourists.

One day I was walking down the boardwalk with Linda

when this English guy, who was selling second-hand clothing out of a stall, basically overheard me talking. I'm looking all rock 'n' roll, you know, tight pants, spiky hair, so I guess I stood out from the crowd, even down there. He said, 'Are you English?' and we started chatting. Turns out he was selling seconds from the Gap, boxer shorts and T-shirts and stuff like that, and, long story short, he offered me a weekend job. 'I'll pay you $10 a day. I basically need you to hawk and bring people into the booth and help sell shit.'

So that was my first 'proper' job in America, ten bucks a day, albeit only weekends at first. It was all 'Step right up, get your seconds from the Gap, buy one for ten, two for fifteen', that sort of thing . . . I took to that fairly naturally, and I can see that the confidence to do the sales pitch probably came from my grandad, who, as you know, was a market trader for ever. I believe that's where my instinct to sell and chat to people and enjoy that experience came from. Plus my mum's ability to do a hard day's work in any type of environment. That market trader, entrepreneurial spirit from way back in Sheffield was helping me out on the sunny boardwalk of Venice Beach.

I would cycle to the boardwalk on Saturday and Sunday to work long hours and always took pride in my work. I had no interest in the clothes I was selling, but it was paying me money. I was never afraid of hard work. There was a woman I met around the boardwalk who needed her house painting, so I ended up doing that as well, but I found that quite depressing. I was working very hard but not earning much from this woman, who wasn't very pleasant to work for. At the time, I wrote a postcard to Mum and said: 'I've been working on the same house for almost four months virtually on my own every day, which is often quite lonely and depressing . . .' Fortunately, I enjoyed my job selling this English guy's jeans at the weekends and I was getting close with Linda, to the point where I then moved in with her in Venice.

The pivotal part of the story at this point was not selling the 'crap from the Gap', it was seeing a guy on the next-door pitch to me who was selling second-hand clothing that just seemed way cooler. He was from New Mexico and was selling a little bit of everything but mostly Levi's, jean jackets, Western shirts, thrift-store stock. That gave me an idea: *Why not buy my own stuff and try selling it down here? How bad can it be, right?* Another postcard I sent to my mum at the time said: 'I would really like to start selling second-hand Levi's down the beach, which I think could be quite profitable at ten-to-twelve dollars a pair . . . although working down the beach means exposure to the sun, which is not good for my schoolboy complexion.'

With Linda being a bit of a hippy and me being a bit of a rocker-hippy, we liked to go to thrift stores and yard sales anyway, so during the week I'd go with Linda to the Salvation Army, places like that, trying to find cool stuff to sell ourselves. Venice Beach is super-packed on the weekend, but during the week the vending stalls or pitches, which were basically just plots in a car park, were mostly empty. You'd make 10 per cent of the money during the week that you did on the weekends, so I rented a stall for $10 a day and just had a clothing rack with a couple of pairs of Levi's on it, some old hippy paisley dresses, a couple of floral shirts – just a few items that we'd bought from thrift stores. Levi's had always been in demand. Levi's 501s were hugely popular in the early eighties in England when I was back in Sheffield. That popularity was a global phenomenon, and quite a cult had developed around certain types of Levi's – there were guys on the boardwalk that only sold Levi's and they'd grade them A, B, C or 1, 2, 3 depending on whether they were ripped up or not, were they 501s or were they zip fly, or were they Big Es or Redlines? It was all very specific, and there were collectors who knew all about these details. The prices basically went from, let's say, ten bucks to thirty bucks depending on how desirable they were.

Like I said, Venice Beach was very popular, so there might have been a hundred thousand people walking up and down each day at weekends, not just buying fake Ray-Bans but also buying these $10, $15, $30 Levi's. So I knew there was a market. However, there were also a lot of stalls selling a lot of clothes. So we had to offer something different . . . which is exactly what we did.

How?

We started putting patches on them.

On our first day, we made one hundred and fifty bucks.

Light-bulb moment.

I was like, *Fuck! This is better than working for the other guy for ten bucks a day!* Pretty quickly, my mind was racing. Suddenly, there seemed to be a thousand ideas and opportunities, and before long it wasn't just Levi's that we were customizing. For example, I bought a bedspread which was covered in jets and rocket ships and graphics like that. What I didn't realize was that it was a Peter Max bedspread, this renowned artist from the sixties who has painted for

51

presidents and is widely regarded as an icon of pop art. Among other styles, he was famous for doing these sort of psychedelic collages, very trippy, incredibly bold and striking. I bought this bedspread at a Salvation Army for like three bucks, cut it up and made patches for all these jeans. Remember, as a kid, I'd been into all those heavy-metal bands and I was always putting patches on my jeans and jackets, so this all felt very natural to me. Except this time around it was much more about Americana, inspired by my love of Evel Knievel, the *Dukes of Hazzard*, Captain America, the red, white and blue.

We also started buying old dashiki shirts with all these beautiful patterns, as well as vintage paisley cowboy shirts and dresses. The clothes we were making also tapped into a classic west-coast rocker look, so there were velvet pants, that southern look, Lynyrd Skynyrd, floppy hats and so on. This fitted in well with the whole atmosphere of Venice Beach, which at that time was still very much on the whole a Grateful Dead/Black Crowes vibe, mixed in with a splash of the Janis Joplin/Haight-Ashbury hippy shit.

Before we could blink, we were sewing constantly, selling tons of clothes and working very long hours. We were buying all these thrift-store items, putting patches on them and selling them on . . . and they were proving to be *very* popular. I was buying Levi's for fifty cents, a dollar, dollar-fifty, sometimes two dollars, at either yard sales or Salvation Army thrift stores. We'd do the rounds on the weekends, Mondays and Tuesdays, rarely spending more than twenty, thirty bucks, then go back to Linda's flat in Venice and start cutting them up and sewing patches on to jeans that we would then

sell for twenty-five bucks a pair. We were doing all this ourselves. Linda had a sewing machine, and we could probably
do a batch in an hour that would cost us no more than five
bucks in total, plus our time.

It all happened so quickly that there was a lot of trial and
error. We were throwing around ideas and changing price points
all the time. You know, 'We could've sold those for $25; let's put
some more patches on and see how they sell.' We'd find the Levi's
somewhere else cheaper, or maybe get a bulk discount, try a
different style – some ideas worked, others didn't.

All of a sudden, on some days we were completely out of
stock. At the time, I wrote another letter home to Mum,
saying:

> Finally found the motivation to put pen to paper, life for me
> is busy and rewarding and quite stimulating although some-
> times working at home can become a little bit intense,
> especially when the whole house is covered in fabric and pins
> and stuff . . . Hoping to start selling the jeans and select items
> of clothing to expensive vintage clothing shops soon.

Another postcard to my parents revealed just how quickly it
was escalating: 'Well, kids, almost a week and a half has
passed since I last wrote that card and the jeans business . . .
is almost to the point where we are now selling them quicker
than we can make them.'

That's when I first started to realize that if you work hard,
stay motivated, are creative and have your own individual
sense of style, you can achieve whatever you want to do.

Something was happening . . .

*

In quite a short time frame, the boardwalk stall was making good money and we were super-busy, selling a lot of jeans. When we weren't selling on the boardwalk, we'd put them in a duffel bag and go down Melrose and start selling to actual stores. There was no making an appointment to see the buyer, no formalities; we'd just walk right in with our bag of clothing and they'd pick what they liked. We might have been selling them for between twenty and thirty bucks on the boardwalk, so we'd wholesale them for like ten to fifteen bucks to these stores. That proved pretty popular, too, so the business was growing organically, and quickly. Within six months, we went from $150 on that first day to doing $500 during the week. We started renting a booth for the whole week, and that cost us somewhere in the region of a thousand bucks for the month, but on the weekends we were doing a grand a day, sometimes two grand a day. All cash.

One day, someone asked us if we could make a 'Cat in the Hat'-style hat. Truth be told, I didn't really know what they meant, because I hadn't read any of the Dr. Seuss books. But I got the book and thought to myself, *That looks pretty easy* . . . so we started making a pattern influenced by that request. At the time, there was a vogue for lining these big floppy hats with cheap black satin, but I just thought that was a bit simple. I figured if we could line it with something cool inside, then it would be reversible, which in turn would double its appeal.

Along the boardwalk there were also these people selling Guatemalan tams and caps, and one day I bought a floppy velvet renaissance hat, kinda like a court-jester style, and I started wearing that on the boardwalk. I bought one of those Guatemalan ones, too, for ten bucks, but then took it apart piece by piece and made a bigger, exaggerated version. I essentially just added like an inch to each panel, oversized the look. Then we started making these little hats that were reversible, but instead of doing them in the Guatemalan fabrics, we'd do them in velvets, kinda like an *Alice in Wonderland* vibe. Before you know it, we had a range of these big exaggerated floppy hats, as many as twenty-five different styles. Pretty quickly, that sort of became our niche. One of the hat tags from that range said: 'The exaggerated, whimsical shape is our distinctive trademark . . . to enjoy this hat at its best, wear it at all times and don't leave home without it.' We advertised the reversible hats as flexible enough 'to switch depending on which side of town you are on'. Aside from the patched jeans, we were selling these reversible hats for $12.50, top hats were $20, hooded jackets were $75 and velvet trousers were $50.

Our timing was fortunate because around 1988 and 1989 the rave scene hit. Back in the UK, bands such as the Happy Mondays and the Inspiral Carpets were at the forefront of rave culture, which centred around the so-called 'Madchester' scene. Rave was not a mainstream genre in the USA, but on the underground, certainly where I was, it was huge. There were all these fashion and merchandise companies that would do loud soap-box-style graphic print T-shirts with slogans saying, 'Rave On' or 'On Drugs' or 'E', and it became this whole big crossover scene that was sort of on the tail end of Burning Man/Grateful Dead/counterculture mashed up with skate/surf – this huge Californian cultural melting pot. They had superstar DJs that would fly in from London to perform at these underground rave warehouse clubs with big elaborate flyers being handed out. You were talking about thousands of people turning up. They were all wearing baggy jeans, overalls, patchwork and, yes, big floppy hats. That scene brought us a substantial volume of sales, so we were appreciative of the timing there, but no one gifted us that success; we had to work hard and act fast to keep up with the demand.

By 1989, we had so many styles and ideas that we needed to produce a catalogue. In that first catalogue, there were about a dozen hats – floppy ones, renaissance, court jesters with three pipes, a Lewis Carroll Mad Hatter short top hat and also a little renaissance cloche. The super-popular 'Cat in the Hat' style came in two sizes, a 12-inch one and a towering 24-inch option which we advertised as having 'enough fabric to cover the Earth . . . to enjoy this garment at its best, chill . . . and shape well before wearing'. They were all full-on whimsical pieces that sort of covered three bases: the Grateful Dead vibe, the southern rock scene and then also rave culture, all at the same time.

About a year into doing all this, we found out about a trade show in New York which could potentially open up our range to a massive new market, effectively nationwide. This was a considerable step up, but I just felt it was worth the risk. You know me by now . . . *Go with your gut instinct, Magnus.*

Linda had a friend who lived in Queens, so we stayed with him and took the train into the Javits Center for this NYC trade fair. Well, long story short, it turned out we were the big hit of the show and believe it or not we took $100,000 worth of orders, including one from the Disneyland theme parks, who bought 144 each of twelve styles. Another postcard at the time told my mum that, 'We are very busy, our trip to New York was great. We took in $70,000 of orders with just the hats. Now we need more sewers.'

We were on to something, but it was still essentially just Linda and me sewing like crazy. As my postcard home had pointed out, the problem was that we were expanding at a faster rate than we could physically cope with. If Disney were ordering 144 dozen hats and the jeans were being sold into certain stores a hundred pairs at a time, then something had to change. The bottom line now was that we couldn't make the gear fast enough to meet orders, so we started to look for a sewing contractor. However, when circumstances in the wider world took a very serious turn, demand for our clothes was about to ratchet up another notch.

Sometimes events in the outside world occur that you have no control over, that you can't plan for but that have repercussions in your own small world. In terms of my story, what happened was that in August 1990 the Gulf War broke out. This was an horrific conflict and naturally it was all over the news. Inevitably, like many conflicts over the years, it led to a surge in patriotism. How did this affect Linda and me? Well, at that time we had three core styles of jeans that were selling: chintzy floral/paisley patterns; the more hard-core, velvet psychedelic stuff; and then these red, white and blue, Stars & Stripes-inspired styles. I'd often be Downtown sourcing printed flag fabric on rolls, Stars & Stripes-style cloth, and we'd designed a number of styles inspired by those colours and styles, such as an Uncle Sam Stars & Stripes hat. Much of the styling and colour palettes were obviously personally inspired by legends from my childhood such as Evel Knievel.

Well, when the war broke out, suddenly people couldn't get enough of this stuff. Whether it was good fortune or not, the reality was that we had these styles already designed and available – we were ahead of the curve. And in business – I have seen this several times – being ahead of the curve is absolutely crucial.

We soon found a sewing contractor and that obviously eased the pressure on the manufacturing side, although conversely it also introduced a greater cost into the business. A typical week might see us buying some grade C Levi's for, let's say, five bucks. Then we were paying someone $5 to put the patches on them and $5 for someone else to sew them. In our apartment in Venice, there'd be a hundred pairs of jeans lined up in different sizes. Then we'd go wash them at the local Laundromat, come back to the apartment and stack them – I guess you could say we were working in our own little sweatshop! Seriously, though, we set up a bench table in the living room, we'd get the fabrics out on there and start cutting and sewing at night, modifying this, trying that, very creative, very enjoyable and, as it turns out, very popular.

We still had the stall on the boardwalk, but we had to employ two people to run that because it was more productive for Linda and me to be out and about sourcing garments and creating new styles than selling the stuff down there. We were still wholesaling to cool stores, and by now we had spread out from LA, too. For example, remember the Royal Oak area of Detroit that I'd enjoyed visiting so much when I was a disillusioned camp counsellor only a few years previously? Well, there was a really cool store there called Incognito that started buying our stuff.

Another great customer was NaNa, which was basically the main distributor of Dr. Martens in the whole of the US. They wholesaled and also had retail stores, and in their stores they carried the patched jeans, the floppy hats, quite a varied inventory of our stock. Within what seemed no time at all, we had over a hundred stores selling our stock.

We were seen as a breath of fresh air, because no one else was doing what we were. For the next couple of years, we kind of had the rule of the roost, we were the stars of the show. Both Linda and I put in some massive hours, neither of us were ever shy of hard work and, besides, this was all so exciting, so creative and very rewarding. I was pretty motivated, to say the least.

Financially, it was also very rewarding. We are talking thousands of dollars in some weeks. In a three-year period, I had gone from sofa-surfing, occasionally stealing a little bit of change and roughing it while watching the pennies, to all of a sudden making quite a lot of cash. We called that first company Venetian Paradise, because we were in Venice and at times that's what it felt like . . . I don't want to call it 'rags to riches', because in a sense that's for someone else to say but, truth be told, it kind of was.

Inevitably, we had to move production out of the apartment. We rented a big garage costing us two hundred bucks a month, which had no phone and no bathroom, so you'd have to go round the corner to use the bathroom. We had four people working for us from that garage, UPS was always coming at the end of the day to pick up these big orders as we shipped stuff out, people were mailing us cheques, stores were phoning up because they'd sold out (again), and we were dropping a few orders off ourselves. We were working hard and learning as we went along. Just because business was booming didn't mean we weren't always looking to keep costs in hand, too. For example, around the corner was a pet-supply place and we used to go there and get their surplus boxes to reuse and recycle, instead of paying for new ones. We never went above our means, so to speak. We were actually beginning to pay a bit of tax, and Venetian Paradise was really flying.

Back then, it was easier to get a social security number and open a bank account, plus I was paying tax and employing people. I kind of felt like, *Fuck, how bad can it be? What is the worst-case scenario? I could get deported . . . okay, I will have to face that if it happens.* That sense of energetic abandonment meant I took more risks than I would have done in England. I want to say I was reckless, but to be fair there was always a very strong sense of purpose. I wasn't just throwing random ideas around or taking loads of time off. I was super-motivated.

If it seems like quite a leap from bumming around the Hollywood scene to suddenly having this clothing business taking off, well, on the one hand I can agree with that. However, to me, there is a logic, a pattern, a common thread. Let me back up. Remember me telling you about doing all that running as a kid at the Hallamshire Harriers, from about nine years old to around thirteen? Well, I was super-motivated when I had that little bit of success. Maybe success isn't actually the right word – I think it's more that I am motivated when I find *something that I like to do*. Back at that young age, it was a simple dynamic – I really liked running, I became pretty good at it and I enjoyed the challenge. I've always liked challenges.

When I arrived in Los Angeles and was sofa-surfing and hanging out with all the rockers, I was having a great time socially, but I wasn't achieving anything or being challenged. Yes, those were good times in a lot of ways, and I don't regret them at all. However, there was no challenge in it for me. So when the clothing thing took off pretty quick, that represented a personal accomplishment. Finally, I was doing something that was successful and fulfilling and creative. This all happened purely organically and out of the blue; suddenly I had success and a job that needed creativity and drive. Fortunately, I teamed up with Linda and we got on great, we were very creative together. Suddenly, I could see a future in America, because I couldn't have sustained that somewhat nomadic, non-structured, temporary lifestyle I had been leading in Hollywood. That can only last for so long.

A huge part of the satisfaction I was getting from the clothing business was that I had made my own identity. I had become 'the crazy English hat guy on the boardwalk' in Venice and people would literally come down specifically to see me. Most days I'd wear a top hat that was eighteen inches tall and patched-up hippy jeans. I was modelling my own product. We even had a flyer that said, 'Look for the big hat!', and I would sign off my postcards and letters home with a little cartoon of a dude in a big hat, too. We started to get a little bit of press – a couple of magazines did pieces on us because everyone writes about Venice Beach. One magazine called us 'one of the hottest hat companies in the country'. The writer John Youngs said that, 'Venetian Paradise hats are slowly but surely working their way into the fabric of American and global culture.' In February 1991, there was an interview in *USA Today* and I even ended up in one of those Californian tourist books. Most importantly, I was doing something I enjoyed and it really was a success. The money was great, but it was more about standing on my own two feet and doing something a little bit different.

As always, I'd been writing back to my mum and earlier on, when I'd been struggling for money and work, she wanted me to come back to Sheffield, you know, 'Maybe it's not meant to be, Magnus . . .' that type of stuff. Just being a caring, concerned mum. However, throughout this whole period I was super-determined and motivated, so I'd just kept sticking it out . . . and now it had turned around. I knew I wasn't in the position I wanted to be *yet*, but I had ideas, dreams and very definite thoughts on how to get there.

Chapter 5

My First Porsche and a Lil' Georgia Peach

I never thought that I would actually physically own a Porsche. Obviously, coming from the working-class Sheffield background that I did, that was a reasonable assumption to make. Okay, I wrote that letter to Porsche when I was ten, but fast-forward into my late teens and early twenties and owning a Porsche was looking increasingly unlikely. Yet here I am, writing a book about my life principally because I am now classed by some people as one of the world's most high-profile Porsche collectors and modifiers. Funny old world, eh?

So let's talk about the story of how I became a Porsche guy. First, we need to backtrack a little. Back in 1988, when I was hanging out in Hollywood with all my musician mates and enjoying my rock 'n' roll phase, I didn't have a car; I didn't even have a driving licence. This was because as a teenager in the UK, my dad wouldn't let me drive his company car, so I actually never learnt to drive back then. I had tried, to be fair. My grandad Joe had a Renault 5 with the stick shift on the steering wheel, and in those days you could go to these old aerodromes on a Sunday and for a couple of quid you could go drive around trying to learn. When I hit seventeen, I took a few driving lessons on the road, but when I took my UK driver's test I actually failed! So from then on I went everywhere on the bus. It was no big deal to be honest; where we lived in Sheffield there was a bus stop just a hundred yards or so from the front door, so I went everywhere on the bus or I walked.

Even when I got to Los Angeles, I didn't initially feel that restricted, despite the fact that LA is really a city where everyone drives everywhere. However, after always having to catch lifts or use the buses in Hollywood, I started to get frustrated. I didn't really have the freedom to do what I wanted to do when I wanted to do it. So I took a driving test at the Santa Monica DMV, and luckily this time I passed. Straight away, I bought a cheap car. No, not a 911, not yet . . .

Remember my mate Johnny who was in the band and let me stay in his spare room? Well, his stepdad worked at Honda of Hollywood, and one day he said this car had come in on trade, so I went down there to take a look. That particular car was no good, but I ended up buying this 1977 Toyota Corolla 2TC instead. It was white, black cloth interior, four speed, not exactly a mechanical marvel, but I thought it was kind of a cool car for two hundred bucks.

I sort of taught myself how to use a left-hooker by driving that car around for a good few months. Back then I was carefree, I went with the flow. Like I say, that Toyota might not have been a rare Porsche, but I tell you what, that car represented freedom to me. All of a sudden, I wasn't waiting for someone to pick me up or having to leave somewhere early because my lift was going home. I loved that Corolla and have very fond memories of it. In fact, the Toyota connection still plays with my mind sometimes, because I have vague notions of one day doing an outlaw Corolla.

Eventually, I sold the Toyota for $200, so it had given me free motoring all that time. By then, I had set my sights a little higher, so I paid $6,000 for a Saab Turbo with the SPG package. Venetian Paradise was making good money at that point, and both Linda and I were working hard, so I was happy to spend that much more. We had a work van and this nice Saab, which was a quirky car. Venice was full of Europeans, so you did tend to see a lot of Volvos and Saabs around, which was kinda cool.

By 1992, the business was really booming. I wasn't going out clubbing any more; it was pretty much a case of working fourteen-plus hours a day, often seven days a week. We were earning real good money. That's when my eye was caught by a 1974 slant-nosed, wide-bodied Porsche 911. I had seen Porsches around Venice; in fact, they were kind of common. As you've seen from the clothing story, Venice is a cultural melting pot, so it was full of people leading alternative lifestyles, lots of creative types, plus transient folk and tourists coming through. There were certainly wealthy people in Venice and quite a few of them owned Porsches.

Now, we need a little historical context here. Buying a car back then was a very different experience to buying one in the modern internet era. Back then it was all about *Sports*

Car Trader and *The Recycler*, print magazines and swap meets. I often went to the Pomona Swap Meet, which is the biggest such event for cars in the area. I loved Pomona and still do. It's everything from VW parts to Chevy parts, probably a thousand acres, maybe a thousand cars. It's not just a 'For Sale' and swap meet, it's a show-and-shine too, so there are all these owners' clubs displaying their pride and joys. It's just a great place for car people to meet up.

That's where I saw this red slant-nose 911. I wasn't necessarily looking for a slant-nose, but it was seventy-five hundred bucks, and I just kind of bought it there on the spot. That was it. That in itself felt great. I was twenty-five. What a moment!

That to me was literally a dream come true, right there. I've spoken about how the clothing had given me that sense of accomplishment, a chance to be creative and work hard to achieve something; well, the Porsche represented a real personal sense of accomplishment, because I genuinely never thought I'd get to own one. This was fifteen years after I fell in love with that Martini Turbo at Earls Court, so to own one in my mid twenties was like, *Wow, I've arrived.*

I couldn't afford a Turbo, because back then they were probably twenty-five-grand cars. A slant-nose is a car that you either love or hate; they really polarize people. Personally, I love them. I think it's kind of this *Miami Vice* throwback vibe from the eighties.

For a while the slant-nose was a very popular look, so a slant-nose wide-bodied conversion of stock 911s was quite a common idea. I've read stories from guys that used to do restorations who had customers bring in a brand-new car that they had just bought and have them put flares on it and slant-nosed front fenders straight away; that was a real big trend during that era. There were the European after-market tuners doing work, such as Gemballa, RUF, DP, Kremer, and for a time it seemed like everyone was doing fibreglass conversions. That is one element of the brand that is so great; unlike other marques, Porsche is ultimately customizable, but we will come back to that idea later. If I recall correctly, DP and Kremer beat Porsche to their own punch and issued a version of that fantastic race car as a street 911. The Porsche Special Wishes programme of customer-ordered modifi-cations didn't really debut the factory slant-nose option until some time later. So the slant-nose was very much of its time.

I just wanted a Turbo-looking slant-nose, and this car was seventy-five hundred dollars. Porsche 911s were affordable back then (I have owned over fifty and, truth be told, only a handful have cost more than twenty-five grand. So I wasn't spending big money. A lot of the cars have been below ten grand and in the mid-teens). The slant-nose car started out as a '74 base 911, then someone had put the Turbo flares on there. So the car had the look, it was wide-bodied, it was Guards red, black interior with these flared arches. Therefore the car wasn't stock to begin with, but I got to customizing and doing a build straight away. It wasn't like I was messing with a matching-numbers car, one with original engine and transmission and so on, something with huge historical provenance. The car was already modified. It still had the original 2-7 motor in it, so it was kind of a little bit . . . I'm not going to say 'all show and no go', but that 2-7 motor is not the most potent power plant, in my opinion. In fact, I think my Saab Turbo might have been as quick, dare I say maybe even quicker.

There was a lovely guy in Venice called John 'Otto' Williamson who was a Porsche expert but is sadly no longer with us. He had an independent Porsche dealership around the corner from Gold's Gym (made famous by Schwarzenegger in the seventies and eighties), and he did the work for me (the best part of ten years later it was Otto who would get me into the Porsche Owners Club, more of which later). This was also one of my first experiences of the world of 'Porsche people', something that I will come back to over the course of my story.

I didn't have to put a three-litre engine in, of course, but to me the 2-7 just didn't seem fast enough. I'm like, *Fuck, this car looks fast but it's not fast*, so literally within a month I'm over to Otto's spending a few grand putting a three-litre SC motor in it. The day the new motor was finished, I do remember driving that car up to San Francisco. The three-litre is just more torque-y than a 2-7, you know. It's not tons of difference, but that was what I could afford. I think it was a four-grand motor swap/install. The car I bought was obviously on a budget, the build was on a budget. I didn't upgrade the suspension or motor, but at the time I was learning and I was in heaven – I had my own Porsche! I also pulled the carpet out and tried some velvet door panels, put on some chrome rims, just trying to customize it, add my own personality. These were pretty stock customizations that everyone was doing, but I immediately enjoyed adding my own touches, just as I had done with the clothing, the jeans, the hats – and would then do with property and much later the Porsche collection. I have always wanted to add my own individuality to anything that I am creatively involved with. I am fiercely passionate about that way of life, being creative with your own ideas in whatever area you want to work in, and that seems to be something that has struck a chord with people.

I kept that car all the way up until 1999, and I was so proud of it. I must admit I did do some spirited driving in that slant-nose. At one point, I got a letter from the DMV saying that, 'Driving was a privilege not a guarantee.' By the time I sold that car, I owned other Porsches, but that first one will always hold very special memories for me.

I'd started off down what I would later call 'the Porsche slippery slope' . . .

At this point, I'm still with Linda, and by then we'd rented a house in Culver City, a cool old 1920s house, so the Porsche was parked in the garage and I was mostly just driving it on the weekends. Still super-focused and motivated with the business, still working very long hours, still enjoying being creative. Venetian Paradise was doing well, but there were an increasing number of challenges. For one, we were no longer able to find enough Levi's jeans for just fifty cents to a coupla bucks, because the wholesale numbers were so high that we needed volume. Once you start struggling to get your source product, that makes life much harder. Then people started copying us. Where we'd be selling them for $25, these people could get them made in China and sell them in the US for $8. Other people started making cheap knock-off versions of our hats – far inferior but much cheaper, and that diluted the market still more. Then the subculture that had adopted our products so quickly and so widely started to change, as street culture always does. Rave started to die off and grunge was taking over, with a whole different look and feel.

This all meant that some of the key elements of why we had initially succeeded started to alter in ways that we couldn't control or even necessarily respond to. We noticed at the trade shows that people would stop coming to visit our booth, because sales had dwindled or you could buy the knock-off version of the cheap hats at a stand elsewhere. So what we needed was a new direction. A rebrand.

We were aware of these changes, so we started moving away a little bit from the patchwork styles and began to produce more of what is known as 'cut and sew'; in other words, making our own clothes. There was still a stylistic thread running through the range, so we had the Black Crowes/Jimi Hendrix/Doctor & the Medics look going on, but now we were creating more original clothing. To a degree, the hats were taking existing ideas as an influence and making them into something different; now we were creating these custom-made clothes from scratch. This was much more intense and creatively demanding, and also the process was far more laborious, but at the same time the end product was being sold for a higher price.

We started to have some success again. A few big-time rappers began wearing our clothes, such as De La Soul, Flavor Flav and Digital Underground. These musicians seemed to like what we were creating. Okay, we weren't musicians ourselves, but they seemed to like our style. Quite a few of these bands and rappers would come to the house in Venice and we'd make custom stuff just for them.

The rebrand went further than just creating more cut-and-sew items. We had been thinking for a while that 'Venetian Paradise' as a brand label was dated, that the business had moved on geographically and also stylistically, and so we decided that the name should change too. One afternoon, a few musicians were round at the house looking at the one-off pieces we were making and one of them said, 'Wow, this is some serious shit!'

That was another light-bulb moment. That's when Serious Clothing was christened.

One of the benefits of all those years of hard work was that we had already established an extensive network of stores and wholesalers that we could approach with the new line. Admittedly, the theme-park orders dropped off because the new clothing was not so much their style, but we replaced that with some pretty big alternatives. For example, we started wholesaling to a chain called Hot Topic, which at that point only had five stores, but in time it would grow to have over five hundred. They were buying our hats already, but now they started buying our clothing, too. So there was a new lease of life injected into the company, and a whole new chapter began.

By 1994, Serious had been going for a year, it was a full-on wholesale operation and we had half a dozen or so employees, including an office bookkeeper and a production guy. We'd moved out of the previous premises and into 760 Gladys in Downtown LA, a 5,000-square-foot warehouse that we rented. This space was where Serious really, really took off and grew pretty big. Plus, it was a cool old building, a converted former church. Once we'd moved Downtown, we became a lot more efficient; we weren't wasting time commuting, people were picking up orders and dropping off supplies, and that helped the business really grow. The Downtown move enabled us to be more productive, which in turn enabled us to be more profitable and spend more time creating stuff, as opposed to wasting time driving around.

I really enjoyed having this renewed success, along with a little bit of notoriety and money in my pocket. I'd got my own apartment (or an apartment in mine and Linda's names), I was paying tax, I'd got a bank account. All those things that I never had in England. Only a few years after I had been scrapping around for loose change in Hollywood, we were wholesaling about half a million bucks a year.

On a personal level, Linda and I had married, but by 1993 we had drifted apart, ultimately leading us to split up and eventually get divorced. I moved out of the apartment we'd previously shared. We had worked really well together but, like I said, over time we sort of drifted apart and ultimately we went our separate ways. Over the next year or so, I basically bought Linda out of the company.

By this point, Serious Clothing had really taken off. That was also the year that I met the love of my life, my beautiful wife Karen, whom I liked to call my lil' Georgia Peach. Let me tell you about how I was lucky enough to meet her. I recall first meeting Karen at the New York boutique show. She came into the booth, but we only had a short conversation. She tells the story where I didn't really give her much attention because I was too busy selling a bunch of clothes to some dude from Miami. But let me tell you, she had certainly caught my eye. How could she not?

Karen was living in Atlanta at the time, she had her own little clothing company called Hooch that was doing well and she was working for an independent designer, too. Hooch is southern slang for whiskey – you know, moonshine. The line was women's fifties glamour, Marilyn Monroe-type cut-and-sew stuff, with a little bit of a punk rock edge, very cool. Karen was super-sexy. She kind of had a little fifties vibe going on, blonde hair, Monroe-esque, just super-hot, super-sexy. She had a little bull ring through her nose and then later she had her eyebrow pierced. The Atlanta scene was different to LA, so she was very flamboyant, part pin-up girl, part rock 'n' roll, part Marilyn Monroe, this amazing southern fusion, this mish-mash of styles. Wow.

By then, I'd been doing trade shows for three years or so and I was a well-known face, established in those circles. The goal at these shows was always to do a killer line, launch it at the trade show, ship it and then sell a new updated version. Just keep rolling, more fuel for the fire. It was a lot of graft, but I used to really enjoy some of those trade shows. Sure, they were hard work, but you met some great people. Everyone was sort of in the alternative arena, they were all similarly aged, mid twenties, successful, making creative stuff, doing pretty well. The buyers for the retail stores were also of a similar age, so of course it was business during the day and then partying at night-time, usually in either New York or Vegas.

So I'd met Karen in New York, then a few months later we did a trade show in Miami called the International Jeanswear

Show, literally a couple of weeks after Kurt Cobain died in the April. That was where we started flirting at a magazine party at some hotel pool. I do remember there was a photo of her and me together at this party in Miami. I think Karen was wearing a little red Marilyn Monroe-style halter dress and she just looked super-hot. I think I told her that I liked her, but we still didn't hook up on that trip. Karen was in a marriage that was falling apart, we were similar ages, I was twenty-seven, Karen was twenty-nine, and she was kind of like the 'It' girl, even though she was relatively new on the scene. A while later, there was another trade show in New York, and that's when Karen and I finally hooked up. We went out clubbing together, just the two of us, and we had the most amazing time.

Not long after that, Karen moved from Atlanta to LA with her friends Liz and Chris. These glamour girls ended up renting a twenty-five-foot U-Haul trailer, and Karen drove that to LA with all their belongings. Let me tell you, they attracted a lot of attention from all the guys in LA! They were like Charlie's Angels; these girls had sort of come from nowhere, we called them the Atlanta Pussy Posse, and everybody wanted to know them. Absolutely *everybody* was hitting on them. For some reason, I was lucky enough that Karen wanted to be with me.

Karen was a lot more extrovert than I was, but we completely clicked. She started off staying with the parents of her friend Liz's boyfriend in Costa Mesa, and soon after relocating she phoned me at the Serious office because I didn't have a cell phone back then. I guess I was a little . . . not aloof on the phone but not quite as chatty as she had expected, and she tells the story that she came off that call and was like, *Well, I guess I misjudged that situation . . .*

What she didn't know was that I didn't want to talk in the office in front of people, so as soon as she put the phone down I pretty much raced out of the building and called her straight back from a payphone around the corner. We arranged to meet that Sunday at this local bar called the Dresden in Los Feliz, at two o'clock. I showed up right on time, which I think impressed her (Karen always liked the fact I was very thorough and prompt with arrangements; she was always really kind about that).

Now, I told you Karen had the most amazing style, right? Well, you'll love what she was driving at the time – an absolutely huge four-door Cadillac from the sixties, which was pretty spunky. Remember, this woman was ninety-five pounds, five foot tall, this petite bombshell riding around in this absolutely massive boat of a Cadillac. Of course, she looked fantastic in it. She showed up in a short miniskirt with some biker boots on and a little T-shirt that said 'Star Fucker'. I went there in my Saab, because even though I had the Porsche at that point, I didn't want to appear like I was showing off; I was trying to be low key. I was wearing black swirl velvet pants with pointy shoes, and I think I had a cowboy shirt on or something similar.

For some reason, the bar was closed, so we parked the Cadillac up and I drove her around doing my infamous LA sightseeing tour. I love to show people around LA. I've always thought I would be a good tour guide, actually! I love showing people the theatres, talking about the glory days of Mary Pickford, Charlie Chaplin, Douglas Fairbanks Jr, United

Artists, all those guys in these elaborate theatres Downtown. Then you can drive to see the Hollywood sign, the Griffith Observatory, all that tourist stuff. That night, Karen really enjoyed the full tour and then we ended up at a bar in West Hollywood that had some sort of happy hour on a Sunday night. We met a few friends and were together all the way through to ten o'clock before Karen had to drive back to Costa Mesa. Essentially, after that first date, that was it – we were *inseparable*.

During those first six months of Karen living with her friend in Costa Mesa, I think she only spent six nights there. She was pretty much spending all her time with me Downtown but still commuting back to Costa Mesa. I was just completely bowled over by her.

She actually moved in with me pretty quickly, around early 1995. We were a similar age and shared similar back-stories, and we were now on the same path, sharing the same mind-set. Pretty soon we were finishing each other's sentences. I will come back to Karen many, many times . . . but for now, let me just say that we were a match made in heaven.

Chapter 6

Serious Gets Serious

As a couple, Karen and I were inseparable, but it quickly became apparent that there was a very natural synergy professionally and creatively, too. Around this time, her business Hooch got a big order with Hot Topic for some leopard-skin pants, the biggest order she'd ever had, and she was obviously all excited. I helped her get them made, but the fucked-up thing was that I guess the pattern was wrong or there was some kind of problem, because after she shipped them to Hot Topic she got a call saying the pants didn't fit, they were too narrow around the ankles. We teamed up together and put a zipper on the sides so that customers could get the pants on, and Hot Topic actually accepted the order. That was the first thing we did together from a business point of view.

Within the first year, Karen decided that it was too much of a struggle with her smaller line and so she basically let Hooch just sort of fade and joined me and my team. That was the beginning of what I like to call 'the glory years' of Serious. In my opinion, up until that point Serious hadn't fully formed its style – it was a little bit all over the place, it had a bit of skate stuff and a little rock 'n' roll but wasn't fully formed. When Karen and I teamed up together, she bought the southern charm and I guess I brought the northern English edge. We designed the line together, bouncing ideas around, all influenced heavily by my and Karen's personalities. I did the men's clothes, Karen designed the women's, but we'd often use the same fabrics on our respective lines and they'd complement each other, co-ordinating separates and details like that. When Karen started working on the women's line at the big warehouse Downtown at Gladys, there was much better cohesion, it all fitted. The women's line quickly began to get a whole lot better and, of course, from a business point of view, that meant sales began to increase.

I believe that part of the key to Serious's success – and this applies to any creative business – is that we designed what we personally wanted to wear. We didn't follow trends. We set trends. A common thread in my life has been the pursuit of two words – *individual style*. I strongly believe that whatever you do, you must try to do it with individual style.

We were both now in our early thirties and we were really cooking. We'd both gone through our respective twenties playing around and working hard, and obviously we'd both come out of broken relationships. We were head over heels in love and enjoying each other's company. We had both gone through a fair share of drama, and I guess the relationship was a breath of fresh air. I had finally found my soulmate, and I think Karen had found hers. It was just a really super-fun, creative period where we got on like a house on fire. We lived together, worked together, partied together, created together – everything just clicked. We were a dream team.

Karen was starting to get a little more edgy, and I remember cutting her hair short and spiky. Then she wanted dreads, and so I did those for her, which she then started dying red and blue and yellow and orange. Meanwhile, I dyed my blond hair black – it was more like Twiggy from Marilyn Manson. At this point, even though we were working really hard on Serious, we were also going out a lot, three or four times a week, every week, and to a degree we became one of Hollywood's rock 'n' roll 'It' couples. We never had to wait in line at a nightclub, we were always whisked in free – 'Hoochy, Magnus, come on in,' you know, drinks tickets at the bar. We felt like we were rock 'n' roll royalty, going to these clubs such as Cherry, Whisky A Go Go and the Pretty Ugly Club on Santa Monica Boulevard (which was run by Taime, the guy who had bought those PVC pants from me way back). We were backstage at every rock show we wanted to go to, hanging out with all our buddies who were in bands, and these various musicians would regularly come down to the warehouse to get clothing – we'd pretty much give clothing away to bands that we liked. By now, nothing was stopping us, we were just on a roll; these were the glory days of going out and nightclubbing until 2 a.m., having fun, working hard and just loving being with each other. People thought we were the cutest couple in town.

These cut-and-sew styles we were creating were proving exceptionally popular, including with a large number of famous people. Actually, a performance artist was one of the first to use our clothes on stage. Soon, there was a real variety of pretty big names wearing our clothing, such as Alice Cooper, Chris Isaak, No Doubt, Social Distortion, Porno for Pyros, White Zombie, Stone Temple Pilots, Stabbing Westward, Nine Inch Nails, Marilyn Manson, plus all the local bands. Our gear was in a lot of music videos, and bands were always coming by the warehouse. During that golden period, we gained a lot of notoriety in fashion magazines, and stylists would be pulling our stuff out all the time. We were on the cover of everything from *Vogue* (on the original British supermodel, Twiggy) to *Axcess* (Gwen Stefani), *Rolling Stone* (featuring Belly all wearing Serious in April 1995), *Just Seventeen* and many more. *Action Retailer* flagged the company up as one of 'Ten Ones To Watch', while *Alternative Press* magazine interviewed me and I was quoted as saying, 'I'm inspired by fast cars, hot rods and rock 'n' roll.' I also said, 'We don't aim to please the masses; we aim to please the individuals who are looking for something different.' This rock 'n' roll edge was reflected in our catalogues and market-ing at the time. The earlier hand-drawn flyers and brochures had been replaced with glossy, professionally produced colour brochures, such as one featuring a page with Johnny Cash, a Dodge Super Bee, the Black Crowes, motorbikes, Nashville Pussy, Karen with her gap-tooth smile and a photo of me.

Away from the party scene and the celebrity clients, the clothing industry back then was quite a close-knit community; there might have been fifty well-known companies, but the top few were Serious, Lip Service and Trip. Serious was considered to be in the top tier. Karen and I were a very tight team. Buyers hated that because they knew when they came

Left: Missing front teeth at an early age, with my brother.

Below: My sister, aged seven.

Above left: 6 Bents Green Road, Sheffield, the last place I lived in before I moved to America.

Above: My mum, brother and me, poolside in the glamorous seventies.

Left: Nether Green Middle School, Sheffield.

Right: Silverdale High School uniform.

Sheffield Federation for School Sports

CROSS COUNTRY
MIDDLE SCHOOLS' CHAMPIONSHIP

SIXTH INDIVIDUAL

19 7

CERTIFICATE AWARD

to Magnus Walker
Nether Green Middle School

SOUTH YORKSHIRE SCHOOLS' A.A.
AFFILIATED TO E.S.A.A.

Cross Country
Championships 1980

Junior Boys

AWARDED TO

Magnus Walker

1st PLACE

TEAM AWARD

Left: Aged ten, getting ready to run with the Hallamshire Harriers.

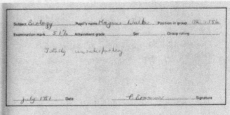

Subject Biology   Pupil's name Magnus Walker   Position in group 11th of 156

Examination mark 5.1%   Attainment grade   Set   Group rating

Totally unsatisfactory

July 1981   Date   P. Lessware   Signature

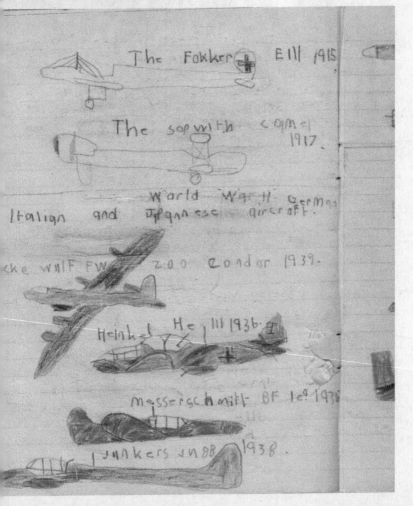

The Fokker E III 1915

The sopwith camel 1917.

World War II German,
Italian and Japanese aircraft.

...cke wulf FW 200 Condor 1939.

Heinkel He III 1936.

messerschmitt BF 1e9 1936

Junkers JN 88 1938.

Above: My class at Silverdale School, 1983.

Right: Camp America acceptance letter, 1986.

CHEERS

PUBLISHED FOR CAMP AMERICA PARTICIPANTS

JULY 1986

ATTENTION CAMP AMERICA PROGRAM PARTICIPANT:

We realize that as much fun as it is, it's a short summer. Many of you have already called us to ask about your return flights. Confirmation of your return flight date is as follows, please note that this is your official confirmation and you must bring it with you to the airport to recieve your flight ticket.

```
001781    CAMP OZANAM
3115      MAGNUS WALKER
EC-22
2
```

Please use the key below to find the date corresponding to the flight number indicated on the label:

EC-24	SUN	AUG 24	EC-16	TUE	SEP 16
EC-27	WED	AUG 27	EC-17	WED	SEP 17
EC-4	THU	SEP 4	EC-19	FRI	SEP 19
EC-8	MON	SEP 8	EC-21	SUN	SEP 21
EC-9	TUE	SEP 9	EC-22	MON	SEP 22
EC-12	FRI	SEP 12	EC-25	THU	SEP 25
EC-14	SUN	SEP 14	EC-28	SUN	SEP 28

OTHER CODES ARE AS FOLLOWS:

EC-200, EC-300, EC-400, EC-500 = You have yet to give us a return date according to our London office.
EC-100 = not returning
EC-200 OT, EC-300 OT, EC-400 OT, EC-500 OT = You have made own travel arrangements and did not come over on a CAMP AMERICA flight.

AMERIPASSES/TRAILWAYS: There are still a number of these passes available through the LONDON OFFICE. Please contact them NOW to order them and make sure to send the extra $1 for recorded delivery as we want to make sure you receive them before leaving camp.

You will find a FLIGHT CHANGE form attached to this newsletter. No change will be considered without the $25 fee and changes will only be made on the basis of availability. If a flight change cannot be granted, your fee will be refunded. The deadline for all flight changes is August 5. IF YOU ARE NOT PLANNING TO RETURN TO LONDON WITH CA, PLEASE LET US KNOW IMMEDIATELY!

US OFFICES: 102 GREENWICH AVENUE   EUROPEAN OFFICES: 37 QUEEN'S GATE
GREENWICH, CONNECTICUT 06830 USA   LONDON S.W.7 5 HR ENGLAND

Left: Venice Beach *c.* 1990–1991, twenty-four years old.

Below: Karen and me, *c.* 1995.

Top: KROQ Weenie Roast 1996, twenty-nine years old.

Above: Serious Clothing patterns.

Above right: Serious Clothing sewing machines.

Clockwise from top left: Serious Clothing catalogues and stickers; Karen, me and Alice Cooper, *c.* 2001.

Right: Karen, me and puppy Skynyrd, *c.* 2002.

Above and right: 1 May 2005, our wedding day, The Hotel, Las Vegas. Karen and I kept it simple and decided to go to Vegas to get married on our own.

to our booth intent on spending just five grand, Karen and I would get a hold of them and they'd end up spending twenty!

On the business side, we had grand plans. Wholesale and trade fairs were great business, but we both wanted our own store. So, in 1996, we opened up a shop on Melrose. This was less than ten years since I was a skint Englishman abroad, walking into Retail Slut, sweating in my $9.99 PVC alligator pants while chatting to Taime. We had some people say that opening our own store was a big risk, but to our way of thinking it was an easy choice. Decisions for Karen and me happened real quick. All the time, we both said, 'Go on gut feelings.' A few of our friends had stores in New York, and they were doing well; owning your own retail space is very good for product development, the margins are better than wholesale, and it's a good way to keep in touch with what the customer likes and how they feel. You get real-time, regular feedback on how your clothes fit, how they hold up, if there are any issues with them or ways they can be improved. A lot of times when you ship something to a wholesaler, you never really get any feedback unless there's a problem. So for us, it was a no-brainer. A lot of work, yes, but not a big risk, at least not in our minds anyway.

Karen had worked in retail before, and I'd sort of worked in retail on the beach, so we had some experience to bring to the plan, too. We outfitted the store with a gothic look, all these leopard-skin fabrics, gold walls and velvet carpets. Here's a nice twist to the story. I just mentioned Taime, the guy from Faster Pussycat who bought those pairs of PVC pants off me when I first landed in LA. Well, by this point his band had started to tour less, so he actually came and worked at the Serious store, which kinda brought that part of the story full circle. I drove down Melrose recently while researching this book and a lot of the stores are vacant now, but back when we opened up the Serious store, on the weekend all the beautiful people were there, handing out flyers, promoting bands, hanging out. It was buzzing.

Karen and I were rarely at the store ourselves because we were too busy focusing on the wholesale side of the business. At first, we only sold our own range of clothing, but after a while we started stocking alternative labels, because we figured not everyone wanted just the Serious brand and it felt important to offer people variety. What we tended to do was buy stock from our friends' lines, which was real fun and created a lot of goodwill. So we were learning all the time as the business evolved. I think you have to maintain that interest, that curiosity to learn, always.

The store being on Melrose was great brand exposure for us, because every rock 'n' roll band that played in LA would go down Melrose shopping for wardrobe, so that sort of opened the door to outfitting yet more big names. The retail store became a popular destination for some of these rock stars. Those guys would often come down to the warehouse, but sometimes if they were only in Hollywood for a day, maybe staying on the Sunset Strip and playing somewhere nearby, it was just easier to go down to the store on Melrose. Sometimes we'd even have bands playing small sets in the store.

I've had people say they wouldn't want to deal with all the pressure and overheads of a retail business like that. But it was never really an issue and wasn't something that stressed me out. Sure, it was busy and you had to be on top of your game, but we were never really 'five-year-business-plan' type of people. We just dove straight in and built it, and this thing grew organically. We put the effort in, the hard work and the dedication; we were both super-focused. We saw an opportunity and we just kept going at it, on and on and on . . .

The second half of the nineties were great years. We were still going out a lot, maybe three times a week around town, and to be fair that was great exposure for our brand, because we were wearing Serious clothes and hanging out with high-profile people. Meanwhile, the shop was selling a *lot* of clothing, and the wholesale side of the business was very busy, too. We were fully in our stride back then, we had a couple of sales reps, an office manager, two production people, we were doing a thousand pieces of this, a thousand pieces of that, selling three to five thousand units to Hot Topic on one order and so on. Serious was really cooking. After three years of trading on Melrose, we moved to a better location further down the street. Essentially, we were selling the same merchandise, but the new location was outfitted in more of a sixties pop-art style, with big Plexiglas backlit display cabinets and a really cool vibe. We spent a lot of money fitting that store out, but the company was doing super-well. By the mid to late nineties, we were doing more business than we had ever managed before, probably up to three million bucks a year.

There was always a buzz of energy in the warehouse when Serious was at its peak. There was a great team who were all focused on the same goal. Every day, there was excitement, anticipation, people buzzing around, we'd be shipping boxes out, designing new ranges, getting clothes manufactured, the steam would be hissing off the irons, the sewing machines would be rattling away, Karen and I would be doing a little bit of everything – designing, trying to sell stuff, on the phones making sure fabric was coming in – it was non-stop. The building has a creative vibe and Serious filled that space with creative individuals, all working hard and for a common goal.

By this point, I'd been in the US for around ten years. Serious was running at full steam, we'd opened the retail stores, we were a top-five company in our sector, doing great. We were doing tons of wholesale, making good money, selling a thousand hats a week at one point. Yet I couldn't fly home to Sheffield because I didn't have a green card. Believe it or not, I actually missed my brother's wedding because I didn't have my paperwork in order, which meant it wasn't a certainty that I'd be able to get back into the country if I flew to the UK for the ceremony. That was too big a risk – Serious was really exploding, and everything I had was here in LA. I didn't want to get deported – fuck, that would not have been cool.

Luckily, I did get to see my family occasionally – my parents and close family had come out a couple of times to stay with me at what I called 'Hotel California', because we had a big loft and plenty of room. I became a pretty polished tour guide.

Even though I had overstayed my official welcome, I had a social security number, a bank account, I had been paying tax and I employed around six people at the time. Although if I left the country I might not get back in, they weren't going to come looking for me. However, I had to protect myself at that point, so I applied for a green card through a system that's known as 'first preference', where essentially they issue them to individuals who can show some degree of artistic merit, in other words people who are contributing creatively and positively to the USA. They don't want you taking jobs off Americans; in reality, I was creating jobs for Americans, but I still had to go through this very lengthy process.

Proving I had artistic talent meant getting letters of recommendation from my peers. As you now know, Serious had been pretty successful, with our clothing used in music videos and on MTV, on the covers of *Rolling Stone* and *Italian Vogue* and all these magazines, so I wrote to hundreds of people I'd done business with, asking for a reference. This wasn't something that happened overnight, it took months and months of perseverance, but we eventually managed to collate references from the likes of Alice Cooper, Chris Isaak, *Glamour* magazine, Walt Disney TV and MTV among literally dozens of others, with people saying things like, 'Magnus is sterling, he is liked and respected for his integrity, loyalty and professionalism throughout the industry.' In the end I'd dotted all my i's and crossed all my t's and documented this in a huge folder, along with press clippings, articles and catalogues. It was a real substantial piece of work, a massive undertaking. I still have all those letters of reference, and they are something I am very proud of.

I finally had my interview for the green card in the basement of this vast immigration services building, like something out of *The X-Files*. On the day itself, I distinctly remember that staff there were not particularly helpful. I was very apprehensive, because I didn't really know what was going to happen and this was a pivotal, life-changing moment. I remember the guy that did the interview just had no personality; it was almost like these people enjoyed putting me through misery. I remember him saying to me at one point, 'What makes you so special?' I said, 'Well, I never said I was special . . . but here is the documentation showing that I have qualified in these ten categories that the green-card system is based on'. If they'd said 'No', I don't know what I would've done. I'd worked for years with the clothing companies, then spent months and months compiling this folder of documents and then this painful interview, then I was just sitting there waiting for a decision.

Thank fuck that in the end they said I'd passed. I was so pleased, I can't tell you. I asked where I could go and pick up my green card, and they said, 'We'll post it to you.' I was like, 'What? Can't you UPS it or something?' At that point, the loft we were living in wasn't necessarily getting mail all the time. I wanted to get my hands on this card, but, no, that was not how it worked. I said, 'What happens if it gets lost?' and he goes, 'Well, that's not our responsibility. We mail it to the address you supply, but once it leaves here it's not our responsibility.' So that's what they did, they just mailed it. The funny thing was, when it arrived (thank God) I remember it came in a handwritten envelope!

There's a funny postscript to the whole green-card story. After I got it, we started doing trade shows in the UK because I was able to fly there and be sure that I was definitely going to get back in the country. This one trip, Karen and I went off, worked really hard and had a great time in England, as usual. When it came time to fly home, we headed for Heathrow and I was feeling completely relaxed, my green card safely in my pocket. Now, the reality is that after I'd ripped open that handwritten envelope from Immigration, I'd never looked at my green card again. You never really need to; it's not something that you carry around every day like your driver's licence. The green card goes with your passport, and if you don't travel for a year or two, you don't look at it. So we get to Passport Control at Heathrow and they ask for my documents. I pull out the green card and hand it to the guy in charge.

'Sir, this green card has expired.'

Shit!

'Is that a problem?'

'You can't board the plane without a valid green card, sir.'

Fuck!

This was a Friday and then they told me that the embassy wasn't open until the Monday morning. 'You are going to have to apply for a temporary replacement green card and that could take up to two weeks.' *Shit!* Obviously, we were panicking, Karen was really worried and we just didn't know what to do. They were really helpful, to be fair, and called over this American Homeland Security guy to chat to us. We explained to him what was going on. Long story short, no word of a lie, turns out he was a Porsche guy! We were chatting away about Porsches and cars and then, after ages talking about 911s, he issued me with a twenty-four-hour emergency green card.

'Safe flight, sir. Enjoy those cars when you get back home.'

Porsche people, eh?!

Of all the famous faces who became our customers at Serious, one of our all-time favourites was Alice Cooper. We first met him through a friend of a friend who was his guitar player, Ryan Roxie. They called us up basically wanting some clothing, and we were like, 'Sure! Come on down, no problem.' We gave clothing away to people that we liked. It didn't matter about money – these people were going to wear our stuff, it was great exposure. So we first outfitted Ryan, and then Alice himself came down. Bearing in mind my love of rock music, you can imagine how exciting that was for me. This one Saturday afternoon, Alice Cooper just walked into the warehouse with his personal assistant and, I've gotta say, he was really nice. After that first visit, we started personalizing and making custom clothes for him. It was a lot of effort making custom clothes for individual customers. From a commercial point of view, we'd sooner be selling a thousand of one style rather than making a single bespoke piece. However, when Alice Cooper asks for your clothing, you create some cool stuff for him! He will wear that gear and give you fantastic exposure, plus we loved the thrill of the opportunity . . . *Shit! We're making clothes for Alice Cooper!* Imagine if I'd known that all those years ago when I was getting into Rebels in Sheffield for free and sipping on my 50p pint.

We started collaborating with Alice and making a sizeable part of his wardrobe – his pants and jackets. He'd come in and say, 'I really love those pants, but I kinda would love them more *Mad Max: Road Warrior* style . . .' At the time, we were doing a lot of this *Mad Max*-inspired, vinyl, leather-looking distressed clothing with bullet holders and patches. It looked kind of like a combination of *Alien*-meets-*Mad-Max*-meets-biker. Alice was very collaborative and so it was pretty straightforward to create clothing for him. We knew what size he was, we had a bespoke Alice Cooper pattern, he was a relatively slim guy. Super-easy to work with.

My favourite ever Alice Cooper moment was when I was lucky enough to actually go on the road with him. He kept saying, 'You've got to come on tour with us,' and I'm like, 'Sure, why not?!' So Karen and I flew to Vegas, saw his show and then Karen went back to LA while I jumped on the tour bus and rode with the guys from Vegas to New Mexico and then from New Mexico to Denver on the next leg of the tour. They were offstage by 10.30 or 11 p.m., but backstage was no longer the rock 'n' roll party lifestyle that it was in the seventies. Everyone was basically clean and sober. They played a lot of cards on the bus. Now, I don't necessarily play cards, but if Alice Cooper invites you to play cards, you go play cards! Eventually, you'd climb into your bunk, sleep for three or four hours, then arrive at the next gig and start all over again. Alice would often go and play golf or shop; in New Mexico, I remember going thrift-store shopping with him. That was all great, real fun memories.

Alice was always super-duper cool and always went out of his way to look after us. This is how nice Alice is – in my warehouse, I have a cool leather jacket that he signed and gave to us. This isn't something that we made for him; this was his own personal jacket from the seventies that he wore around the *Billion Dollar Babies* era. Alice Cooper is just so down-to-earth. A very cool guy.

Other stars we had little or no contact with. A friend of ours was a stylist and had bought some clothing for Madonna that apparently she liked, which gave us a buzz. We ended up having to make a dozen of the same outfit so that she could have enough for the whole tour. She had several costume changes during that show and we provided the punk rock style costume that she needed.

LA, the land of opportunity, eh?

Chapter 7

A Diamond in the Rough

By the late nineties, Karen and I were in our early thirties and really enjoying life. We were living in a good-sized rented loft in Downtown LA, around 3,500 square foot. We were also renting a 5,000-plus-square-foot warehouse to run Serious Clothing from. So we were, in effect, paying two other people's mortgages. We had credit at the bank, we were making good money, the business was established and profitable, all our bills were paid on time . . . but we didn't physically own any property. So we felt that we needed to take the next step and get our own building. To be fair, Karen pushed for that. She'd owned a house in Atlanta, so she sensed that we needed to own property together.

One day Karen came back and said she'd seen an old warehouse on Willow, Downtown LA, that she really liked. I went over to take a look and, truth be told, at first I didn't necessarily fall in love with the building. So we passed on it and kept searching for the right place. Looking back, Karen maybe had more of the vision for the building than I did. She was exceptionally clever.

At one point, we were house-hunting in Hancock Park, but a couple of months passed by and we still hadn't found a place we both loved enough to buy. Then one day I just thought, *Fuck it, I'll call the broker and see if that warehouse on Willow is still for sale.* Ironically, they had actually put the price of the building up a little bit since our first viewing. We were already approved by the bank for the finance we'd need to buy the place, so, without telling Karen, I viewed the warehouse again . . . and I bought it. That night I went home and said, 'Hey, Karen, guess what I did today? I just bought us Willow!'

Just like the store on Melrose, buying the warehouse was another leap of faith – one of many I have taken with Karen at crucial times in my life. I would recommend that if your gut instinct is telling you to go for it, then you should do that, too (I will come back to that idea because it is very important). At the time, people thought we were crazy because back then Downtown LA was not the trendy, artsy, bohemian place that it has since become. In the mid eighties, when I moved to LA, nobody really came Downtown. There was the jewellery district and the shops, but at night-time there was nothing really going on. There certainly weren't organic delicatessens where a bunch of sandwiches will cost you fifty dollars and a coffee is five bucks. Far from it. It was a desolate landscape of industrial warehouses, with abandoned shopping carts tipped over at the side of the road. Not especially dangerous, but there were a ton of transient homeless people living in tents under the bridges, prostitutes giving blow jobs to truckers. It was not uncommon to see homeless people sat on a milk crate taking a shit on the side of the road. It was that type of neighbourhood. However, for us the warehouse had great bones, we had a shared vision and we loved projects. This was a blank canvas. A challenge. The decision to buy a huge run-down warehouse in the middle of such an area wasn't something that seemed overwhelming. We were just firing on all cylinders, in unison, with this attitude of, *Fuck it, we can conquer anything, we can take on the world, nothing's going to stop us.* We were like a steamroller, full speed ahead.

The finances stacked up, too. The new mortgage didn't cost us much more than the two sets of rent we had been paying, so we went for it. Just like the retail store in Melrose, we didn't really overthink it. At the time, truth be told, the warehouse did feel expensive, but that was partly because we'd never bought anywhere before. Yet fifteen years later, at the time of writing, it's probably worth fifteen times what we paid for it. That's a pretty good return on our investment. I'm not sure I can claim our crystal ball was *that* polished, but it is safe to say that the decision came from a gut instinct that we were brave enough to act on . . . and it's paid off.

But I'm getting ahead of myself. We bought the building in 2000, then moved Serious in during the September, and then in the summer of 2001 we moved into upstairs as our home. The plan had always been to use the warehouse as a traditional live/work loft. There was absolutely no intention of the space becoming a rentable asset – which I will get to in a moment – we just wanted somewhere cool to live and work that we actually owned ourselves.

Before we could do any of that, though, we had to refurbish and renovate the building. The warehouse was built in 1902 and it's big, over 26,000 square feet, essentially spread across three continuous buildings (the core is 1902, then more was added in 1928 and finally the garage where I store most of my cars was built in the fifties). It had always been an industrial building and warehouse space, and it was used for storing truck parts at one point. We bought it from a Korean garment guy who was using it as a denim jeans cutting facility. He'd bought it maybe ten or so years previously, probably for next to nothing. Before that at some point, we believe it was unofficially converted lofts, but it is quite hard to ascertain the exact history of the building over the decades. There weren't necessarily squatters in there, but it wasn't correctly zoned for residential living, it was more of a commercial industrial space. At some point, believe it or not, it seems that Madonna shot one of her very early videos there, which was interesting given what the warehouse would later evolve into.

As I've said, the bare bones of the warehouse were sound; we really liked the carcass, so to speak. Inside, however, there was a huge amount of work to be done. Due to its industrial history, the building had a lot of deferred maintenance issues. So although the warehouse had good structure and was fully sprinklered (plus it had been retro-fitted to meet all the existing earthquake safety standards), it suffered from ageing problems, for example the roof was very battered and leaky, and there was a hole in one corner upstairs that would leak all the way down to the floor below. There were dead rats everywhere. It had one bathroom but that was like the one in

Trainspotting. It was just a pigsty, a little bit of a flop house. What we did was convert it legally through a specific housing policy – back then the city was open to the adaptive reuse of former industrial property. This was essentially the first phase of LA's inner-city gentrification boom.

We began fitting the warehouse out as our dream live/work space, so there was no compromise. We were very happy to put a lot of money into the property to create our own vision, so it was no holds barred. We started off by sandblasting everything to get rid of all the paint – everything was painted either white or grey. All the brick upstairs was painted, the floors were painted, the skylights were covered, it was coat after coat of thick industrial paint that had been caked on over decades. The skylights were tarred over and covered in garbage bags to stop any leaks. The sandblasting was laborious and very invasive, so we hired a specialist crew; the mess was insane, but it left us with acres of exposed brick and beams, which looked cool.

Karen and I became project managers. We weren't really swinging hammers ourselves; we'd bring people in for that while we oversaw and designed the build. Every week, we were writing cheque after cheque after cheque, but we were firing on all cylinders, so we just blasted through it all. If something feels right, we invest in it. Whether it's time, energy, money or all of the above. The warehouse is kind of the perfect example of the way we worked, I think.

We would put duct tape on the floor of these huge open spaces to mark out where the partition walls might go – 'This is where the bedroom is, we'll put the kitchen here, this will be the living room.' The construction crew that we had working at the retail store in Melrose used a French carpenter who we then just kept on for almost another year. There was some very complex and detailed carpentry work, because it was being done out of passion and as a labour of love. To do that properly takes time. For example, the library alone took three months. We weren't going to stop/start, stop/start, because that's what a lot of people do and consequently projects never get finished. Create your vision, get on with it and don't stop till it's finished – no compromise, no holds barred, stay motivated. I guess the message here is to be persistent and never give up. We wanted to make sure that once we started, the warehouse project was definitely going to get completed.

We still had our rented loft down the road, but we gave up the warehouse that Serious rented across town and, despite all the ongoing renovation work, we moved the clothing business in downstairs pretty quickly, probably within three months. Then we spent a year fine-tuning how we wanted the upstairs to look. The fact that we were running Serious Clothing from the ground floor meant that we didn't have to run across town to check up on construction; we were at Willow all the time. The clothing company was still going pretty strong at this point, we were still doing all the rock stars and high-profile stuff as well as the wholesale, and by then we were doing a ton of business with Hot Topic on a pretty big scale, 200,000 units a year at one point, so those were good times. We had around eight employees downstairs, where we set up the sewing machines and these huge long cutting tables lit by big overhead industrial lighting rigs and surrounded by big steel industrial racks for all the fabrics. It all looked cool and was actually hugely practical.

Upstairs was to be our home. The style of the warehouse is very eclectic, but essentially it's *our* style, Karen and me. The design plan was to make it sort of our take on an English country home, mini-Hearst Castle meets mid-century pop art. In theory, those styles don't go together, but actually, in my opinion, they kind of blend pretty well in Willow. Overall, it's got this semi-English country house, semi-gothic theme going on throughout. It's got elements of pop art and mid-century modernism as well as slices of various other art movements, too. It's a combination of everything that we liked, all mixed up together. The master bedroom has a dramatic gothic arch with a huge red stained-glass door. There's also a stained-glass window from a church in Harlem. The open-truss ceilings are huge, there's an enclosed modern kitchen, a dining room, a library, a master bedroom, a guest bedroom – it's pretty vast. Some of the ideas were inspired by my mum hauling me around all those National Trust houses when I was a kid. There's French religious carvings near some Indonesian imported furniture. There are some fibreglass inserts we found at the Rose Bowl Flea Market, probably some movie props, which we ended up building an entire wall around. There's a bunch of semi-religious artefacts, outdoor lights, some genuine antiques, some reproduction stuff – you know, it all kind of goes together. Some of the features are quite high end and some of them are from flea markets and yard sales, but everything kind of fits. It's a huge melting pot of ideas and personalities.

The modernist theme is mixed with older pieces. There are some genuinely vintage pieces, such as an eighteenth-century

English oak chest. There are some beautiful Balinese import pieces, there's some Tibetan furniture, there's some reproduction antiques. There are some church gargoyles and Moroccan imports. The design ideas even took in the previously rat-infested alley, which we transformed into an alley garden with jasmine and other herbs and a fountain. We also added windows along the east and west walls to let in more light.

We sourced the interior-design elements from all over the place; one day we'd be in IKEA, the next we'd be in a thrift store or at a yard sale. There were no real rules other than if it looked cool and fitted into our vision, then we'd buy it. Cheap, expensive, new, old, whatever. We like shopping, we like thrift stores, we like yard sales, we like furniture, we like architecture, we like designing. Constantly staying creative. We like to mix and match. If you look in the kitchen, perfect example. Talk about putting stuff in the blender. So it is a combination of some functional and inexpensive pieces from IKEA, mixed with tasty high-end designer pieces like a prestige Philippe Starck sink. A lot of the furniture was customized, too. So, for example, we didn't buy desks, we made them. We had some old aluminium pipes, fitted them to a Formica top, then we just had a guy laminate them in the whole red, white and blue theme, so there was continuity . . . Evel Knievel, Captain America, Stars & Stripes again. So it's form and function, mix and match.

On the ground floor, we relocated stairs so that we wouldn't have to walk through the warehouse to get upstairs, because we wanted to separate the live/work spaces properly. On the one hand, living and working there was great, but it could sometimes create a bit of cabin fever because you might not leave for a couple of days. However, generally it was a fantastic space to live and work in – one obvious upside was that if you woke up at three in the morning with an idea, you could just go downstairs and start working on it.

The downstairs office was equally personalized. I have my signed guitars and various pieces of rock 'n' roll memorabilia in there. The walls are covered with posters of Keith Richards and Led Zeppelin as well as all the Serious artwork and, obviously, quite a few pictures and photos of Porsches.

Sure, it is a mish-mash of styles, but that's exactly the same as with the clothing. We took elements that didn't necessarily go together, threw them in the blender, shook 'em up and what came out is what you see. So we had the vision and that was worked on religiously for a long time. It either feels right or it doesn't, but I've never been the type of person who asks for other people's opinions, because if you do that then you get sidetracked; you start listening to other people's ideas and not your own. I never want to be that guy that says 'I should've, could've, would've'.

I think the result is that we created a very vibrant and exciting place to be – everyone that comes in this building remarks how it's got a good vibe, it's a creative space. A high-profile book on loft living, *L.A. Lofts* by Barbara Thornburg, called the warehouse 'surreal . . . like a mothballed set for *Citizen Kane*'. That sort of reaction, as it turned out, was shortly to mean that Willow would lead to a totally unexpected and exciting new chapter in our lives.

In September 2001, only a couple of weeks after 9/11, the *Los Angeles Times* called us up and said they were writing a piece on urban loft gentrification and would we be interested in being interviewed? The article was all about the first wave of what was called the adaptive reuse of former industrial structures that were getting converted into loft spaces. Truth be told, to some degree this process has been happening all over the world since the fifties and sixties, in places like Soho in London and New York, among others. LA was just kind of behind the curve a little bit. The article was entitled 'Explorers of the Lost City' and interviewed all these different people who lived in lofts in the early days of that lifestyle. There were probably a dozen or so featured lofts, some of which just got one page. Well, we got a centre spread, it was a brilliant piece and we were very proud.

So, I've talked about opportunities presenting themselves to you and how you react to those moments. Well, had this article never happened, we may never have got into the film business. Within a very short space of time of that article coming out, we got a phone call totally out of the blue from a production company saying, 'Hey, I saw you in the *LA Times*, would you be interested in renting your loft out for a music video?' Now, we'd seen people filming Downtown all the time, everything from *Batman* to *Terminator* and *Gone in 60 Seconds*. This was nothing new, this was the arts district, they'd been filming here since the fifties. That was just a part of LA life. DTLA was a popular location, but at that point we had nothing to do with that industry. It certainly never occurred to us that we could actually make money out of filming ourselves, not least because we'd never previously owned a property. So even though we'd been around that world when pop stars had come into the warehouse looking for clothing for videos and promo films, the idea of location filming had never occurred to us. We didn't build the warehouse in Willow as a film location. We built it as our dream live/work space and poured all our heart and soul and every ounce of creativity into that idea.

However, out of nowhere an opportunity had presented itself; it was just a case of what would we do with that opportunity?

So back to that phone call. The guy says, 'We need somewhere to shoot a video for a rap star's new single, and your place looks ideal. Would you be interested in us hiring it as a location?'

Well, you know me well enough by now . . .

'Sure, why not.'

How bad can it be, right?

I often say, 'If it feels sort of scary, you should do it.' Everyone has goals and dreams, and sometimes a moment will come along in your life and how you react can define where you go from there. Remember when you were a kid and you climbed to the top of the high diving board at the swimming pool? When you get to the top, you either jump or you don't jump. Some people will clamber back down the stairs because they can't jump. Not everyone jumps. Some people don't even climb the stairs. Those are the moments.

We had some discussions with this production company about the fees, and the day rates sounded pretty good. We were obviously completely new to the whole situation, but we had been running a very successful clothing business for many years, so we were able to learn fast and work out the best way to do this. We were pretty street-smart. By the time we struck the deal to have the first ever video shoot at Willow, we were both excited and looking forward to this new adventure.

On the day of the shoot, I turned up at 6 a.m. as the site manager/Mr Hard-Working Man, if you like. Remember, this was our home as well as our place of business. The plan was for them to just shoot upstairs. Everything started off well, then in the afternoon they said, 'Can we just film a little scene in the office, please?' I felt like, *Sure, why not? What goes around comes around.*

Well, four hours later there's another thirty people on set and I was starting to think, *What is going on here?* Then it transpires they were shooting a commercial off the back of the original music video. Well, they had never told us that. So, lesson number one: give an inch, they take a mile. Then they asked about using the garage. Now, at the time I only had a few cars in there, and they said it was ideal for a night-club scene, so I agreed that they could use it. So I moved the cars out, they start shooting the nightclub scene in there and all of a sudden there's fifty extras all over the space; I'm like, *What the fuck is this? No one told me about this many people.*

Long story short, by midnight we had been going for over fourteen hours, they were already way over their agreed twelve-hour limit, but they reassured me that overtime was time and a half. By one o'clock in the morning, I'm starting to get irritated, I'm waiting for these guys to go, I've been up since 6 a.m., I'm fed up, tired, I've had enough but . . . 'Just be another hour, Magnus.' By nearly 2 a.m., I'm like, 'I really don't give a fuck, you're now over eighteen hours.' They tell me it's double time now, and I was like, 'I don't give a fuck. You need to stop.' In reality, it should have been a two-day shoot, and I felt they had taken advantage of my good nature. Finally, they started breaking down to finish the shoot. They were physically done by 4 a.m., so I had been up for twenty-two hours. Karen was pissed off, I was pissed off and we both said we'd never do that again. We let the dust settle, then when Monday rolled around, we looked at the pay-cheque and realized, *Wow, we just earnt three times what we thought we were going to earn!* That five-grand day became a fifteen-grand day, so now we were going, 'Oh wow, maybe we'll do this again!'

That one day was the best and worst first day ever, and although it proved to be very lucrative, it also taught us to set boundaries, to make it clear exactly what we had agreed to. With regard to the film business, you have to have an attitude that at times goes against my nature: it's best to not really go out of your way to do favours. In life, that is something that I will always try to do – help people, do favours, always attempt to make people's lives easier – because I am a big believer in what goes around comes around. However, the film business is an extremely commercial world, and we learnt that lesson very quickly. Those guys were obviously trying to make their shoot as efficient and productive as possible, and that is understandable; we just needed to learn the lessons and move forward.

We decided to see where the location business would take us. So we signed up with about six agents who – in theory – would go and scout out some business for our location. Then, of course, very early on we were smart enough to realize that no one could sell the space as well as us, so we decided to build our own website. Karen took photos of the building and had some brochures designed and printed up, drawing on our experience of having to produce fairly lavish catalogues for Serious for all those years. We started taking calls and fairly soon about 70 per cent of the business was coming direct.

Over the next three years, we probably filmed on average fifteen to twenty days a year. Remember, this was still a part-time business – we were actually renting out our home. Sometimes we would have to move out altogether, so the production company would put us up in a hotel, with two cats and our dog Skynyrd, and let me tell you that got tiring very, very quickly.

Then came a real turning point. Again, this wasn't something we chased or planned, it just came to us organically and we reacted instinctively. We ended up landing this 2004 Bruce Willis movie called *The Whole Ten Yards*, also starring Matthew Perry, Amanda Peet and a whole bunch of big names. It was a big-budget movie, so they were at Willow for a month. They paid us a boat-load of dough and rented us a house in the Hollywood Hills for four weeks. That's when the light bulb flashed again, *Wow, I bet if we didn't physically live there, we could film all the time.* So after the Bruce Willis film had finished, we rented a house right next door to the one in the Hollywood Hills where we'd been staying. Again, it was essentially trial and error, literally saying, 'Let's move out and see how it goes.' Well, it went pretty well, because two years later, with the Willow film business thriving, we were still renting that house.

That was great fun at first, for about six months. It stayed pretty good for a year, but then to be honest the novelty started to wear off. We actually tried to buy the house in the hills, but that didn't happen. Long story short, two years later we decided we wanted to move back Downtown. So, in 2005, we bought a loft round the corner from Willow. With the warehouse still fully available for filming, we really hit our stride and business was booming. So that became the next segment of our lives, this ten-year film-location cycle.

By then, on average we were filming a hundred days a year, and on a couple of occasions we did over one hundred and twenty days. Everything from shows like *CSI: New York* to commercials for pretty much anything – cell phones, fast food, beer, party scenes – as well as music videos, films, whatever. We started doing a lot of reality shows, like *America's Next Top Model*. They would come in and be there for eight weeks: two weeks of prep, build out, remodel, set dress, three to four weeks of reality filming, then two weeks of striking out. That particular crew moved in like a well-oiled machine; they were like an army. The average reality show probably had fifty people on staff who were at the warehouse all the time. They would break down to a skeleton crew at night, but during the day there'd be fifty or so people in there. One aspect of the warehouse that they seemed to like was its flexibility – it was a very versatile space; there were a lot of different looks under one roof. We ended up doing about fifteen reality shows all told.

I've mentioned that we learnt lessons from that first shoot. Pretty quickly, we realized we needed a site rep, we needed to make sure we'd got a security deposit in case these crews scratched the floors or broke something. We needed to protect our investment. At the same time, we cultivated a reputation for being film-friendly. For example, say you rent a mansion in the hills and during the shoot someone scratches an oak floor. Let's say it's a $500 scratch, but the owner insists you have to refinish all his floors, so now it's a $20,000 scratch. Those people don't get work that often. So we'd have a little floor fund. If the scratch was really bad, okay, here's five hundred bucks, it goes in the floor kitty. At the end of the year, we'll refinish the floors. We were always very, very fair. So we developed a reputation for not only having a great film location but also for being really, really film-friendly.

At the same time, I was never going to be a pushover. You have to strike a balance. If you step over the line with me, I can become what I call 'the Sexy Beast', where I just blow my top. To a certain point I'm the nicest guy, but when you push me too far the Sexy Beast comes out. So some shoots I'd be like, 'You know, you've asked me five times and I've told you no.' Then they'd ask me again and I'd be like, 'Dude, which part of "No" don't you get?' If they continued to ignore my position and kept pestering, I'd say, 'There's an option here where you can walk away or you can ask me one more time and I'm going to tell you to go fuck yourself and find another place to film.' That usually did the trick.

The recipe seemed to really work, and the location business continued to boom. We even had a phase when people were asking us to go in and design their interiors for them, you know, like designers for hire. That never happened; it didn't seem natural for us. What works for us wouldn't necessarily work for someone else and, more to the point, we always thrived off creating with passion, rather than for a cheque.

*

It was a busy time. We were running Serious on the ground floor and renting out the warehouse for location shooting. Truth be told, by then Serious was starting to wind down a little. We were no longer doing the big-volume clothing sales, the business was still making money, but it was a smaller concern. By contrast, the location business was expanding. The film money was really easy compared to the clothing money. One big upside of the location business was that we didn't have to make a product; we'd already created this space that people wanted to use, so it was more a case of hiring it out, agreeing terms, organizing the deal. Sometimes they might paint a few walls or move a bit of furniture around, but other than that it was a very efficient business model. By contrast, if you think of clothing and fashion, twice a year people come out with a whole new season, these big ranges where the designer has to keep reinventing the wheel. We didn't have to do that with Willow.

And it wasn't just the film-location business that we took a chance on during this period. In terms of property generally, we were also pretty active. From 2005, we were doing really well and quite aggressively acquiring property and land. For instance, we bought what I call 'the chop shop', a unit over the road from Willow that allows me to have part-assembled and semi-scrap cars scattered around and some of the more rough-and-ready work going on in another premises. We also bought a building in East LA, a former Masons Lodge, another leap of faith. We even bought a bunch of land under the Fourth Street Bridge that wasn't even actually for sale. We had seen what had happened around Borough Market in

London and all those places that utilized disused railway arches and spaces, and thought we could do that here in LA. Under almost every railroad and train line in London is either a café stand or brickyard or a builder's supplier or a taxicab stand or nightclub or garage. That's thinking outside the box. Our real-estate broker knew this parcel of land under the bridge was railroad property, but there was no legal title, so we contacted the railroad company who were based in Texas and they didn't even really know where it was. We kind of had a crystal-ball feeling, a sense that the neighbourhood was going to become this desirable residential area that it's evolved into; we had that vision early. The railroad company had no use for that parcel of land under the bridge, it was all very makeshift, ramshackle tents, lots of petty crime, drug dealers, prostitution. Obviously, the bridge runs over it and has an easement in place, so it was a real complicated piece of property to buy.

Undeterred, we picked our way through the legal minefield over about nine months and eventually acquired that property. Karen never, ever gave up. Never wavered. She was incredible. Then we had renderings and architect's drawings commissioned for a development offering these enclosed glass pods, basically renting or selling these cocoons as individual spaces, just like in London. We also often used that land for film crews' parking. If crews were filming at Willow, they might commonly need a hundred car parking spaces, so there you go, fifteen hundred bucks a day right around the corner, we can give you parking. One-stop shop.

We were probably five years ahead of the developers, but after articles in the press and various other bits of media coverage, the property companies started hungrily buying big, undervalued industrial properties in the area and then converting them to lofts. This was pre-financial meltdown, when elements of the banking industry were often funding people who couldn't really afford to buy property. Well, we'd seen that happening and we knew that it was only a matter of time before all these buildings were converted to residential, and what happens after that? Well . . . coffee shops, art galleries, expensive condos. That's coming to fruition now. The gentrification is continuing. Five years before I wrote this book, you wouldn't have seen a single crane in the centre of Downtown LA; now they are building everywhere. Lofts, converted offices, shops, all these previously empty and at times derelict spaces are being converted into expensive properties. Just down the road from Willow there is a huge shopping mall being built as we speak, and there are organic coffee houses and CrossFit gyms springing up all over the place. It's so different to when Karen and I first moved in. In terms of inner-city gentrification, LA was just behind the curve. Karen and I weren't property developers in the sense of marketing, financing and selling condos, but we had the means to acquire property, and that's what we did. That took some courage and self-belief. I'd like to think that history shows that Karen and I were, in terms of property in the Downtown area of LA, ahead of the curve.

By this part of the story, Karen and I had done the clothing business for the best part of fifteen years and were now in our late thirties, early forties. We were not going out on the scene three nights a week, we were not really listening to new music so hungrily and truth be told we didn't really care what kids were wearing because, for my part at least, I'm pretty much wearing the same thing every day. So the mantra of 'we only design what we like to wear' started changing a little bit. Perhaps inevitably, sales started slipping. We were no longer doing the $2 million–$3 million a year; that dropped to a million and then below a million and then eventually we were losing money. We still had staff, but neither of us could bring ourselves to let them go because, you know, they were family, we had built that business up together, so we just couldn't do it. We'd sooner be losing money. Clearly, that isn't a viable commercial reality in the longer term. Then a couple of people quit and finally, unavoidably, we let one or two go and scaled back to where it was a much smaller operation. By then, we were really miserable, because on top of all that we were doing something we were no longer passionate about.

Meanwhile, the film money was really good, and we were acquiring the property that I've told you about. So we sat down and talked about what to do with Serious. We knew the passion had gone. We chatted about what our definition of 'success' was, and we decided that meant being able to do whatever we wanted to do. Therefore, why were we doing something that we were no longer enjoying? Karen was sick of doing payroll and workman's comp, or spending all day paying the bills. I was not as focused on Serious because I was doing more with the film-location side of things, showing people around and doing the contracts, because that was still fresh and exciting and you never knew who was going to be filming there next.

People pick up on a business that is run without passion.

People saw it in our clothing line. It wasn't quite as creative. We weren't putting the effort in; we weren't quite as excited about selling it. Passion goes a long way. You can have all the education and business qualifications in the world, but without passion for what you are doing . . . where is it going?

So we stopped designing the Serious line, we stopped going to trade shows, and then, after about a year of dwindling sales, we said, you know what, that's it. Serious is no more. The film-location side of things was generating enough revenue for us to feel secure that we could pay the mortgage, although we didn't actually know for sure where the money was going to come from next. However, we took that leap of faith just like we always did, just like when I started selling hats, when Karen and I got together and we started to partner up, when we opened up the store in Melrose, when we bought the building. You have to have that courage.

Closing down Serious was a hard decision. This was our baby that we'd worked on together for all those years. Some people thought we should have closed Serious down earlier, but in reality now, looking back, the timing was right. Some years were good financially, some years were bad. A few people said we should have sold up when it was making money, but we never wanted to sell. Some people build a business up and develop a brand and then sell it; they have what the management consultants like to call 'an exit strategy'. We never had that kind of business plan. We were doing something that was our passion, not following a business strategy. No spreadsheets, just gut instinct and a ton of passion and energy.

*

111

We had some great times with the film-location business; you can imagine some of the characters that turned up at our door. That's one of the great things that I love about LA. Take Bruce Willis. As I mentioned, he was at Willow doing *The Whole Ten Yards*, a movie being made with his own production company, which was proving to be very successful. They set up three trailers on site, one for Bruce, one for his friend and one for a gym. Bruce was the star of the film, of course. We were really interested to see how this panned out, because obviously he is one of the biggest movie stars in the world.

It was very common for people to be so taken with the warehouse that they'd ask who owned it. It was also very common for them to be completely surprised when their site manager would say, 'You know that rock 'n' roll couple you saw walking round, the tattooed guy with the dreadlocks and that super-cool, beautiful rock chick? That's them.' That happened numerous times. People didn't seem able to quite understand it. So anyway, during *The Whole Ten Yards* shoot, we got summoned to go meet Bruce Willis. Jokingly, he told us he wanted to buy our building and we replied, 'Sorry, Bruce, not for sale'. He was cool about that and to be fair wanted to know the back-story of the warehouse, how we came to own it, all about how we fitted it out; he was very curious. Cool guy.

We went upstairs and watched him direct his own scenes on set. Bruce was telling the director how he thought this particular footage should be shot, the director wanted to shoot a different way, so we watched them do this one scene which literally took all day. We used to joke about how the film industry was 'hurry up and wait'. Trust me, you've never seen anything like it. Bruce was a very motivated, dedicated kinda guy, and he was really nice to us. It was fascinating to watch and because it was our building, they couldn't really tell us that we couldn't be there. If any location manager ever asked us to move out of a room, I would politely say, 'You guys are renting the building, you are not owning the building. We can be here.'

Another big plus of the location shooting was that I got to meet a lot of cool bands. As you've heard, as a kid I was massively into my rock music. At that age, if you are lucky enough to somehow get backstage to meet your heroes, most likely they might shake your hand, sign a piece of paper and then move on; it's all over in, say, ten seconds. You're in their space, you're just one of five hundred kids coming up saying, 'Great show, I'm a big fan!', so they sign and move on; there's not a lot of interaction. Well, with the warehouse, the difference was that when these rock stars came to film, they were in *my* space. For example, in 2004 we did a shoot with Van Halen, and it's a perfect example of how the warehouse could be a great equalizer. This is after Eddie Van Halen had recovered from cancer, and they were shooting a promo video for their new tour. They all rock up, Eddie, Alex and Sammy Hagar. Bearing in mind what you know about my heavy-metal days as a kid and young adult, what happened next was a seriously magical moment: Eddie Van Halen walks into the kitchen area and *starts playing my guitar*, along with Sammy Hagar strumming away. That was a big buzz for me, so I went into the kitchen and you could see they checked me out, they saw I looked like a rock 'n' roller, and they were obviously a little puzzled. You could see them thinking, *Who is this guy? What's his story?* When that happens, even with absolutely huge stars like them, it sorta levels the playing field. I'm not saying they are uncomfortable in my space, but the dynamic has shifted a little bit, they are intrigued by me because they don't know who I am. Of course, I know everything about them, so then I pull out the 'Love you guys, I saw you twenty years ago', all that stuff. I'd just come back from England and brought all these concert programmes back with me from home in Sheffield. So, I dig those out and, of course, they can't believe it. One of the programmes was from 1984, which was perhaps the biggest year that band had ever seen. The massive single 'Jump' had just come out the previous December, and they were on top of the world. It turned out Alex Van Halen was a Porsche guy, so we started talking about all that, too (Porsche people, again). They were there all day long, so that was a real treat for me.

Now let me tell you my Lemmy story. Motörhead was a pretty big part of any rock fan's life in the seventies and eighties. So, you can imagine how excited I was to find out that Motörhead were going to film part of a BBC documentary at the warehouse. We had Geezer Butler and Bill Ward of Black Sabbath and Lemmy from Motörhead shooting this programme about the history of British heavy metal. A few feet away from the keyboard that I am typing this book on, there's a bottle of Jack Daniel's that Lemmy drank from, which is now one of my most cherished possessions. He was here for about four hours and I sat off-camera about ten feet away listening to him talk about his whole history, from roadying for Jimi Hendrix in the sixties through being in

Hawkwind in the mid seventies to forming Motörhead – the whole story. You have to remember that, for me, Motörhead has been much more than just a band and some brilliant albums. It has been a lifestyle, an example of a real 'fuck-you' attitude, of doing things your own way, a way of life, so you can imagine how special that experience with Lemmy in the warehouse was.

A little while after the Lemmy shoot, one day we get a call saying that Prince is working on an unscripted project. He's writing a play, there is no script and he wants to rent the loft for three days. He sends his people down to scout the loft, which is fine, so they come down and really like it, but a few days later they go, 'Yeah, Prince loves it, but you've got to remove all the demonic and satanic gargoyles or cover them up, because Prince doesn't want to be distracted on set. And you know when Prince comes in, you can't look at him.' I swear to God they told us this. 'Oh . . . and everyone needs to wear either a black or white T-shirt.'

On the day of the shoot, Prince walked in with a 6 ft 10 in., 400 lb bodyguard. Of course, I have to look at him and say, 'Hey, Prince, nice to meet you, I'm Magnus,' and to be fair he was totally cool. Later in the day, he walked away from the set because he was a very strict vegan and someone had ordered chicken when apparently the building was supposed to be a meat-free zone. Prince found out and never came back.

We also had a fashion shoot with Victoria Beckham, Posh Spice, for a Japanese jeans company. Two days before the scheduled start of the shoot, her personal bodyguard comes down. This guy was an ex-SWAT/SAS/MI5 type of guy. Real nice guy, super-professional, and off he goes checking out the facility. I asked him, 'What's all the scrutiny for?' and he goes, 'For Victoria.' I explained that we'd had all sorts of big names come through there, and he said, 'This is different. I need to check the perimeters and various other aspects.' For example, he asked us how long it took for the electronic gate to slide shut on the main entrance to the street. So we really didn't know what to expect when she was due. But do you know what? Full-on respect for her, the day arrives and she drives herself to the set in a white Bentley, no entourage whatsoever, she's not chauffeured in a town car, she just drives herself right in, followed by the bodyguard in a black car (thankfully the gate closed right on cue . . .).

When we met Victoria, she was super-nice, I mean super-friendly. We thought she'd be there probably for an hour – she was there eight hours. She was perhaps one of the biggest celebrities of the time back then, and she was here all day long, really lovely to absolutely everyone, hard-working, polite, friendly, and we were like, 'Fuck, she was proper salt of the earth.'

It was only when we were chatting that we realized she was being followed by five or six paparazzi all the time; this was right when her husband David had moved to LA to do the Galaxy soccer thing. The paparazzi had been using roofing ladders, trying to climb walls, all that stuff. So the security guy obviously knew what was going on, and he had a job to do.

We filmed all sorts of rock stars here . . . I can't even remember all of them; if you are filming a hundred days a year for fourteen years, that's one thousand four hundred days. The amount of people that have been through here . . . and Karen and I never documented anything. We didn't want to be like the Chinese restaurant with all these cheesy photos of us with our arms around celebrities, so we never took any pictures. The other day, someone said, 'Yeah, remember when Jay Z was filming?' and I was like, 'Jay Z was here?!'

Happy memories. Obviously, none of those experiences would have happened if I had stayed in Sheffield. This was a very LA part of our lives. And even then, living in LA or not, those stories wouldn't have occurred if we hadn't bought the building in Willow. So the warehouse, I often say, is a pivotal part of my story because it gave us the freedom to close down Serious and got us into a business that we'd never, ever have thought about, which was actually quite lucrative.

And it allowed me to have more Porsches than I actually need . . .

URBAN
OUTLAW

Chapter 8

Wheels of Steel

One of the most frequent questions I get asked is 'Why Porsche?' Well, it's a pretty simple answer, but I'll get to that in a moment. First, I need to rewind a little and tell you the back-story to my car collection which really began in the mid nineties. I spoke about my very first car, a Toyota Corolla, and my second car, the Saab. The third car was my very first Porsche, the slant-nose car that I told you all about. After that, well . . . how can I put it . . . Karen and I . . . we just liked buying shit. Business was good, as a couple and a company we were on fire, designing and selling cool clothes, all these famous people were digging what we did, the money was great, it was good times.

Like I said, we just liked buying shit . . .

At one time, we had a '65 Mustang GT350R replica, a '67 Series 1 E-Type Jag, two '69 Dodge Super Bees, a '73 Lotus Europa, a '79 308 GTB Ferrari and three or four Porsches.

That was from 1995 through probably 2005, so roughly a ten-year period. At that point, my car collection was a lot more diverse, so taking in Porsche but also American muscle cars, European sports cars – a much broader selection of stuff. I've always been a Porsche diehard, but I am also open to other ideas. Not all Porsche guys are like that. I know that might seem an odd thing to say when my garage is, at the time of writing, full of around twenty 911s. But remember, I was a kid growing up in the seventies, so I was well aware of all these other marques. I saw Jim Rockford's Firebird, the *Dukes of Hazzard* car, James Bond's Esprit, Colin Chapman and Lotus on the track, famous Ferraris, the Jags – all those cars.

The Mustang is an iconic car and an all-time American classic. We loved that car and even featured it in some of the Serious catalogues. The problem for me was that it didn't stop very well and didn't really go around corners. As for the E-Type, well, Enzo Ferrari said it was the most beautiful car in the world, and it was. However, the E-Type Jag really wasn't a reliable car, you know. We paid twenty grand for a restored E-Type, which was a considerable step up in terms of the money we were spending on cars; I think at the time we'd never spent more than $10,000. The funniest part of this story is that we actually flew up to Sacramento with $20,000 in a backpack, met the owner at the airport and then drove the car back home! We got within two hundred yards of our loft when the clutch went. Welcome to the world of E-Type Jag ownership. Maybe it hadn't been that well restored. Maybe we were a bit naïve back then, but we just wanted a cool car. And the E-Type is certainly that. Remember my uncle Mick, the market trader who owned an E-Type? Since then, I'd always wanted one. So I'd ticked that box, but that car was unreliable; we upgraded to a bigger radiator, all that stuff, but we'd seldom drive it. So it was in the garage a lot, just sitting there. Then sometimes at a weekend we'd go, 'Why don't we drive the E-Type? It's so cool,' and then you'd go for a drive and it would break down and we'd go, 'Oh, that's why we don't drive the E-Type.' I have to say, the great thing about the E-Type Jag is that no one ever said a bad word about it. People would sometimes give you the finger in a Ferrari and maybe look down their nose at the muscle cars like the Mustang, but the E-Type Jag was loved by everyone.

Super Bees . . . we loved them, had two of those. Hell, I've even got a '69 Super Bee tattoo. We had a 383 four-speed and a 440 automatic, both just brute raw power. In essence, that was the *Dukes of Hazzard* car, same body style. So I ticked that off the list. One time, we were leaving the warehouse, driving through Downtown, I was in the Super Bee, and I think Karen was following behind in a Jag XJ6. Basically, I must have been displaying what some might call 'an exhibition of speed' in the Super Bee; problem was, I didn't realize that there was a cop behind me when I was gunning it. Suddenly, I saw the flashing lights of the cop car and so I made a right turn and then a left and pulled over. The cop got on his walkie-talkie and then gets out of the car. Then he comes over to me, gets me out of the Super Bee, puts my hands above my head, and I'm spread-eagled on the front of the car. At this moment, Karen came around the corner and couldn't believe what was going on in front of her! She got out of her car, but the cop told her to step back. Karen basically said,

'No, that's my boyfriend, what are you doing with him?' This cop said, 'We're holding him for questioning.' He asked me where I was going, so I said, 'I'm going home.' He replied, 'Well, you were driving a little quick, what are you doing Downtown?' To be fair, the neighbourhood was sketchy back then, he probably saw my tattoos and dreadlocks and jumped to the wrong conclusions. I think the cop must have thought I was Downtown trying to score drugs. I explained that we worked there and were in the clothing business, and it wasn't until I pulled out my ID and driver's licence that he started to back off. Being Downtown in a fast car in the nineties was not quite as enjoyable as it is now!

Anyway, back to my other cars. Next up, a '73 Lotus Europa with a burnt-sand paint job, a beige/copper metallic colour. Back in the pre-internet days, I would religiously get *Sports Car Trader* on a Wednesday night and trawl through it looking for Porsches and muscle cars. I wasn't looking for a Lotus Europa, but one week there was this car. I thought, *That's kind of quirky*; my uncle David had that Lotus Type 47 that he worked on with Dad. I thought, *Fuck it, this one's not a Type 47, but it's still a Europa – same thing*. The car was for sale in Walnut Creek, northern California, near San Francisco. I called the guy up, told him I was interested in the car, long story short, he says, 'My cousin lives in Orange County, I'll drive the car down next week. You can take a look at it.' I said, 'Fair enough, that saves me flying up to you. You know what? If the car makes it, I'll buy it.' The car made it, so I bought it. Sadly, I never really clicked with that car, though.

I bought the '79 308 GTB Ferrari for twenty grand in

1995. Again, probably ticking the box after my uncle had one. And that car was kind of nice and reliable, believe it or not. We only ever changed a water pump on that. It did break down on us once, though, coming back from Vegas along with my buddy in his Viper.

So, you can see, I have owned plenty of cars other than Porsches in my time. I have some great memories of those cars, too. However, that is not what my garage is full of at this very moment, nor is it what I am well known for.

So back to the question: why Porsche?

Like I said, it's a pretty simple answer. As great as all those other cars were, they were maybe good at one or two things. The Mustang was pretty fast but didn't stop or go around corners. The E-Type Jag looked good but was very unreliable. Also, as great as the E-Type is, I was not a fan of the 'famed' handling – that's kind of a myth in my opinion. The Ferrari was great, but that isn't a car you put high mileage on; you just don't see a lot of high-mileage Ferraris or Lamborghinis. They are either not reliable or they don't get driven that much because people just collect them and get all paranoid about racking up the mileage.

In addition, I have always found the world of 'Porsche people' absolutely fascinating; there are so many different characters, individuals, people from completely contrasting backgrounds and lives, yet somehow we all have this common interest, these cars, and that has opened me up to some great experiences over the years that otherwise would not have happened.

For these reasons, over time I gradually started to sell off anything that wasn't Porsche. The last non-Porsche that we kept was the E-Type Jag, which finally sold in 2011 (coincidentally that was the fiftieth anniversary of the E-Type, so luckily that car had gone up in value). I'm certainly not dissing all these great cars; I'm just trying to explain how I came to own over fifty Porsches. The bottom line is that while other cars were good at a few things, the Porsches excelled at *everything*.

At this point, I was driving these cars only on the streets – fairly aggressive, 'spirited' street driving, shall we say. However, I realized that this wasn't necessarily the safest way to enjoy the cars, so it was perhaps inevitable that my obsession moved up a notch. In late 2001, I joined the Porsche Owners Club along with its 115,000 members and took my spirited driving to the track. Over the next six years or so, I honed my driving ability and became increasingly fixated on racing.

It was John Williamson at Otto's (the repair shop in Venice who worked on my first Porsche) who first got me into the Porsche Owners Club. I remember doing my first track day and it was perhaps the only time Karen ever went to the track. She went out in this short miniskirt, all rock 'n' roll, looking beautiful, but it was in Willow Springs, the high desert in the middle of nowhere, over a hundred miles from our home. There was nothing else to do, it was a hundred degrees, just this bunch of gearhead guys talking about cars and racing (these were real 'dedicated' Porsche people!). Karen was bored stiff by lunchtime, ready to go home. She said, 'Magnus, that's the last time I'm ever going to the track with you!'

For me, the experience was altogether different. That was the beginning of what I like to call the Porsche slippery slope, sliding down towards modification. I just dove in at the deep end. I did my first track day at the first event of the year in 2002. You had to do four short track events to get what's called your short track licence, which I did within two months. Then I moved on to getting my time trial licence straight away, such that by June I had progressed to the big track at Willow Springs.

I started competing and did relatively well in that quite quickly. Between 2002 and 2007, I was tearing around tracks such as Willow Springs, Thunderhill, Laguna Seca, California Speedway, Las Vegas Speedway and Phoenix Speedway, honing my skills and always tweaking the cars I was driving. I'd like to think I earnt the respect of my racing peers, and certainly I have quite a few trophies and race wins to show for my efforts. Some people would turn up with their race cars on trailers, but I would always drive the car to the track, thrash it around and then drive it back home. That's what old-school racers back in the twenties and thirties did, characters such as the Bentley Boys and all their old-school contemporaries, so for me that was just the natural thing to do. And besides, it was usually a 911, so it was easy; these cars are very adaptable.

I was winning races and earning trophies and plaques – in 2004, I won my class championship and placed second in that year's HP Time Trial Series. I still have the Porsche Owners Club year-end review book for that season. I am in there as the short track champ and there's a little interview with me. The writer asked me if I had any advice for upcoming racers and I said:

Get real comfortable with your car and drive it as often as you can, try to resist the urge to spend money to go faster right away, ask other drivers about their lines around the track, if possible drive with them. Always set yourself a reasonable goal and try to achieve it. Take little steps, remember smooth is quick, buy some good tyres, paint some racing stripes on your car . . . it just feels faster.

They then asked, 'How does Magnus balance racing and real life?' to which I replied, 'Being nice to my wife Karen certainly helps, always trying to drive home at night from the events.' In the same interview, I described my racing as a matter of self-preservation: 'You can only go so fast and get so many speeding tickets on the street before you realize fast is better attempted in a controlled track environment.' (Truth be told, I was still doing quite a lot of spirited driving on the streets and getting a lot of speeding tickets.) I also told the interviewer that my lucky charm was my Serious Number 1 patch and the Union Jack flag on my helmet. My parting words to fellow racers and competitors were, 'Stay Motivated.'

At that same time, I was also doing a lot of coaching, so I became a Porsche Owners Club instructor. By then, I had gone through the whole programme (short track licence, time trial licence, club race licence), so to make the day go real quick and to get more experience, I'd instruct students. I didn't view that as a chore; I saw it as a way to get more seat time even when I wasn't driving. I was seeing different parts of the track and also learning from coaching someone else.

By the middle of the decade, I was doing forty to fifty track days a year – that's as good as one a week. Each event is a whole weekend, and I was instructing too. The problem was that the more competitive the racing became, the more pressure was introduced and the more costly it became, too. Thunderhill was five hundred miles away and there were other away days like Laguna Seca, Phoenix and the Las Vegas Motor Speedway. Those events would be a Friday, Saturday, Sunday at the track, meaning you'd have to leave on a Thursday to get there. That's four days away, three nights in a hotel. Most likely you are flying there. Someone's shipping your car and you're buying a set of tyres – that's a thousand bucks. At the same time, you are modifying, upgrading brakes, suspension – you know, it's a thousand bucks here, two thousand bucks there, three thousand bucks at times. Then there's entry fees, etc., and you better hope you don't break the car. It was getting so expensive. Let's say a track day is a minimum of a thousand bucks. If you are doing fifty a year, do the math.

Over time, as the racing became more serious, I found myself enjoying it less. The pressure was greater, the costs were higher, but I wasn't necessarily having a better time. So around 2008 I started withdrawing a little from that scene, racing less, going to fewer track weekends. The attraction was wearing off, and I started to think I could have more fun buying, selling and modifying cars instead. That's when I started putting all the money I had spent racing into acquiring Porsches. Karen would always say, 'You love buying cars, you are great at buying cars' – that was one of her famous lines. Then she said, 'But you need to become great at selling them as well.' She had a point. Karen was always thinking about our situation, scoping it out; she was super-intelligent. That kept me focused.

So I got myself on Craigslist and *Auto Trader* and started buying these project 911s – five grand here, six grand there, real inexpensive cars. I remember the very first one pretty well. It was a matching-numbers '69 911T that barely ran. I bought it for five grand here in LA, and then my buddy Sergio, who works with me, and I attempted to restore it ourselves. We didn't get the five-hundred-dollar paint job, we went for the thousand-dollar paint job, and, to be fair, the end result was half-decent. Sergio and I stripped all the interior and did the headliner ourselves, the seats and carpet, changed the wheels, too. I think we were probably into that car for maybe twelve grand when we were done. So it was a real budget restoration. We sold it for twenty, so we actually made money on the car and that felt great! Often it wasn't easy money, though. There was another car I remember well, a '74 911 Carrera that I bought for eighty-five hundred bucks It needed a bit of work, some paint correction. The Porsche market was quieter back then, so I had a really hard time selling that car, finally offloading it for twenty grand in about 2009.

We were kind of learning as we went along, trial and error. Early Porsches are pretty easy to modify and upgrade. We figured out how best to get stuff chrome plated, powder coated, cad plated. We scouted around for the best paint jobs, the different ways to work on the interior, all these various details and methods. Essentially, I am completely self-taught. The great thing about these online forums is that you can just Google an issue you are faced with, maybe how to strip paint off a Porsche, restore a certain part or whatever, and people will help you. Ask questions, be nice, be grateful, treat people with respect. They will enjoy helping you and you can learn so much.

Then I found a painter called Jose who worked out of his backyard down in Vernon. He was painting cars for three grand but to a really high standard, so gradually the quality of the restorations went up, even though to start off with we were still buying rust-bucket 911s. I did a couple of 912s, too. Over the period from 2008 to 2011, the quality of the cars I was working on continually improved. At that point, however, truth be told, my personality wasn't on the cars. Quite a few of these earlier cars are now cropping up for sale as 'an ex-Magnus Walker 911' because I registered and titled them to me. Yet a lot of those early cars have little or no elements of my personality or signature touches whatsoever; those are stock cars that were just restored and flipped. Even though I've owned them, they are not cars that I have outlawed.

I started to document the process a little bit. You may or may not have heard of Pelican Parts. It's a comprehensive website and parts supplier, and their online forums are really great. So, around 2010 I started a thread, nothing headline-grabbing, just a few words about my cars and Porsche stuff. I called it 'Porsche Collection – Out of Control Hobby'. It was the first time I'd ever done that, because even though I had been on the Pelican Parts forum since 2004, I had never really posted anything. I'm not one of those guys that is necessarily computer savvy, I didn't have an iPhone, this stuff didn't necessarily come naturally to me – still doesn't to be honest. I think you are either a tech/computer guy or you're not, and I was never one of those guys that had to rush out and get the latest iPhone. In fact, at that point I was still on a Motorola Razr flip phone. Did me fine.

So I had this little thread going on both Pelican Parts and the Early S Registry, which is more early Porsche specific. The 'Out of Control Hobby' vibe and my posts seemed to tweak people's interest and began attracting quite a lot of attention and views. I was having fun posting about the cars that I was assembling and building, all the time documenting my work with photos, and so that was, essentially, my first little bit of exposure. Before that, I wasn't really known other than probably in the local community and around the streets of southern California and on those track days as, like I say, a spirited Porsche driver.

By now, I'd moved away from the complete basket-case five-grand cars and I'm buying cars in the teens. Some of these I'm actually just selling on, making a little bit of money. So that's how I've got through over fifty-odd cars. We were still not making much money at this point, barely breaking even on some of them, but this was not about money for me. The location filming at Willow was bringing in a good income, but more to the point, the car builds were all about the process and the education, and it was something I loved to do. I'm very passionate about it. Losing money on a car or making a grand or two didn't matter to me. This was purely a hobby.

Like I said, it was a hobby that was getting out of control . . .

The real turning point came when I started injecting a little more personality into the cars. What people now call my signature touches. The louvred deck lid for example. You will find those on a lot of hot rods but not many Porsches. Also, other little touches such as two-tone hoods, drilled door handles, integrated turn signals, central filler caps, chrome-faced gauge bezels and Plexiglas bubble windows. I became a lot more detail orientated. By then, I had a buddy from the Porsche Owners Club called Phil who was helping, too. Now that we were able to do most of the work in-house, I started to learn a whole lot more, the quality went up again and, crucially, the costs went down. I always pride myself on the way things fit. Take a bumper, for example. You can put a bumper on in ten minutes, but it won't necessarily fit perfectly. Sometimes you can literally spend all day getting the bumper to fit, so if you are at an independent shop and they are charging you one hundred bucks an hour, that's not good.

I slowly began to modify in my own unique style. This led me to develop what I call 'Street-able track cars'. The 68R was arguably the first signature build that gained widespread notoriety. That was a serious, defining build. I'd worked on that car back in 2009 – I had a guy doing metalwork across the road and some of the build was done in-house. Then I get this email from a dude called Liam Howlett. Classic example of Porsche people vibing with each other. Turns out he has a band called the Prodigy, whom I was obviously aware of. He'd seen an STR that I was working on around the same time, which I will come to in a moment. Long story short, he shot me an email and said, 'Love your work, seen you on Pelican and a couple of magazines, I would love you to build me a car.'

I'd long since realized I didn't have the time, energy and

passion to just work on cars and then sell them on, so I said, 'Dude, with all due respect I don't build cars for people, I don't do customer cars, it's not my business. I just like to build forty-year-old street-able track cars.'

He goes, 'Well, I have never owned a short-wheelbase car, and I really love your 68R.'

I had a think about where I was at and eventually I said, 'Okay, I'll sell you that car.' So he comes back at me with, 'Can you do me one favour? Could you do your integrated turn signals?' (He'd seen those on the STR.) Initially, the 68R didn't have integrated turn signals, or rather it had them on the front but not the rear. You might think that's a relatively small request but, hey, far from it. In fact, I actually ended up repainting the entire car again to get it exactly right. I didn't charge him any more money though; I stuck to the deal, even though some guys might have charged many thousands of dollars for the extra paint work. Liam bought the car and at a good price. I think he bought well! He was a cool guy, and I actually asked him if I could keep the car for a short while as I had a film project coming up that I wanted the 68R to feature in – but I am getting ahead of myself again.

Like I said, around the time of the 68R I had previously been building my first STR. It began life with me as a non-running, non-matching-numbers 1972 roller. It had a 2.7MFI motor built from the remains of some other parts. What I built was aggressive, very sharply focused on style, performance and detail. When I decided to sell it, I threw out a price and it sold very quickly for sixty-five grand. In retrospect, that was probably too low, but this was still a steep learning curve.

These later cars with more personal detail and precision were starting to put me on the map, building my reputation. Then I started getting attention from the media. The first article I ever had written about me was in a Dutch magazine called *RS Porsche* by this guy Erik Kouwenhoven. Before that point, I had kind of shunned editorial coverage for some reason, I don't quite know why. I just didn't feel comfortable, the timing wasn't right – that was what my instinct was telling me. But Erik had seen me on Pelican and that interested him enough to write this article in early 2011.

That same year, I had got an email from a Dutch guy called Maurice van den Tillard, a former BMX rider who works in the Dutch Air Force as a mechanic on fighter jets, a clever guy. Anyway, he is an automotive enthusiast and a great photographer, and he wanted to document the So-Cal scene, mostly based around hot rods, BMX bikes and choppers, for his blog called Dutchman Photos. He'd already done articles for magazines in those scenes and with various So-Cal bike builders, but now he was looking to get into the Porsche world a little bit. He wasn't a Porsche owner himself, but he'd seen the Pelican Parts thread and was interested in what I was creating, so he contacted me.

I met him at the Rennsport Reunion, this great Porsche heritage event, at Laguna Seca in 2011. We had a chat, then he drove down to LA and we kind of clicked, you know. He's a little bit younger than me but also comes from a punk rock background, so not your typical Porsche person. He ended up writing an article which went into Issue 83 of *Total 911*, England's number-one independent Porsche magazine. The article was all about me building these unconventional

Porsches. Maurice's article introduced me with the words: 'Meet Magnus Walker, the Urban Outlaw . . .'

I didn't come up with the term 'outlaw'. That had been around a long time. The obvious Porsche connection is from the fifties when people were customizing 356s back in the James Dean era, but the essence of the idea goes back much further. Guys had been rodding cars when they returned from the Second World War in the late forties and early fifties, you know, old flat-top Fords and cars like that. Remember, the car-culture scene in southern California has been around for ever. Less than a mile down the road from where I am writing these words there is an old Ford Motor Company plant, opposite where I used to live, which is now being converted into apartments. Cars and California are just inseparable.

If you look up the definition of 'outlaw', it means someone who is beyond the normal confines of the law, 'a person who refuses to be governed by the established rules or practices of any group; a rebel, a non-conformist'. That term has evolved beyond the history of renegades and criminals and into more of a general description of an attitude and a lifestyle. With regards to cars, it was applied to people who were taking stock vehicles and working on them in a way that was outside of the norm, outside of the boundaries of standard factory specifications.

Like I said, for many years the term 'outlaw' was very frequently used with Porsche 356s. Rod Emory and his company, Emory Motorsports, are arguably the most renowned proponents of that particular art. However, the outlaw instinct is the same regardless of what marques you are talking about – essentially what I'm doing with my Porsches is adding hot-rod touches and elements of customization that people have been doing for decades. That's the creative lineage that *Total 911* saw. In that particular article, Maurice said, 'I am sure that we will see a lot more of these beauties in the future . . .'

And so the seed was sown.

Chapter 9

277

The one car that everyone always asks me about is 277. Truth be told, that's kinda funny because it's a car that has so few of my signature touches. Yet it seems to have captured people's imaginations and is always first on the list when magazines and websites want to photograph my collection. 277 is the second 911 I ever bought, and it is a one-off car, very much the sum of its parts. If you are after a matching-numbers, factory-stock car, 277 is not your 911. It's a '71 911T, which I first saw at the Pomona Swap Meet in 1999, the greatest place ever for this sort of story. There are so many cars, the air is full of the smell of oil and petrol, the occasional squeal of tyres. People are chatting passionately about their cars, and there's a real buzz and energy.

The guy who owned 277 was actually an aerospace engineer who worked at Lockheed Boeing. I paid seventy-five hundred dollars for the car, which had already been modified, with a

2-7 motor in it, but it was still narrow bodied, it hadn't been flared. The car was originally gold, although it had been painted green and then various shades of white. It was a great running, driving car, so I paid the money and brought it home.

Straight away, I wanted to build my interpretation of a '73 RS replica. I have never lusted after an actual '73 RS. They made 1,580 of those and when I bought 277 for seventy-five hundred bucks, a '73 RS was probably a fifty-grand car (at the time of writing, a great RS is now a million-dollar car). The point being, back then fifty grand may as well have been a million bucks to me, because under ten grand was where I was at.

I ended up buying real RS flares for seven hundred and fifty bucks, and they were butt welded on to the car within three months of me owning it. Then I got the '73 RS Carrera fibreglass ducktail, repainted the car white and put black Fuchs on it, so within six months it was a '71T that looked like a '73 RS.

I did my first track day at Willow Springs in that car. My obsession with racing meant that I very quickly made more and more modifications to the car, always searching for better performance. The modification side was not something I did to make the cars look good; it all began when I went to the track with a somewhat basic car and then you get a dose of the need for speed, so I started doing performance modifications which were generally suspension, brakes, wheels and stickier tyres. When I moved up to the next level in the Porsche Owners Club series of bigger tracks, a number of safety requirements came with that escalation. So I put a roll bar in it, bought some cheap Momo bucket seats for two hundred bucks, fitted a five-point harness, fire extinguisher – you know, safety first. The fact that the car is a '71 made it 'pre-smog', so it didn't have to be tested for catalytic emissions. That's one of the many great aspects of these early Porsches, I say it all the time, everything is interchangeable. So I could put a 3-6 motor in and it still wouldn't have to go through smog, because it's built before the smog cut-off of '76. Like I said, these were not modifications for style or looks; I was doing all this so that I could continue to progress on the track. That was sort of the step from street car to track car but, saying that, 277 has always been what I call a 'street-able' track car, meaning that I drive it to the track and back, it was always street legal.

For the first couple of years, the car was number 731, just a random number that I was given by the POC. Then I put it on wider rims, lowered it, did some suspension work, inserted thicker, heavier torsion bars, some race spindles and really set it up as an aggressive, canyon carver/street-able track car.

Around 2004 I painted the Brumos stripes on the car. Brumos is my favourite race team and car dealership, one that has been in business for over fifty years. Their number-one driver Hurley Heywood won Daytona five times and Le Mans three times, and when I later met him, a genuine legend, it was a real 'pinch-yourself' moment for me. So 277's colour scheme was Brumos-inspired. Of course, the red, white and blue Brumos livery also ties into my love of Americana, Evel Knievel, all that stuff I have already talked about.

For some reason, at one stage the POC gave me a new number. You could pick any number (if it was available), and

I just wanted a low-digit number with sevens in it because I was born 7/7/67. People always say, 'What's 277 mean? What's the significance?' There is no real significance; it was just as simple as that. Besides, 007 would have been perfect, but guess what? Yeah, that was taken.

The car has had four motors in the back, with the last 2-6 one being heavily modified. The initial 2-7 motor it had when I bought the car started getting a little bit tired, so I put in a 2-4S spec motor which I'd bought used. Eventually, that motor started getting a little bit weak, but this is a car that I've never spent big money on, so I'm not spending thirty grand to have someone build me a whammy motor. I'm finding used motors online. So then I had a 2-5 motor put in it that I'd bought for eight grand. I've always been one for just driving all my cars, you know, 'plug and play', enjoy the cars with the motors for a couple of years, then change them if they get tired. Whenever a motor got tired and started excessively leaking, instead of rebuilding it I would just put an ad online: 'Wanted: plug and play motor'. It doesn't have to be pretty, ideally some sort of combination of short-stroke, twin-plug 2-4, 2-5, 2-6. I never wanted a big motor. It doesn't really matter if you don't know the differences between all these engine specs – the point is I am happy to swap an engine as soon as I think it's getting tired. Plus, I don't need some huge amount of power, that's just not what these cars are about, in my opinion. Some guys love putting big motors in cars, 3-2, 3-4, 3-6, 3-8, because they do drop right in. However, 277 has always been a small displacement, momentum car, because I believe that makes you a better driver. I used to love hounding faster cars on the track, where, fair enough, they'd pull you on the straight, but you'd outdrive them on the turns. I had buddies who'd say, 'Why don't you just put a 3-6 in it? Why are you dicking around with these small motors?' Well, it's not really going to make me any faster, truth be told, because I can't physically keep my foot planted with 277's short-stroke, twin-plug 2-6 motor with about 230 horsepower, so why do I need 300 horsepower? I'm not going to be going that much faster with a big motor than in a small displacement, momentum car that is really well balanced and set up. I describe 277 as a 'flat-foot car', meaning I can keep my foot planted on the accelerator most of the time. You can't really keep your foot planted in some of these huge-engined cars, they are just too brutally powerful for that. In 277, you can keep your foot planted all the time, and I enjoy that.

Around 2006, the Brumos-inspired livery on 277 evolved into the current well-known livery, when I swapped the original striped steel hood for a fibreglass hood that just happened to be red. I was like, *Don't bother painting it, just put it on, it looks cool.* Then I painted the bumpers blue and replaced the whale tail with a louvred deck lid.

It's still running torsion bars and shocks, the car never got converted to coil-overs; it's still running the original steel trailing arms. I didn't upgrade to lightweight aluminium trailing arms, although the brakes were upgraded to SC brakes. That was another thing, a lot of guys were always upgrading to more powerful turbo brakes which are heavier, but when the car only weighs 2,200 lb you don't necessarily need a lot of stopping power because I'm on super sticky Hoosiers – fantastic, very grippy tyres. In essence, the sum of the parts of 277 – certainly by today's standards – is nothing special. In fact, given that the car has been developed over many years, many of the parts are dead-old components now. So it's not the latest, greatest, state-of-the-art racing machine; it's more of a basic, even somewhat antiquated approach.

As anyone who has seen the car in the metal will testify, along the way 277 has got plenty of road rash and patina. I describe it as my favourite pair of old shoes, it's an old war-horse. People always say to me, 'What's your favourite car?' and I go, 'Without a doubt, 277.' Why? Well, *everything* . . . aside from what I said about 277 being a flat-foot car, I love the patina – the more chips and cracks the better, those are all *memorable moments*. As great as a brand-new custom build or hot-rod 911 is, there's no personality on those cars yet; they're essentially brand-new vehicles. To me, 277 is perfection in a different way. Perfection doesn't necessarily mean a shiny paint job. I don't even know how many miles I've got on that car, I don't know really how much money I've got in that car, it's a classic case of five grand here, three grand here, two grand there. Frankly, I don't care.

People don't always understand my view of 277 and the idea that a car with patina and personality is often far more appealing than a concours perfect specimen. Let me give you an example. At one point, I was approached by Sparco and Recaro, who very kindly wanted to give me new seats for 277. Now up to this point I have never taken anything for free, I have never asked for a discount, I've never gone down that route. So I thanked them but said to these guys, 'If I wanted a new seat, it's six hundred bucks, I'd buy one myself. Why would I put a new seat in the car?'

I don't like new jeans, I don't really like new shoes, so why would I put a brand-new seat in it? One guy asked me why the driver's seat is Sparco and the passenger's seat is Momo, and suggested maybe he could give me a new one so that they matched. However, that driver's side seat is the one I've done all my races in, that's why it's ripped up and damaged, it's scuffed from the seatbelt harness. The $250 T-bucket Momo seat on the other side used to be the driver's seat before I could afford to get the Sparco. I did actually have a pair of them, but I gave the passenger seat to a buddy who couldn't afford to buy one. That's when I bought the Sparco and I moved the Momo over to the passenger side. So why would I take them out of the car? They've been in the car since 2002 when I went club racing with the Porsche. That's the DNA of the car, that's its personality. A funny aside, the number plate is 71T24S. Sometimes people stand next to the car and say, 'What year is it?' I'm always like, 'Dude, look at the number plate, it kinda gives you a clue!'

Sometimes 277 needs work for reasons other than modification. In 2015, I was at a press event when I took a journalist out in 277, spun on the road and hit a truck. That was the first time I've ever crashed a car, believe it or not, the only time. My first thought was, *Is she okay?* Thankfully, she was, and I walked away without a scratch. The car took a heavy hit, but luckily the impact was right by the roll bar and that dissipated most of the energy. Most people would have totalled that car; I didn't even run it through insurance. I paid for it myself. Shortly afterwards, I took the repaired car to the Rennsport Reunion and people were saying, 'Dude, that can't be the same car, there's no way!' I just said, 'It is, trust me, I drove it here. This is 277.' The car is the same as it was before the crash, but now it's got even more stories to tell, more memories to think about.

277 has become the 'go to' car, it's the car I'm most associated with, that I'm most recognized in. As I've started to get more publicity for my builds, it's the car that's been in most of the videos, magazines, websites . . . it has grown to be inseparable from me, really. It has become a celebrity in its own right, in a way. I once got invited to the opening of an independent Porsche place in Tokyo and there was a guy there who had replicated 277 in minute detail; there are probably a dozen replicated 277 cars out there. I'm not talking in the virtual world of people building them online; I'm talking about actual cars that look exactly like 277. As I said, that's kinda ironic because the car actually has so few of my signature touches. Other than the louvred deck lid, it doesn't have integrated turn signals, louvred fenders, channelled hoods, drilled door handles. Why? Because 277 preceded all that; the car came before I was building outlaw Porsches.

Like I say, the sum of 277's parts is nothing really special, but it's the memorable miles, the moments, the smiles, the stories, all the people that have been in that car, the experiences I've had sitting behind that steering wheel. I think it's fair to say that 277 has become pretty iconic. It's irreplaceable.

Chapter 10

Urban Outlaw

Urban Outlaw is a portrait of Magnus Walker, the rebel Porsche customizer who turned a hobby into an obsession, and an obsession into a successful business ... He obsessively harvests fragments from donor 911s, grafting them onto vintage frames to create one-off automobiles with the spirit of Ferdinand Porsche but an ethos entirely of his own.

An extract from the press release for *Urban Outlaw*, 2012.

By this point in my story, you can see that I've had a modest amount of publicity – the Venetian Paradise coverage, the Serious days when Karen and I were sometimes featured but also, of course, when rock stars and celebrities were wearing our clothes on magazine covers, and then the building and film-location business at Willow. I'd even had those handful of articles about my Porsche builds that I just mentioned. However, nothing could have prepared me for what happened next . . . the thirty-two-minute short documentary film, *Urban Outlaw*, released in 2012 by Tamir Moscovici.

This film pretty much changed my entire life.

The story starts with just an email in late 2011 from this Canadian guy called Tamir. Basically words to the effect of . . . 'Been following your story, I'm a commercial film director, I'm thinking that you'd be great subject matter for a short documentary film, any interest in that?'

Now, remember, I'd been in the film business for ten years at this point, and over that time as the cars had evolved we started to get loads of people offering to make videos of me driving. I had always turned that sort of stuff down and so – aside from those few articles – in terms of my cars, I was pretty much under the radar. You might think *Why turn down someone wanting to film you?*, but I guess ultimately I just didn't click with the people who had previously been asking. I'm all about relationships. Some fast-talking film dude might have been shooting something at the warehouse and he'd like my cars, so at some point in the day he'd say, 'Hey, let's strap a camera on your car and we'll shoot some footage . . .' but I wasn't really clicking with that. It's all about people – whatever you are doing, you have to click with the people involved.

However, when Tamir got in touch, there was just something about his email, I just got a vibe that hadn't been there all the previous times when the other film guys had machine-gunned the idea of filming the cars. So instead of emailing him back, I actually called him. I always talk better than I text or type; you can get a lot more across in a verbal conversation than you can in an email chain. So I phoned him, we had a conversation and kinda instantly clicked. I think the fact that Tamir wasn't part of the Hollywood set was a major factor.

Turns out a copy of *Total 911* had made its way into the hands of Tamir over in Canada. Now, he was already a Porsche guy, he has a 993 and was an enthusiast. He had also been loosely following my thread on Pelican Parts, then he read the *Total 911* article and shot me this email.

Initially, his goal was to create something a little bit more edgy for his commercial film reel; he was looking to branch out beyond doing beer and fast-food commercials. With that in mind, he'd already done three pieces, including a short five-minute film on a tattoo guy, as well as a documentary with Honda on Indy racing called *Between the Walls*. He shot me some links and they were cool, stylish, cinematic, very well done and, yes, edgy. I'd watched a lot of these reality car-building TV shows, and in my opinion they always come off slightly cheesy and not that well shot, but Tamir's material had such a cinematic blend.

At first, he just wanted to shoot a three-to-five-minute short YouTube documentary. We knew that momentum was really building with the car collection and my profile in that world, so I said to Karen, 'What do you think?' She was also of the view that it felt right. We'd dipped our foot in the water with Maurice, Erik and *Total 911*, so now it felt like the right time and with the right person to dive in with Tamir. Gut instinct again. I know I keep saying that, but it's so true. Our logic was, 'We'll get some great footage, probably some images to put on a blog . . . fuck . . . what's the worst that can happen?'

When Tamir arrived to film the documentary, I'd never even met him face to face. He flew down using his frequent-flyer miles on a Wednesday ahead of a meeting at the warehouse on the Thursday morning for a four-day shoot. He hired a very talented crew here in LA. Luckily, these people were all available, such as Anthony Arendt as the Director of Photography who'd worked with Tamir on a brilliant biker build film. The film crew arrived before Tamir, and again we all just kind of clicked. So it quickly felt like the stars were aligning – everything just slotted into place.

Tamir has his own production company, Supplemental, and he'd been able to raise the funding through that for the film, so it was essentially a very independent passion project (the actual press release for the film would use those exact words). The whole *Urban Outlaw* documentary, as it would become known, was shot on a low budget. I don't actually know what the cost was, truth be told, but it was essentially shot on two Canon 5DSs. It was the first filming I had ever done. Obviously, I'd been around film crews at the warehouse for ten years, but I'd never been the subject matter myself. In terms of being on the other side of the lens, I didn't know anything about the process, so it was super-exciting. I was pretty eager and keen, but I didn't really know how it was going to go . . . you quickly learn. Over the next four days, we basically hung out for twelve hours every day, spoke about Porsche and drove the cars as the story evolved.

When we had location shooting going on at the warehouse, Karen and I used to joke about how it was all, 'Hurry up and wait', like that time I told you about with Bruce Willis. It takes for ever to set up a shot that might only last a few seconds. Well, very quickly I got a different vibe from these guys, a relatively small team, only eight people or so. Tamir and his crew were super-efficient. Not quick for the sake of it or because they weren't being precise, far from it. They were just very, very efficient.

Even though this was the first on-screen interview I'd done, I said to Tamir, 'Don't bother showing me any questions, I don't want to think about it, just ask me.' Therefore the whole documentary is completely unscripted. Also, we didn't pull a single permit, the whole film was shot bootleg-style, meaning there was no traffic control, no police officers co-ordinating traffic, we didn't have any film permits. It was guerrilla film-making at its finest. Looking back, I guess it was pretty intense, but I think I tapped into my inner reserve and put 110 per cent in; I gave it my all. Karen was completely involved, and it was a spectacular time for us both.

Truth be told, there was a spell around day three when I was getting a bit restless. There were elements that I found mildly tedious. I had hit my stride by this point, but we still hadn't really shot anything to do with fast driving. Believe it or not, Tamir and I actually got in a little bit of an argument, and I'm like, 'Dude, when are we doing the fucking fast driving?! This is all bullshit talking . . .' but I didn't understand his vision. I was naïve, I didn't see the bigger picture. I was just impulsive; I wanted to go and do some spirited driving. So I'm not gonna lie, there was a little bit of tension building during that third day, but other than that we got on like a house on fire.

There were three cars featured in *Urban Outlaw*. The period correct '66 Irish Green 911, the '68R (Liam Howlett's car) and then obviously 277. I'd asked Liam if I could keep the 68R a little longer so that Tamir could film it, and he was cool with that. The 68R is kinda the hero car in the film.

There was a lot of talking and a lot of driving; it was a really enjoyable experience. Tamir would say, 'What does Porsche mean to you?' and I'd ramble on for like twenty minutes. Being a real talented guy, Tamir knew how to make me look good on camera, and obviously later on I realized it is all in the editing.

On the fourth day, after we'd finished, we threw ourselves a little wrap party at the bar next door and realized we'd probably shot at least twenty hours of great footage. Tamir had obviously been looking at the footage at night-time – the dailies and the raw footage – and he had started to believe that there was more to my story than a short five-minute documentary. Tamir sensed he had captured something a little bit special. He was somehow able to bring this story out of me and that coincided with me being ready to open up. That night at the bar there was talk of a longer film, which was obviously really exciting. That film is not just a Porsche story. It's the story of me coming to America, about never giving up on my dream, about going with my gut instinct, taking risks, working hard, being creative and individual, about everything that I have spoken of here in this book. Tamir, I think, had seen some spark in me that went beyond just talking about my story and the passion for Porsche. It was a perfect storm.

Then Tamir flew home to Canada and I didn't hear from him for two months . . .

*

Hurry up and wait again, I guess. I just left him to it. I didn't want to rush him; I wasn't bugging him for footage. He might occasionally have emailed a couple of little fifteen-second teasers, but otherwise I kept out of the way. Then he sent us a three-minute trailer, which was subsequently posted on his social-media channel in June 2012.

That's when it all started to go completely crazy.

By that summer, I'd finally got on Facebook, although I wouldn't say I was exactly an expert at that point. I still didn't have an iPhone. I'd only signed up because a guy called Brian who was doing graphics for us said I should be on Facebook in case this thing took off. It was essentially still just my thread on Pelican Parts and the S Registry; I didn't even have a website at this point.

With Tamir being an inspired film guy and a great story-teller, he had pieced together a very compelling three-minute trailer. I posted the trailer on Pelican and the S Registry, as well as my Facebook page, and Maurice had helped me set up my magnuswalker911 blog, so it was posted on there too, but I had absolutely no idea how many people were going to view this mini-clip. No idea whatsoever . . . a hundred, a thousand, maybe three thousand? Who knows?

The trailer went live around 8 a.m. and by nine o'clock I think it already had five thousand views. I remember calling Karen and she said, 'It's unbelievable . . . what's happening here, Magnus?' By lunchtime, it was up to twenty-five thousand views and we were like, 'What is going on here?' Well, either it was a quiet news day or people had connected with what we were doing.

Then *Top Gear* picked up on it and events got really crazy.

That was a special moment in a very memorable day for me.

On their site, they said I was 'The most un-Porsche Porsche enthusiast'. I am a big fan of that show, so I couldn't even believe I was on *Top Gear* in any form. Over the next couple of days, it was just unbelievable, the social-media coverage went crazy. At the time, I'd probably got around a thousand followers on Facebook, then suddenly I'm coming in each day and there's five hundred friend requests . . . just from Spain. I'm like, *Fuck! What's going on in Spain?* Normally, I'd get a couple of requests at a time.

Turns out this Spanish automotive blog had picked up on *Top Gear*, but that was the tip of the iceberg . . . over the next week or so the trailer just went viral around the world. I was getting friend requests from Turkey, Russia, Poland, Australia, all over the place. So the initial *Top Gear* posting had generated massive attention, then all these countries around the world had picked up on the clip, and also every automotive blog, as well as magazines including *Road & Track*, Jalopnik, *Car and Driver*. It was going nuts.

You see, Tamir was ahead of the game. Obviously, people had been making documentaries about Porsches for a long time, but nothing like this had really been done before. It was the first film of its kind. It was Porsche-related, yes, with someone like me that was unknown and . . . let's just say unconventional. It was filmed in a really stylish way, and there was a wider story that just seemed to hit a chord with so many people worldwide. That initial trailer went on to get over two million views.

Then I got an email from this guy called Sandy Bodecker, who is the vice president of Nike Action Sports Division. He is a very successful businessman and a Porsche guy (he had a GT2). He told me he had seen the trailer, loved my story and my passion and asked if I would be interested in talking at one of Nike's huge design/merchandizing/branding summits that they hold for their staff several times a year. The idea soon evolved, and they actually held that event in the warehouse in Willow, a full two-day summit at the loft. Remember, the full documentary by Tamir hadn't even come out yet. This was all off the back of just the trailer. They even rented Soho House in Hollywood, which has a screening room, and showed a very rough cut of the film to the Nike employees, who were in fact the very first people outside of my immediate circle to see more of the documentary. What an honour, right? Nike was coming to me. This seemed completely bizarre. I was starting to think that maybe something very special was happening.

By now, there was a lot of anticipation for the release of the whole documentary. I was getting messages all the time asking about when the film was coming out – the trailer had simply ended with a 'Coming Soon' tease. Well, at this point, editing of the film wasn't even finished. Then, around September, Tamir sent me the thirty-two-minute documentary on a private Vimeo channel.

Obviously, I watched it with Karen straight away, with great excitement and anticipation.

First impressions?

Truth be told, I didn't actually like it.

I was just expecting something a little . . . well . . . *faster*. I thought it was going to be all reckless abandonment, racing, speed, just this blur of fast cars and spirited driving. I didn't phone Tamir back for a day, and he's since told me that (understandably) he was getting worried.

But then I watched the film a second time . . . and I started to see what he had done. I began to see the bigger picture, understand his vision. I watched it again and by the third time I was completely hooked. This wasn't just a film about cars; what Tamir had done was tell *my story*, and to do that there needed to be so much more than just fast cars. Some of my favourite scenes are the ones where I'm just sitting quietly working at a sewing machine. Tamir – being the smarter guy and the storyteller – had edited all the footage into a much wider narrative; he'd blended this melting pot of clips into a cinematic statement. There's not necessarily a lot of dialogue, but it creates a very powerful vibe. And I'd like to think people watch that and get inspired.

There were quite a few spontaneous little moments that happened while filming the documentary that just worked brilliantly but were completely unscripted. There's a point in the film where I talk about having a 'Porsche passion'. Well, I'd never used those words before. It just came out in the film. You see that look in my eyes, 'What does Porsche mean to you?' . . . 'Porsche passion'. There's also a scene where I'm catching a bit of sunshine, lying on a wall, when suddenly a beautiful Porsche 356 drives past. We never did find out who that was, we didn't know the car or the owner, he just happened to be driving by. In another scene, you see these people on a street corner taking photos of my car on their phones as I drive around at speed. Those were just some guys who happened to be there, probably heard the car coming and turned their phone cameras on. Then there's the scene where the camera pans out to the LA skyline as I exit 6th Street on the 110 South, and in the dark sky there's a searchlight in the background. That isn't added digitally, nor was it planned by us. It just so happened that the Oscars were on in that area of LA at the same time, so they had these big Batman-like searchlights sweeping the LA skyline. Like I said, the stars definitely aligned.

If I was blown away by what had happened so far, then I was in for more shocks. Tamir was always one step ahead of the game. He submitted *Urban Outlaw* to various film festivals like Toronto, Sundance, Tribeca, and, much to our amazement, next thing we know we get a phone call from him – we couldn't believe it! – the documentary had been accepted for the London Raindance Film Festival. We were like, 'Fuck, now we're in a film festival!' We were just happy that we'd had a documentary made, let alone been included in the rainy version of Sundance. The film was due to be screened in London's West End in late September. So now all of a sudden Karen and I were going to London. It was all just so exciting . . . genuinely hard to believe.

Tamir and his wife flew to London, too, then various people that had been following my threads online decided they were going to fly over from Europe. Porsche passion, see? Porsche is first and foremost about people – so, for example, there's a guy called Joost Hermès (who helped me find my '64 911, more on which later) who has become a real pen-pal buddy, he flew over from the Netherlands. Then Liam Howlett from the Prodigy, who bought the 68R that featured in the opening shot of *Urban Outlaw*, came down as well. There was a bunch of us who all met up and had a little pre-screening party at the St Martins Lane Hotel in Covent Garden where Karen and I were staying. My mum came down, my brother and sister-in-law and my sister, too. I remember my brother was all excited to meet Liam because he is a Prodigy fan. One of the journalists from *Total 911* was there as well as a couple of other members of the UK motoring press, because there was a real buzz about the film. It was just an unbelievably memorable night. From my point of view, I was like, *When do you get to go to a film premiere in central London on a Friday night? Never mind the premiere of my own film!* It was crazy. What a memory.

After those pre-screening drinks, about twenty of us walked through Leicester Square to the Odeon in Lower Regent Street for the film, which was sold out. It didn't matter that there were only two hundred seats in the theatre, it was sold out. I walked in there feeling like a rock star, just floated in, amazing.

We watched a few other short films first, and then *Urban Outlaw* came on. It was unbelievable, people were shouting and cheering as the credits rolled and the film came on. At this point, we'd never seen the documentary on the big screen; I'd only ever seen it on my computer, not even on a TV. I think at the time my monitor was like 14-inch, proper old-school, none of these big high-def jobs. So to see it on the big screen for the first time at a film-festival premiere was emotional; truth be told, I almost cried. After the screening, we went to a pub right around the corner; it was just an unbelievable experience, you know. Then we hung out in London for a few days and eventually went back to Los Angeles.

*

One of the very few sad moments from this exciting period was that my father passed away just a month after the London film festival. After the premiere and before we flew home, we'd travelled up to Sheffield and shown him the DVD of *Urban Outlaw*, but he was struggling. He'd had throat cancer for eighteen months, and when I saw him I came away crying. I said to Karen, 'This will be the last time we see him alive.' Remember everything I've told you about those turbulent teenage years when I clashed with my dad? Well, as we both got older we had become closer. He had obviously given up on the 'cut your hair and get a real job' and was proud of my success. My parents had started to come out to LA, sometimes for as long as a month, which was great. One of the most memorable trips was around 2007 when he came out with me in the Irish Green 911. He and I took that car out and we drove probably two hundred miles to go look at some rust-bucket piece of crap car in the desert, but the point was it was him and me together all day long, just the two of us. That is a very fond memory.

The fact that he saw the film and was really proud of it was real special, but then six weeks later he was gone and we were back in England for the funeral. Looking back, I think of all those times in my childhood when we went to see motor shows and cars and motor racing, and I can see that Dad was a very big influence on certain parts of my life. Driving round LA in the Irish Green 911 was almost as if our relationship had come back around full circle.

Back in LA and with the release of *Urban Outlaw* fast approaching, I knew that I had to get a few things in order – a logo, my website, some merchandise, just generally a bigger presence online. I'd always liked the TAG Heuer logo, so essentially the Urban Outlaw artwork is very much influenced by that, just 'Urban Outlaw' with my name on top and the Union Jack added. I doodled the basic idea on a napkin and then had a graphics buddy draw it up. Then we launched the Urban Outlaw retail store ahead of *Urban Outlaw* being officially released on 15 October 2012.

When that happened, everything went even more crazy, and I knew that my life would never be the same again . . .

URBAN
OUTLAW

Chapter 11

How Bad Can It Be, Right?

The roller coaster had begun. In the immediate aftermath of *Urban Outlaw*'s release, some incredible things started happening. For example, every fall, usually early November, there's a huge car show in Vegas called SEMA. It's a big aftermarket auto show, with hot rods and custom cars. It's fast and furious, it's muscle cars, sports import tuners, Ken Block, drift cars, every major car manufacturer, every independent guy, every distributor – it's an unbelievable show. I'd wanted to go there for ever but for a variety of reasons had never made it happen. To be fair, these were not generally Porsche people; if there were over two thousand cars on show in a typical year at SEMA, there might be ten Porsches there, tops.

Tamir's documentary had only been out for two weeks at this point, everyone online had been buzzing about it and the link for the film had been blogged and reblogged all over the place. However, that autumn's SEMA was my first indication of the real-world impact of *Urban Outlaw*. First off, I didn't actually have a pass to even get into the show. SEMA is an industry show and I don't actually have a car business, so . . . no pass. Undeterred, I flew in to Vegas on a 7 a.m. flight out of Burbank, got there at 8 a.m., borrowed this guy's pass and kinda blagged my way in. I was there early and had to wait for the show to start, but even before the doors had opened people were coming up to me to talk about the film. All sorts of characters were saying how much they loved the film and, like I said, these were not Porsche-centric people. They were just car enthusiasts, bike enthusiasts, hot-rod enthusiasts . . . a huge variety of people who had seen the film and connected with it.

However, the real crazy part of that first day at SEMA was in the early morning when my phone rang and it was this guy called Robert Angelo. He introduced himself as the producer of *Jay Leno's Garage*, one of the most popular car shows in the world, presented by one of the biggest collectors and, obviously, a huge name in the world of entertainment. He said Jay had seen *Urban Outlaw*, really enjoyed it and would love to have me on his show. I was just gobsmacked, standing there at SEMA, trying to take this all in. Then the kicker was he said, 'We have availability for filming this Saturday if you are around?' I didn't know if Jay had actually seen the film or if this guy was just blowing smoke, but I was like, 'Sure, I'll go.' You know the drill by now – how bad can it be, right? I'd only gone to SEMA for a day and chanced my arm to get a pass, now I'm taking calls about appearing on Jay Leno's show four days later. I phoned Karen and told her what had

Above: Porsche memorabilia in the garage. [*Larry Chen*]

Left: Sat at my desk surrounded by organized chaos. [*Larry Chen*]

Below: POC racing plaques and awards. [*Larry Chen*]

Above left: I never throw anything away. The back room behind the garage . . . leftover tyres. [*Maurice van del Tillard*]

Above right: I collect steering wheels. [*Maurice van del Tillard*]

Right: Fenders and window frames, everything is interchangeable – the great thing about Porsches. [*Maurice van del Tillard*]

Right: Me taping off the very first 52 Outlaw wheels. [*Jon White*]

Right: Swapping rims on the '78 SCHR. [*Larry Chen*]

'67 SRT work in progress, *c.* 2012. [*Maurice van del Tillard*]

Donor parts cars – you never know when you may need that piece of sheet metal. [*Maurice van del Tillard*]

'72 STR 3.2 short-stroke motor, built by Aaron Burnham. [*Sean Klingelhoefer*]

My holy grail car: a '64 911. [*Maurice van del Tillard*]

Above: Turbo fever: '76 and '77 930 Turbos, stay boosted.

Below: Into the red and beyond. [*Larry Chen*]

Above: '78 SCHR. [*Andrew Ritter*]

Above: '68R – the hero car of the *Urban Outlaw* film.

Above: '78 SCHR in DTLA [*Sean Klingelhoefer*]

Above: '76 930 black Turbo. [*Andrew Ritter*]

Right: '78 SCHR on Lower Grand Street. [*Sean Klingelhoefer*]

Above: 277 and the '72 STR under the iconic 6th Street bridge.

Below: '72 STR. [*Sean Klingelhoefer*]

Above: Shark Werks 997 GT2 at the Queen Mary in Long Beach. [*Larry Chen*]

Above: A real honour to have my own signature Momo steering wheel.

Left: '76 930 Minerva Blue Turbo on the 6th Street Bridge. [*Larry Chen*]

Below: '67S in the DTLA Arts District. [*Andrew Ritter*]

Above and above right: Behind the scenes of filming the *Urban Outlaw* documentary film.

Right: Walking towards 277. [*Andrew Ritter*]

Right: Anthony Arendt, me and Tamir Moscovici reviewing footage during the filming of *Urban Outlaw*.

Below: It's a wrap! Finished filming *Urban Outlaw*, February 2012.

Left: 15 October 2012. Without Tamir Moscovici's award-winning documentary film, the past five years of my life would have been very different.

Below: 1990 964, my most performance-orientated build to date. [*Larry Chen*]

Bottom left: My favourite car, 277. [*Jon White*]

Bottom right: Karen and Jay Leno, *c.* 2013.

Above: My parents.

Right: Karen and me at the Hollywood sign.

Below right: Karen, my brother St. John and his wife Nicky at the *Urban Outlaw* premiere.

Below: With Karen and her family, in Atlanta, Georgia.

Below: Karen kicking my ass – she always used to keep me in line [*Larry Chen*]

happened; she was as shocked as I was, it was just crazy.

That Saturday, Karen and I drove 277 over to Jay Leno's garage at Burbank. Jay Leno is such a car enthusiast, an icon. He has about 100,000 square feet of the most diverse and incredible car collection, perhaps even better than the Petersen Museum, it is that good. He has collected well over a hundred and fifty cars and motorcycles, some of which he uses as daily drivers and some are the very rarest of pieces that deserve a place in any museum. It's everything from a 1902 steam car to the latest McLaren to genuine exotics, as well as unexpected cars like Renault 5s, Citroens and oddball stuff. He loves McLaren for the technology, precision, performance and engineering, really loves McLaren. The F1 is one of his all-time favourite cars. I would describe him as a full-on British gearhead – he's got Morgans, Austin-Healeys, E-Types, Astons, various Jags – he is a real fanatic about British cars. He is also an Italian sports car fan, for example he loves Lamborghini for the drama, so he's got a Countach and two Miuras. He loves American muscle cars, he's got numerous Mercedes . . . the list is endless. It's not just the vehicles, it's the posters, the memorabilia, the artefacts. He is a true gear-head, petrol-head, motor-head, car enthusiast, call it what you will. You can sense he appreciates 911s, but he is not really a Porsche guy. When I first went there, he only had two Porsches –a Speedster and a Carrera GT, no 911.

Anyway, we were looking at all these cars while waiting for Jay to show and then suddenly he just turned up, driving himself, no entourage whatsoever. He is just in this denim outfit, no fanfare, and he comes over, shakes my hand, gives Karen a hug and says some really nice things about the film.

It was immediately apparent that apart from being a super-knowledgeable car expert, he was also very down to earth and just totally genuine.

Then suddenly, boom, we were filming. Jay's talking about how great the internet is for discovering interesting stuff online and how 'unlike TV, I can find stuff I actually wanna watch'. He said that he'd stumbled across *Urban Outlaw* and gives this little summary about me, all while I'm standing off-camera thinking, *This is not what I was expecting to do this Saturday!* Then he said, 'Let's meet him . . .' It all felt very strange. Remember, working with Tamir had been the very first time I'd ever been filmed. Appearing on *Jay Leno's Garage* was the second. And in between the two there'd been a nine-month gap!

Before you know it, Jay and I are chatting, completely unrehearsed and unscripted. We stood next to 277 and talked about the car and then we went for a drive. We filmed for probably two hours, and later Jay sent his crew down to do a little bit of footage at the warehouse. It was just the most incredible experience.

Of course, Jay drove 277. That was very bizarre. I'm sitting in the passenger seat of my car and Jay Leno is driving us down the freeway. I was just thinking, *How did I get here?* But as you know by now, I like to go with the flow, so I'm trying not to talk over Jay, because he's just such a seasoned pro. Everything is just one take, there are no retakes, no chances for mistakes. We cracked a couple of little jokes, and I would say we got on pretty well – it was just cool to be with him.

We headed back to the garage, and he took us around some

more of the collection. Then he showed us around his own workshop. He's got this crew of guys working on various complex restoration projects and maintaining the collection, too. He's even got his own CNC precision engineering machines and a factory-standard paint booth.

Then it got even better – Jay fucking Leno says, 'You guys want something to eat?' So he orders a dozen pizzas and we are all eating this food, chatting away with him and his crew. Then – and here's the coolest part – he starts cooking up some pasta for everybody. Karen and I are just looking at each other, pinching ourselves. Karen offers to do the dishes, so Jay loves that. At one point, I went to the bathroom and there's pictures of Jay Leno and Bill Clinton and all these super-famous people on the walls. Nothing's really off limits with him. I don't know if he's like this with everybody, although I think he might be, because I got the impression he's just that type of guy.

He wasn't finished yet. Next up he says, 'You ever been in a steam car, Magnus?' I mentioned a real English character called Fred Dibnah, this old Yorkshire dude who was a famous northerner and considered a world expert on certain elements of Britain's industrial heritage, and Jay had met him! Turns out they'd met because Jay had half a dozen Stanley and White steam cars from the early twentieth century.

So, next thing we know, Karen and I are sitting in a century-old steam car, being driven around Burbank Airport by Jay Leno. Now, you don't just turn the key in a steam car, so he's got this mechanic getting the thing started. They fill it up with water and then they stoke the boiler and it comes up to temperature about twenty minutes later, then Jay, me and this other guy push it out there. It makes pressure, but then it develops a leak, so they were like, 'Oh, we can't take this one,' so they start again with another priceless steam car he also owns.

Now, not only are these steam cars pretty laborious to get started, they are also not the fastest vehicles out there, so we are doing about 5mph around Burbank Airport. You can imagine the scene: we are stopping at lights in this one-hundred-year-old steam car, the world-famous talk-show host Jay Leno is driving, I'm sitting there with my dreadlocks and tattoos just grinning and Karen's looking beautiful and also somewhat bemused in the back. We were completely dumbfounded to be honest; people were taking photographs, shouting hello, it was just the most incredible experience. I just kept thinking, *How the fuck did we get here?!*

Two weeks later, the Jay Leno episode came out and, before you know it, we had over 200,000 views to add to the rapidly escalating online figures for *Urban Outlaw*. If Tamir opened the door and *Top Gear* fired that movie off around the internet, then *Jay Leno's Garage* opened up my story to the non-Porsche audience on a global scale. At the time of writing, Jay's fourteen-minute clip has had over 500,000 views. That's a lot of eyeballs. To finish up with this part of the tale, I ended up doing two other appearances on *Jay Leno's Garage*, one with my follow-up build, the STR, which I will talk about later.

The craziness wasn't just online or on TV shows either. The magazine coverage was insane, and I am talking about all around the world and not just in Porsche magazines either. There was plenty of non-Porsche coverage through people like Jalopnik and Speed Hunters, which really took more of a car culture/lifestyle angle. Those types of blogs appear to have picked up on the customization and personalization vibe, because, as I always say, true car guys have that in common – you may not drive the same car, you each pick your own poison, but ultimately it doesn't matter what you drive, we all share the same passion. Real car enthusiasts share the same DNA. Part of the appeal to magazines and journalists, I suspect, is that when these media people come to LA, I am close by, it's an interesting building, there's an unusual back-story and also some great driving to be had.

The year 2013 was just unbelievable. There were so many magical moments. If you've seen the *Urban Outlaw* film, you will know there's a moment where I talk about that letter I wrote to Porsche when I was just ten years old. It's a night-time driving scene in the 68R in Downtown LA, it's not particularly fast footage, you see the lights flashing and the skyline driving by, and Tamir asks me what I thought Porsche would make of my outlaw builds thirty-five years after I sent that first letter, and I respond by saying, 'I would hope they'd be smiling . . .' Bear in mind, I'd had no contact with Porsche until the film came out. I've always been about old Porsches, never, ever owned a new one. I didn't go to dealers to buy parts; I just never went into a Porsche dealership at all. So my interaction with anything officially Porsche-related was non-existent.

Well, a week or two after the film came out, I get a letter from Porsche's PR department, saying:

Dear Mr Walker

In the last few months, we read numerous stories about your incredible collection. One can feel enthusiasm and real adoration for our brand and especially our 911. Having such a fan like you out there really fills us with pride. With a twinkle in our eye, we also read about the loss of your invitation to Zuffenhausen many years ago.

The best part was that they then invited me to a guided tour of their factory in Stuttgart. I couldn't believe it.

I'd only ever been to Germany once, running in that athletics competition as a kid. Now I was going back as a guest of Porsche. Unbelievable. I travelled to Stuttgart as their guest, and they treated me like a rock star. They drove me from Frankfurt to Stuttgart, put me up in a hotel and gave me a private behind-the-scenes tour of the Porsche factory and headquarters. I got to spend time with the lovely Dieter Landenberger, who is the curator and historian of the Porsche archives, and I took the opportunity to show him some information on what I believe is the first US-production Turbo ever sold, my '76 930 Turbo. I was thrilled that he validated my theory using the factory archive. He showed me all the documentation that most people never get to see – the build certificate, everything – it was fascinating. Porsche treated me like royalty.

Another nice Porsche twist came when a guy called Chalmers Niemeyer, who is a very senior marketing manager for Porsche, sent me a Porsche shield with a letter saying, 'Here's something for your garage wall.' Funnily enough, he was actually a friend of Karen's from Atlanta, and I had met him ten years earlier when he wasn't at Porsche but was instead working in the fashion industry. Then we lost contact with him, but he'd seen *Urban Outlaw* and got back in touch. He couldn't believe that I had gone from this Serious Clothing dude whom he'd met in New York at a fashion trade show years earlier to this guy in a short documentary film with a renowned passion for Porsche. Porsche people again, see. I talk all the time about Porsche being a language – doesn't matter whether you speak English, German or Japanese, Porsche is the bond that brings everyone together. No matter where you are in the world, you can all relate to the car; you don't have to speak the same language, you can walk around the car and point at elements and without talking know what you are both saying. In my opinion, it's also a great equalizer of social standing. I've met billionaire Porsche owners who are down to earth and relate to what I'm doing. I would never have met those guys if it wasn't for the connection with Porsche. It's my drug, it's my religion, it's what brings people together. Like I said, Porsche passion.

Perhaps inevitably, I was then approached about being more involved with Porsche officially. With Tamir being Canadian, the very first Porsche event I did was around a month after the film came out, for Porsche Cars Canada in November 2012 when they debuted the Panamera for the US market at my warehouse, in conjunction with the LA Auto Show. Detlev von Platen, the president of Porsche North America, came by; he'd seen *Urban Outlaw* and really enjoyed the film. He sat in my '64 911 with me, signed the certificate of authenticity and I'd like to think I really clicked with this guy. I remember him sending me a Christmas card. I also got a Christmas card from Michael Mauer, the chief designer at Porsche, who very kindly sketched 277 on the front.

Since then, I've worked with Porsche on many occasions. Sometimes I appear at events, other times they come to my garage for launches. For example, they once did a dealer event where all their worldwide distributors held a workshop at the loft. Another time, Porsche Classic actually had me involved doing a little motivational talk in the workshop. I've also been to the Goodwood Festival, the Revival and the Techno Classica in Essen with them too, among many other events. I also got approached by an agent to be in a Porsche commercial for the new Macan. Essentially, the idea behind the advert was to show that there is a Porsche for every type of person. That said, I'm the only guy in this advert driving a car that's not actually for sale in the Porsche line-up, because I'm driving 277, so I guess I'm in there as the Porsche rebel. That was such an honour to be asked, especially as they wanted 277 in there. Remember, I have no agent, no PR, no marketing advisers, no nothing. I would have done it for free, but they ended up paying me a shitload of dough for like a day of work. They shipped the car to San Francisco, flew us up there first class and yet I'm only in the video for about five seconds.

I shot two more videos that year with Porsche, one at the factory in Zuffenhausen talking about the fortieth anniversary of the Turbo for Porsche GB. That was filmed with the brilliant Porsche designer Tony Hatter, who is a real nice guy; it was a total honour. I also shot another video with Porsche at the Goodwood Revival. At one point, there was even talk of a 277-liveried 991-911. Not just the livery though, actually a combination of two of my favourite limited-edition, high-performance 911s: a Sport Classic and a GT3. There was even enough interest to generate some verbal orders. That would have been incredible, but it hasn't happened yet. I'm still hopeful it might eventually work out though, so watch this space! If it does ever happen, that will be the ultimate realization of my dream to design for Porsche, which I had written about as a ten-year-old in that letter after Earls Court. Despite all the crazy things that have happened since that day nearly four decades ago, I've never lost sight of where I came from and the dreams I had back then, so getting the chance to work with Porsche always gives me an incredible buzz.

Of course, 2013 was a huge year for Porsche themselves, completely unrelated to anything I was doing. This was because it was the fiftieth anniversary of the 911. The first model rolled off the production line in 1964, but the car itself was launched at the Frankfurt Auto Show in 1963. So fifty years later, the timing of *Urban Outlaw* was ideal because the whole world was talking about the 911. The stars aligned – like I say, sometimes opportunities present themselves, and when they do you have to seize them because that set of events might not come along again. The 911 is, I believe, the third-oldest still-in-continuous-production sports car in existence. The world's longest in-production sports car is in fact the Chevy Corvette, which came out in '53 as a '54-year model, so that predated the 911 by ten years. In '64, the Ford Mustang came out. Although I've also owned a Mustang as well as my 911s, the two cars in a sense couldn't be more different. One's German, one's American; one's rear-engined, one's front-engined; one's air-cooled, one's water-cooled. Completely different, but they have both been in production since 1964 and more importantly have similarly fanatical fan bases, with cultures where people either cherish stock vehicles or alternatively heavily customize them.

Anyway, I'm getting distracted. Back to the story. So, all these magazines and websites were running articles on the anniversary of the 911, and my story seemed to appeal to so many of them. I guess it was a twist, something unusual to add. Consequently, lots of the press I gained that year was based around the fiftieth-anniversary celebrations.

I think part of the appeal was also that I'm not an independent dealer, I'm not selling cars; this is just my collection. It's a diverse collection as well, and the story of how it got to that point was pretty complex. Some of these articles touched on the warehouse, the location filming and the clothing, and went beyond the purely automotive. So my tale was then pitched as a lifestyle story, with a lot of fashion and lifestyle magazines buying into it. On a similar vibe, I am also always really pleased to receive so many emails from girlfriends and wives who've seen and enjoyed *Urban Outlaw* – that is indicative of a lot of non-automotive people who connected to the film because it's a story about passion, staying motivated and never giving up on your dreams.

Events started gathering even more momentum when I presented my next big build, the second STR. This was the car that I had been working on during the filming of *Urban Outlaw*. I combined my two favourite Porsches – the R and ST icons from the late sixties and early seventies – into my own version, which I call the STR02. As a consequence of the film's success, there was now an awful lot of attention and anticipation for my next build. I went back on *Jay Leno's Garage* for the second time to debut the STR02 in March 2013. At that point, I would say the STR02 was my definitive build. That car went on to be on the cover of *Road & Track* during the 911's fiftieth-anniversary celebrations. That was unbelievable, a no-name independent enthusiast making the cover of *Road & Track*, rather than a classic or stock car by Porsche themselves or some famous tuning house. Inside, among a feature on various high-profile Porsche people, I was listed as 'The Fanatic'. The STR02 was also on the cover of *Total 911* when they very kindly asked me to be the guest editor for an issue . . . they called the car 'The New Legend'. Later, for the hundredth edition of *Total 911*, I was invited to write the intro and the back-page closing piece, while they also did a full feature on the STR02 and then had me pick my top twenty-five Porsches.

In 2013, I also started doing what media types call 'appearances'. If you recall, a lot of the Dutch guys on the scene had been incredibly supportive, like my buddy Joost Hermès, Erik Kouwenhoven who had done the first article, my photographer friend Maurice, *RS Porsche* magazine; that whole contingent of European guys had in essence sparked the very first interest in what I was doing. The producers of *RS Porsche* magazine had an event called 'Porsche Fest' and invited me to appear. They picked me up at the airport, we did a Rotterdam tunnel run, which was perhaps one of the first of what came to be christened 'Outlaw Gatherings', then met up at a Porsche dealership.

Urban Outlaw hasn't just led to exciting tie-ups with Porsche. I've also ended up working with some other pretty massive global brands including Mobil 1, Pirelli, Volvo, Bentley and Oakley. Remember when I had to sneak into SEMA 2012 on someone else's pass? Well, eventually I would find myself invited by Mobil 1 to show two cars at their stand in 2014. Mobil 1 only had three cars in their booth and two of them were mine – 277 and the 67S. I drove 277 there, which in itself is unusual for cars on show, which are normally trailered in. But why would you want to put 277 on a trailer when you can go and drive her all the way there? Makes no sense to me. Gotta tell you though, 277 was leaking oil on the Mobil 1 stand, which is kinda ironic, especially when you consider I gave them the tag line 'Stay lubricated'.

I enjoy those shows. It takes me back to the glory days of doing all the fashion trade fairs with Karen for Serious. I do these autograph signings and really enjoy meeting fans and car people. Right after *Urban Outlaw* came out, people would come up to me and ask for my autograph and, truth be told, it was kind of awkward at first, because I was just thinking, *What do you want my autograph for?* But it kind of became more awkward not to do it, because otherwise you have to say, 'No, sorry I'm not into doing autographs,' and then you're seen as this wanker.

I try to spend as much time as I can with people who queue to meet me and say hello. Why would you not? I'm literally the first person there and last person to leave. I treated that SEMA show – and all the subsequent ones I've been to – as a chance to give back to all the people that have supported me over these recent years, spending their time watching my videos and all the online support. In the end, the autograph session that day at SEMA went on for three hours. At one point, after two hours, the people at Mobil said, 'Do you want to stop? We only really expected you to stay for an hour.' I said, 'Well, the queue's not finished and we've still got spare posters, so let's keep going.' I never want to be that idiot that says, 'Sorry, man, I'm done, I'm too busy.'

I did that for four days at SEMA. One of the guys at Mobil complimented me on my work ethic, saying, 'We have brand ambassadors turn up, sign for half an hour then dash off, but you've been here for hours every day!'

For me, it's pretty simple: always remember your roots, where you came from. Imagine my mum seeing me letting fans down who'd queued for hours to meet me? Not good enough. At heart, I am still a hard-grafting, working-class northern boy, so never give up, and wait till the last person's been sorted.

Like I said, I had experienced a degree of notoriety before on a lesser scale with Serious, and I felt reasonably well equipped to handle the exposure and attention that followed Tamir's documentary. So those glitzy car shows were just me getting back to grafting with Karen at fashion trade shows, or back further still to the market traders in my family across the Pond in Sheffield, my grandparents, my roots. (Talking of roots, when I appeared at one Porsche event, I got my dread-locks stuck in the door of their 918 supercar, much to everyone's amusement!)

A small but nevertheless very telling example of how much *Urban Outlaw* has changed my landscape often happens at these personal appearances. In the past, when Serious was at its height, people used to come up to me at trade shows or when I was out and about and say, 'Hey, aren't you the singer Rob Zombie?' I wish I had a dollar for every time that happened. In fact, when I was feeling mischievous, I sometimes used to say, 'No, I'm his brother.' However, from 2013 that stopped and people would come up and say, 'Hey, aren't you that Porsche guy?'

Another way I get to meet fans and more Porsche people is when we organize Porsche runs. I've been involved in quite a few outlaw runs now. We did a meet at the famous Ace Cafe on London's North Circular Road, we did one on Boxing Day of 2015, we've done one in Switzerland, at the castle where my cousin lived, and in various other countries. I love doing those runs, and I look forward to meeting you on one of them in the future.

There were so many highlights in 2013 it's almost hard to remember and list them all, but one of the absolute best, not least for what it represented, was when I got the unexpected and tempting opportunity through Gooding & Company auctioneers to put the STR up for sale at the Monterey Historics in Pebble Beach, which was celebrating the 911's fiftieth. I often talk about things lining up organically, well, you know my set-up now – there is no PR team behind this, these opportunities were just coming in direct to me and I reacted to them on instinct. Gooding reached out to me and gave me a time slot late on the Saturday night at Pebble Beach to auction the STR.

At this point, remember, the whole car world and beyond had seen Leno drive the STR, it'd been on *Fifth Gear*, on

Road & Track's cover, all these other magazines, all over the internet – this had become a very well-known 911. It was also my defining build to date, the best car I'd created. It was kind of a weird experience in the three or so weeks leading up to the auction, like some mad goldfish bowl. People come from all over the world to this prestigious five-day event, and the auctions are one of the biggest dates in the high-end car-lover's calendar. Everyone was asking what the car was going to sell for, and it was one of the most talked-about vehicles that was going up for sale. Remember, in some ways I am effectively an unknown builder. So they put no reserve on the car, with an estimate of around $125,000. At that point, a completely ordinary '72 911T would probably have fetched around $30,000 unrestored, but no more than say $60,000–$70,000 all sorted.

Lot 61, my STR, ended up hammering down for a little over three hundred grand.

It's hard to know what cars are worth sometimes – in that case, I knew it was worth over $150,000, more likely over $200,000, but I didn't realize it was worth three hundred plus.

This caused a big stir in the Porsche scene, and indeed across the wider car world. For starters, the car was bought by a wonderful couple called the Ingrams. They have one of the most incredible car collections you will ever see and famously all factory originals of dozens of marques. I believe they have one of the top-three collections in the USA, everything from a Gmünd Coupe to a 918, one of every RS – theirs is a serious assortment of cars. They'd reached out to me relatively soon after *Urban Outlaw* came out, seen the film, said they were fans, we'd naturally just connected and went on to form a good friendship. They are super-down-to-earth people, super-generous, salt of the earth; they even allowed me to drive their Carrera GT and their RSs. Those guys display cars all over the country, and one time they'd invited Karen and me to an event in Pinehurst, North Carolina. They'd also come out to see us during one of the west-coast car shows, and that's when I just briefly told them, 'Hey, I'm going to be selling the STR.' Long story short, they had to have the car.

If the 68R was the build that put me on the map, I think it's fair to say that the STR gained me the most worldwide attention. The key point in all of this is that up until the STR, there was not one single customized car in the Ingrams' collection. Mine was the first. That endorsed my work in a massive way, and I was very proud of that fact. I'm a firm believer that if I had restored that car back to its original stock, it would not have been worth the money it got. Essentially, that car was worth more because it had been hot-rodded.

In the weeks and months after the Gooding auction, there were quite a few articles written about what had happened, and it really made people reconsider their preconceptions about hot-rodded cars. Of course, the money was great, but what was even better was the credibility that it gave my work. That really ruffled the feathers of the industry. The purists questioned it because it was a non-matching-numbers car and obviously heavily modified. I believe Jerry Seinfeld, who is a famous Porsche collector, asked the Ingrams why they'd bought the STR. They explained why and that they were very proud to have the car in their collection. I was super-proud to later be asked to be a part of their own book, *Porsche Unexpected: Discoveries in Collecting*. The Ingrams are just really lovely, genuine people.

There have been some really exciting spin-off projects more directly tied into what I do with my car builds, rather than just personal appearances. I was approached by Matt and Brad from fifteen52, which is an independent boutique wheel manufacturer here in LA that happens to supply wheels to professional rally driver Ken Block. In pretty much every Gymkhana video that Ken Block's ever done, the cars are running on fifteen52 wheels and you are talking about 250 million-plus views. So fifteen52 is an industry-leading boutique wheel house. They approached me about doing a wheel collaboration together, and in all honesty that took a little bit of time because I wasn't quite ready for it. People had been asking me about how to get hold of some of the signature touches that I put on my cars. Folks were asking me would I be selling things such as louvred deck lids, drilled door handles and integrated turn signals, and I really had no interest in that because I didn't want to set up that type of business. I didn't want to water my designs down by mass-producing them. However, the fifteen52 connection really appealed to me.

We started collaborating on designs and, long story short, we launched the first signature 52 Outlaw wheel in June 2014. The design is obviously inspired by the classic Fuchs wheel, but we had to do something different. I mean, every-one's copied the Fuchs, and I'd built my reputation on doing the opposite of conventional. I'm not into copying other people, so the idea was to not replicate the Fuchs but build something that looked like it might have come out of the factory in that same period, late sixties, early seventies. It was great to actually see the process of how the wheels are made out of a single piece of billet aluminium, fascinating. We made a film documenting the manufacture and design process, and the collaboration has done very well.

Now, everyone loves Momo steering wheels, so imagine how pleased I was to one day get a visit from Henrique Cisneros, the owner of that famous brand. He told me he'd seen the film and was also a Porsche fan. So Henrique comes to visit, I give him the tour, he sees that half of my Porsches are not running stock wheels but are instead running Momo wheels. In *Urban Outlaw*, I talked about Mario Andretti, Jackie Stewart and the Momo Prototipo wheel. So Henrique sees my passion for the brand and within half an hour we're talking about a collaborative steering wheel. Momo was due to celebrate their fiftieth anniversary in 2014, so we decided to do a signature steering wheel based on my two favourites, the Jackie Stewart thick grip and the Momo Prototipo. Of course, I wanted to do things a little bit differently, so we combined the two into one and the real key is the distressed leather. I didn't want a new Momo steering wheel in my own cars, so why would my signature wheel be a shiny new one? I showed Henrique how we'd done these worn-in leather pants and suggested that it wouldn't be that difficult to hand-distress leather for a steering wheel. I was delighted and very proud to find out that in all their fifty years, Momo had never done a signature wheel with a non-professional race-car driver. So I was in lofty company, alongside racers such as Jackie Stewart, Mario Andretti, Clay Regazzoni, Niki Lauda and numerous other famous racing drivers. How honoured was I? We released the wheel at the Road to Rennsport in September 2015, which was the biggest Porsche event in the world. We invited fifty people, which became a hundred, to take the scenic route from Downtown LA, through Willow Springs, through my favourite road Angeles Crest Highway to Monterey. I drove 277 there, and on arrival at the event it was set up in the Momo tent with a few other cars. I did a really enjoyable meet-and-greet, and I am delighted to say the collaboration, which was limited to just four hundred steering wheels, sold out within a month.

Another fun project was getting my own set of Hot Wheels cars! People generally associate Hot Wheels with hot rods, but not necessarily Porsches. That brand is perhaps the world's biggest toy-car manufacturer and a global phenomenon, so getting the invite to go see those guys down near LAX designing toy models and witnessing the work that goes into them was unbelievable. I've ended up doing five cars for Hot Wheels, and now we are working on some non-Porsche models moving forward. I've also got Schuco 1:43 scale model editions available of 277 and Liam's car, the 68R.

In 2015, I was approached about being in the new *Need for Speed* reboot of the all-conquering video game. Well, truth be told, I'm not actually a video-game guy, but they very kindly asked me to be one of five so-called 'speed icons' featured in this new edition. They suggested that my spirited street driving was very much in keeping with the idea of their game. This is not a professional racing game to see who can go around the Nürburgring the fastest; it's more of a street-racing game. I asked them who the other four icons were and they said, 'Ken Block, the car modifier Nakai-san, the Risky Devil drift crew and Morohoshi-san.' I'm like, *Fuck! Being associated with these guys is great, plus they are expecting to sell a few million video games, so, sure, why wouldn't I be in it?*

We filmed my segments in London and ended up getting 277 in the game itself, where you can build your own inter-pretation of my most famous car and race against me on screen. Although the game is set in a fake world, a lot of the visual inspiration and scenery is pulled from within a mile of where I'm sat writing this chapter. For me, it was an honour to be in *Need for Speed*, and it has certainly introduced me to an audience that probably never knew about me before.

You might think at this point that I've done an awful lot of collaborations in the aftermath of *Urban Outlaw*. Actually, I've been super-selective about who I work with. For example, I must have been approached by three or four watch companies wanting to do a new watch, but I'm a vintage watch guy, TAG Heuer, Omega and stuff like that. A funny side anecdote to all this is that after *Urban Outlaw* came out, I heard that there was a whole thread on some vintage watch forum in England about, 'What watch is Magnus Walker wearing in *Urban Outlaw*?' I'm like, *How do they even see my fuck-ing watch?* Turns out there's one shot where you very briefly see the watch on my wrist as I'm turning the steering wheel. For the record, it's an Omega Speedmaster circa 1972! I have been approached to do sunglasses, but I don't wear them at all, so why would I endorse a range of sunglasses? If I don't believe in a product or feel a connection, I will just politely turn the offer down, because that's not my vibe.

So many new doors opened after *Urban Outlaw*, including the opportunity to do my own TV show. Truth be told, initially it was Karen's idea. We've all seen these car shows and some of them are real good but a lot of them are kinda crappy. The poorer ones are all the same – you know, buy this car today, sell it tomorrow, these guys chasing deals and flipping cars. I had no interest in that. I had kind of become comfortable in front of the camera since *Urban Outlaw*, so I was cool with the idea as long as we could find a format that was interesting. So the idea was conceived to have a show based on the concept of a great American road trip. I've talked about my adventure on that Trailways bus from New York to Detroit, then Detroit to LA in 1986, but I have never actually driven across the country. I've done a lot of driving but never a US tour. So when this idea was put to me, I was like, 'Fuck, let's just go!' Essentially that was the idea: let's go, take a camera with us and do a great American road trip. We figured that along the way we were going to meet car-culture people, chat to them, hear their stories and drive their cars. Everyone's got their favourite car and everyone's got their favourite road. So the plan was for a travel show/car show/talk show, where I was just hanging out with like-minded people, enjoying the open road and chewing the fat.

There were a lot of pitches, a lot of approaches by production companies. These TV shows take a long time to come together; it is a very complex process. The production companies had probably seen the format of various shows like *Fast N' Loud* working pretty well, so a lot of the conversations started off with them wanting to film a car build, but I'd politely say, 'Let me stop you right there . . .' On more than one occasion, we'd meet a team and I'd say, 'Have you seen *Urban Outlaw*?' and they'd reply 'No'! Not really anywhere to go after that, is there?

Eventually, after countless meetings and dead ends, we ended up getting a deal with the History channel to shoot a pilot. Their team loved *Urban Outlaw* because it is so stylish and cinematic – that resonated with them. Filming the show was a lot of hard work, but we had some great guests. We ended up shooting the ex-American footballer and pro-wrestler Bill Goldberg, who has a muscle-car collection – a cool guy. We shot Shooter Jennings, a country and western rock 'n' roller. His story is great because his dad, Waylon Jennings, wrote the fucking theme song to *Dukes of Hazzard*, so that's me on board right there (sadly his segment didn't get included in the pilot). Then we had rally race driver Alex Roy and a three-wheel Morgan, we had Rod Emory, the legendary Porsche 356 outlaw build icon, and also actor and racing car driver Chad McQueen.

We shot this pilot over a month before Christmas 2015. It was really well received, so at the time of writing it will be really interesting to see what happens next in the world of TV. If these shows take off, it can be a very serious business, so let's see . . . how bad can it be, right?

Chapter 12

A Hobby That Got Out of Control

I'm pretty sure that if you are reading my book, then you probably like cars. There's also a good chance that you are a Porsche fan. By this point in my story, I think I need to explain in more detail – from a car point of view at least – why all these magazines, online blogs, TV shows and journalists have been interested in my collection. It's time to take a walk around my garage. So, if you don't like cars or Porsches, I suggest you skip on ahead.

I spoke earlier about how I fell in love with Porsche as a ten-year-old, then it took me fifteen years to acquire that first 911 in 1992, the '74 wide-bodied, slant-nosed conversion that I bought at the Pomona Swap Meet. Well, since that point I have owned over fifty Porsches, so let me pick out a few of the highlights. When it came to working on this chapter, I decided to sit in my garage in Willow, surrounded by the cars, so that hopefully I can give you a flavour of the collection I have been building all these years.

Let me tell you, I never take the cars for granted. No matter what is going on in my world, good or bad in business or pleasure, I can come in here and it always feels fantastic. If I've been travelling and have been away for a couple of weeks, the first thing I do when I get back is come in the garage and just sit in here and vibe it out, you know. Then, of course, I get in a car and go for a drive.

Superficially, this chapter is about cars, then. However, in telling you these stories, I hope you can see that Porsche is actually all about the people. Every vehicle in here has a tale to tell about the people behind that car – that's what I love so much about this marque. Porsche people, shared passion. So let me talk you through a few of my cars, the back-stories behind them and what I did to them once I owned them. Hopefully it will give you a flavour of why I do what I do, how I approach these cars and maybe you might take a few ideas away for your own car project.

Let's start real early. I'm a goal-orientated collector, and I like to collect from the beginning, the early years, so initially the goal was to have one of every year from '64 through '73. That goal was not achieved in chronological order, obviously, but it was eventually completed. In 1964, Porsche made 232 models of the 911. None of them ever came to the States. Technically, they were all '65 year models. For me, to own a '64 911 was the holy grail. I now have one. It took me a long time to find that car. Of the 232 documented, I think there are no more than about sixty or so recorded as surviving. That seems probable, as you have to figure those cars are now well over fifty years old, so they are either rusted, wrecked, crashed, stolen, parted-out or chopped up. Maybe there's a hundred surviving and of those sixty-odd are documented. I think three dozen are in the registry with original motors and transmissions. The one I've got back there in my garage is slate grey with a red interior, a matching-numbers car. So that is the holy-grail car right there.

So how did I find this super-rare 911? Long story. I was running an ad everywhere that simply said, 'Wanted: '64 911', I was writing letters to people on the '64 911 registry saying I was looking for one, but these cars don't just crop up. Sometimes when I'm after a certain car I've run adverts for eighteen months with no joy, then suddenly someone will get in touch. People think the '73 RS Carrera is the holy-grail car, and it is indeed an iconic 911, but they made 1,580 of those. Today, a good '73 RS is about a million bucks, but we could go find a dozen for sale right now. I guarantee you are not going to find a '64 911 for sale right now because they only made 232 and, as I said, maybe only sixty or so survive to this day. Of those 1,580 '73 RSs, there might be, say, 1,000 surviving. So that is a way more common car in that respect.

So anyway, I'm running this advert but getting nowhere fast. Then I get an email from this guy I've mentioned called Joost Hermès, who had been following my thread online on the Pelican Parts post. He said he'd found a '64 911. The great news was that the car was on a non-Porsche-related forum; had it been posted on a 911-specific site, the geeks would have been all over it. It was on some little car blog, like a single paragraph by this guy Chuck Rizzo who was the owner. It was pretty much just a generic post, enquiring about some information on a '64 911. So Joost gave me his email, didn't ask for any finder's fee or anything, just turned the information over to me.

Then I started a three-month-long conversation with the car's owner, Chuck. The car was in Pennsylvania. I say this all the time – it's all about the people. Without the people, there are no car stories, right? Truth be told, probably 70 per cent of the cars that I own or have owned have never been for sale. It's all word of mouth, someone knows someone who is thinking of selling a car. So this process teaches you a lot of lessons, but the number-one lesson you must learn is patience. You *cannot* rush the sale. You have to just let the guy talk. These people are sometimes hugely attached to their cars, and if you rush them they might panic and decide they can't sell after all. Sometimes sellers get remorse and all of a sudden they don't want to let go of the car. You have to respect their story and their relationship with the car.

So Chuck's story was great. This '64 911 was purchased by a US serviceman stationed in Germany somewhere in the middle of the 1960s (I believe I'm only the third or fourth owner of the car, but I haven't fully traced it back). This US serviceman buys the car in Germany while stationed there, brings the car into the country in '69/70, then Chuck buys the car a year or so later. Chuck tells me one of his memorable stories about driving down from Pennsylvania to Florida with his then-girlfriend and getting pulled over by a state trooper after supposedly speeding at a hundred miles an hour. He had to pay the state trooper a fine not to impound the car and let him keep going.

Chuck was a fascinating character and a great guy. He wasn't really a full-on Porsche guy, he was actually more of a Corvette and Harley-Davidson fan, so the 911 wasn't his daily driver. By the mid seventies, he had a wife and kids as well as a business, the Porsche was parked up on blocks in the garage and he hadn't driven it since 1979. Actually, that probably saved the car in terms of it being chopped up or stolen or raced or modified. I chatted with Chuck and he found out my background and where I was coming from. I think he liked the idea of me becoming the next custodian of the car, the 174th 911 ever made.

Once we had agreed on a price, the next problem was that at the time I didn't have enough money to buy it, so I told Chuck I'd put x-amount down as a deposit and pay him the balance over the next two months or so. I don't think I even told Karen I was buying the car because I was probably . . . well, let's just say by then I was probably at the point of having bought just one Porsche too many. The last thing we needed was another car, and this one was a little bit more expensive than the others, though still really well priced, in my opinion (today, the price would be astronomical).

Anyway, during the talks with Chuck, it became apparent that he hadn't been to LA in about twenty years, but he was due to come to town within the next eighteen months, and he said, 'Hey, when I come to LA can I borrow one of your cars?' Sure, no problem. At the time, it was just part of the negotiation, I don't know if I ever really anticipated he'd take me up on the deal, but long story short I got the money together, paid him the balance and bought the '64 911. I didn't hear from him for about a year, but then he did come to LA after all and I let him take out my Irish Green '66. Despite its age and condition, I use the Irish Green a lot; it's kinda the car I jump in to go and get some milk. That was the first time Chuck had driven a 911 since 1979, back when he'd parked the '64. So he spent a whole week in LA driving my car around, fell in love with it and now he is chasing his second Porsche 911! It's that Porsche slippery slope again.

Now, remember how my Dutch buddy Joost turned me on to the '64 car and never wanted a penny for a finder's fee? A lot of people could have bought that car and flipped it for a lot of money. Well, I made sure I took care of Joost. I sent him quite a few things (for example, I did a louvred deck lid for his own 912 and sent him that as a little thank-you gift) and then we became sort of pen-pal buddies, although I'd never met him in person. That's why when *Urban Outlaw* came out and premiered at that Raindance Film Festival in London, who should fly in from the Netherlands but Joost. When I visited Porsche after I got that letter from the factory, I flew to Amsterdam first and who should pick me up at the airport but Joost. Then we did a Rotterdam outlaw run and Joost let me drive his car. Fantastic guy. So when I talk about Porsche I'm really talking about Porsche people. Joost is a perfect example of that, because if it wasn't for his tenaciousness and 'Sherlock Holmes' ability to have sleuthed out a '64 911, I'd never have found that car. But even more importantly I'd never have made the friendship with him.

Just over in the far corner of the warehouse at the moment, I have a '65 911, a silver one that I call the gentleman's racer car, with a Paul Smith stripe. That was another example of a nine-month acquisition project, working on it just to get the guy to sell. That car is the 310th 911 ever made. That's 136 cars later than the '64. What's great about the '65 car is that it was one of the first half a dozen cars that Brumos Porsche (as you know, my favourite Porsche dealer ever) imported into the States. In fact, I made a video about that car for Brumos.

I've spoken about the '69T that I bought in 2008, which was my first restoration project, and how I'd restored that car with Sergio and the help of a few other friends. So once I had the '69T and covered that base, the next part of the collection really was the most iconic Porsche, the car I fell in love with, the one I always talk about: the 911-930 Turbo. Yet again, I started my Turbo collection right at the beginning with what's known as a generation-one, three-litre car, built in '75, '76 and '77. This is the iconic shape. As I scribble down some notes for this chapter, I am sitting right here next to six of them (I've owned seven of them). So, back to the very start – the first one I bought was a silver 1976 930. The Turbo came out in '75 in the rest of the world, but for some reason those early cars didn't meet US emission standards so, believe it or not, America didn't get the Turbo until '76, which is bizarre given that the USA has been Porsche's biggest market for fifty years. So the first Turbo available in the United States was 1976 and I have one. That's a real special car. It's a lifelong California car, never been out of the state (although, to be honest, I never understand adverts that say a car has never seen rain! You have to drive them!). The car was delivered to Bob Smith Porsche, built in October of '75 as a '76 model, and it really works in silver. That history is documented by the factory, and it's VIN number 15, which makes it the very first US-production Porsche Turbo sold. It's not the first one built – there's four prototypes, VIN numbers 11, 12, 13 and 14, and my car is number 15. Number 11 is documented, that's a silver car with red interior; number 14 is documented, I believe it's a green car. Numbers 12 and 13 disappeared, and apparently legend has it that one of them got stolen from a magazine's offices. So the first four '76 US Turbos are sometimes talked about as 'the prototype cars'. I don't think they were really prototypes; they were just four cars that were pulled off the production line. Not everyone would agree with me but, hey, let's not get into that! I had an inkling that mine might be the first ever US Turbo because I knew the VIN number was super-early, but I didn't know the whole history. I was 90 per cent sure and then when I visited the Porsche factory and museum and scoured through their archives in 2013 with Dieter Landenberger, I was shown the handwritten build records of that car.

What is a fact is that those four, the 11, 12, 13, 14 VIN numbers, were press demonstrator show cars, loaned out for PR and publicity. The first one that was publicly sold through a dealer, as documented by Porsche at the factory archive, is my car. I'm the fourth owner. My buddy Marty had worked on that car over a period of twenty years, for the second owner, the third owner and then me. I met Marty through the Porsche Owners Club, and he builds a lot of my transmissions and helps out mechanically; he is *the* Turbo guy.

My car is now forty years old and it's got an interesting back-story; in fact, Marty told me a little bit of great history that's undocumented. Rumour has it that the car was ordered by the actor Robert Redford, who apparently never actually took delivery of it, so the Turbo was never titled in his name (whether he took delivery of it or not can never be proved, this is hearsay). That doesn't mean Bob Smith Porsche didn't bring it in, give it to Robert Redford and for some reason he never bought or titled it. Frankly, who knows what went on. Now, you may be aware I made a video called *Turbo Fever* where I touch base a little bit about that story. Well, when I was at the SEMA show in 2014, this guy came up to me out of the blue, said he'd seen *Turbo Fever* and told me a story about how he'd run into Robert Redford in a silver Turbo somewhere in Colorado in '76. True story. So even if that guy was making this incident up, I don't think my buddy Marty would do that because he's effectively been with the car for the past twenty years. Was it the same car? In a sense, it doesn't matter because Redford's name was never on the title. It doesn't matter to me, but it's kind of an interesting story . . . yet again, it's about the people. For me, the most special thing about that car is that it's the first Turbo I ever bought and it's the first US-production 930.

So the first Turbo I bought was the '76, America's first. I was immediately really taken with the whole Turbo vibe, and so at one time I owned five Turbos – three '76s and two '77s – but I didn't have the holy grail of Turbos, the '75, the first ever year of production. That car was the missing piece to my puzzle. The '75 Turbo is almost as rare as the '64 911 because they only made 284 of those cars in 1975. However, unlike the '64 911, the Turbo was notorious for people driving it off the showroom floor and wrapping it around a tree in the first week – you know, lifting off the throttle, oversteering or having the boost come on and then someone bails out or their talent doesn't back up the performance of the car. So those really early Turbos were notorious for either being crashed, stolen, parted out or upgraded. People wanted to upgrade to the later edition with bigger motors and bigger brakes, so finding an unmolested early Turbo is pretty hard.

So I was on this quest for a '75 and they were already getting pretty expensive, but fortunately I was still ahead of the curve. One of the things I've been lucky at is being ahead of the curve when it comes to collecting early cars. For example, I've had five '67Ss, although only two of them were matching-numbers cars. One of them I bought for nine thousand five hundred bucks. Another one I bought for eighteen grand. Today, those cars are worth ten times that. Everything in my garage has been bought really inexpensively. I really want to make this point: I'm not some rich guy with loads of money just writing out cheques for any car he vaguely fancies. I like to research the cars I want, enjoy the whole experience, find the right car, show some restraint. When I started looking, early Turbos were twenty to thirty grand cars in the US. Nobody wanted them. So that's how I've been able to get six of them.

Anyway, so I am on this quest to find a '75 Turbo and I get on the beautiful thing known as the worldwide web, where you can sit in your home and find cars all over the world. I missed one in Japan but remained undeterred. After months of looking, I find a right-hand drive '75 Turbo in, of all places, Australia. At first I was like, *Fuck, Australia, the other side of the world, really?!* However, you know me, it doesn't really matter where the car is; I'm not afraid of shipping them all over the world. Besides, a lot of people were put off with this car being in Australia. It was a right-hand drive car, but I couldn't get hold of the seller. The car was on some Australian car website where, frustratingly, the guy's phone number and email wasn't displayed, so you had to log in and put an Australian phone number in to even be able to contact this guy. Well, I didn't have an Australian number, so I'm trying to put a US number in . . . it's not working . . . long story short, I never got hold of the guy.

Fast-forward six months, I looked again and the car was still advertised for sale. A couple of months earlier, I had met these guys from Autohaus Hamilton near Sydney when they visited me during a trip to California. So I called them up, told them about the car, and they'd already seen it but also couldn't get hold of the guy. Anyway, I guess one day this elusive seller picked up the phone and they had a conversation, so I sort of hired Autohaus to go inspect the car for me. This is the only car I've ever done a pre-purchase inspection on, and I did it because I couldn't get hold of the guy and didn't have much to go on. While I'm on that subject, let me veer off a moment: sometimes when I am in England and around people buying 911s, they are very restricted and guarded, all worried about provenance and mileage and what it's going to be worth when they sell it. I always end up saying, 'Guys, loosen the fuck up a bit, you know. If it feels right, just buy and enjoy the car.'

So, anyway, getting back to the story of this '75 Turbo. We knew what the price was, Autohaus took a little margin on the car, naturally, for taking a look at it and helping me, and they ended up buying the car on my behalf. Then I simply shipped it from Australia. It's copper-brown metallic, although that's not the original colour. Apparently, it is a former UK car that left England in 1980 and went to Australia and then it came back to me in the States in 2014. I believe they only made seventeen right-hand drive Turbos that year, so how many do you think exist today? I would suggest less than ten. So that is a really, really rare car. I don't know any collectors that own both the right-hand drive and left-hand drive '75 Turbo.

Sitting next to that car to my right is Turbo number twenty-seven for the US, a black one that also looks super-cool. If you do the maths, if car fifteen was the first one sold then car twenty-seven is still only the thirteenth car (they don't actually necessarily sell in chronological order, of course). Another of my favourite Turbos is the European Minerva blue car that we featured in *Outlaw Fever*, where we debuted the fifteen52 collaborative Urban Outlaw signature wheel. That's a car that people seem to have connected with a lot. I also acquired a '77 ice-green metallic one with tartan interior. That's also a pretty special car.

You've seen how patient you have to sometimes be when you are buying cars, and also how much investigative work you might need to do. I'd also like to think this next story proves there is such a thing as Porsche karma. One day I get an email from a guy asking if I have any interest in a '75 Turbo roller, namely a car missing the transmission and motor. I'm like, 'Sure, of course I do.' This guy told me the story of how he found the car behind a tow yard in Albuquerque, where it had been under a tarp. Apparently, the car had lost its motor, the engine somehow becoming separated from the vehicle. Again, listen, be patient, this guy's not necessarily looking to sell, but he's definitely looking to see what my interest level is. Then he made the mistake of telling me what he paid for the car, and it was peanuts. I asked him what he wanted for it now, and, of course, he replied with the answer I always hate, 'Make an offer.' Well, I knew what he'd paid for it, so I just doubled what he'd paid and made him the offer, which was still pretty low ball. He didn't take that, so I offered him another five grand. He didn't take that offer and then I offered him another ten grand, but he still didn't take that offer. So then I backed off. A lot of people call me up or email me out of the blue trying to offer me cars. Some sellers don't really want to sell, they think they've got a car that is the holy grail, but for me it didn't really matter, this particular Turbo was always going to be a non-matching-numbers car . . . at that point.

So three months go by, during which I also buy a red '70s Turbo wide-bodied-looking car with a '75 Turbo motor and transmission. Then I went back to the guy with the '75 Turbo roller, but obviously I didn't tell him I'd found a donor motor and trans.

I asked him again, 'What do you want for the car?'

He goes, 'Well, really I just want a Turbo-looking car.'

I had an idea.

'How about this red car I've got here, it's all Turbo-looking, minus the motor, would you be interested in trading that?' He was, so we did the deal. So now I own the '75 Turbo roller, which has no engine in there.

Then I get this email saying that someone has found the original motor for this '75 roller that I've just bought. This particular guy had actually tried to buy the roller too, but when that went to me, he did some what I like to call Porsche sleuthing and realized that he knew where the original engine was. So, all of a sudden, I have the rolling gear for a '75 Turbo and I know where the matching-numbers engine is. Without going into all the detail, I made contact with the person who had the motor and after quite a lot of back and forth, negotiations and agreements, I finally get the motor for the '75 Turbo roller. So the original motor was fitted back into the matching car that had carried that engine when it was first produced way back in 1975. Therefore, it was now a matching-numbers 1975 Turbo, which is obviously worth a lot more than a non-matching-numbers car. Talk about finding a needle in a haystack!

You might think that would be a one-off, a once-in-a-lifetime occurrence. Not so. I've found the needle in the haystack three times, or, let me rephrase it, the motors have found me. You might ask why such a valuable car has the motor or trans ripped out? Well, 911s haven't always been so valuable, for a start. Practically too, transmissions get damaged, broken, people swap them out. Thirty years ago, when a '65 was worth nothing, some guy blows a motor or the engine gets damaged, let's say hypothetically it's five grand to rebuild that motor. So he goes to the local Porsche garage and the guy in the shop suggests, 'I've got a 2-2T motor there in the corner I can put in the car for fifteen hundred bucks and you can have it next week.' That happened all the time with these early 911s. Or people say, 'You know what? Why am I running around in a two-litre with 130 horsepower when I can put that 3.2 in it with 230?' So out comes the original two-litre motor, in goes a three-litre or 3.2 because the guy's building his race car or whatever, then the '65 motor is for-gotten and separated from the car. Then the car goes through five owners, it's still only a five-grand car, ten-grand car . . . but then thirty years later, when the car's worth two hundred grand, someone's trying to find the original motor, right? Times have changed. That's how it happens – like I said, common story.

So, how about another needle in a haystack and car 1036? I'd bought it for like eleven grand or something, sat on it for a while, then sold it for fifteen grand, made a few bucks, thought nothing of it. Just moved it on. This was when I was buying and selling a few cars and also when I used to be more active on the online forums. One day I get an email from this guy, and he goes, 'You're not going to believe this, I've got the motor that was in your 1036!' Turns out the motor was on Craigslist in a shop in LA. So it's kind of comical because I'd never looked for the motor, but all along it was here in LA. So I said, 'Well, I've sold the car, but I'm still in contact with the owner. Let me put you in touch.' So, long story short, I put them in touch, and I think the guy ended up paying more to buy the matching motor than he did for the car! He ended up with a matching-numbers 1036, which he later sold at Pebble Beach; it was even listed as an 'ex-Magnus Walker car'. Anyway, it sold for quite a significant sum of money.

Then, in 2014, I was at the US Grand Prix in Austin, Texas, with my buddy Helmut. Even though I'd been watching Formula 1 since the seventies, this was actually the first time I'd ever gone to an F1 race. While we were there, this French dude walks up to me and says, 'I have one of your former cars.' Turns out the guy was Nicolas Todt, son of Jean Todt (former rally driver and now president of the Fédération Internationale de l'Automobile) and he'd bought car 1036 with the matching engine back in there. That was nice – it kinda brought the story full circle.

The third time this has happened to me was with the 365th 911 ever made. I had it on sale on eBay for some reason. Anyway, long story short, and with four days left before the auction closed, this guy contacts me and says, 'I have the motor to your car.' I ended up trading the guy . . . so three times the needle in the haystack found me, two of them on very, very early '65 911s and one very early '75 Turbo. The Porsche gods have shined down on me quite a few times.

Now, let's talk about one of my highest-profile Porsches, the car known in some circles as 'the Religion 911'. I'd got the Turbo collection going, so then I moved on to G-bodied cars, which essentially means '74 through '89, covering the 911 from '74 through '77, the '78 through '83 SC and then the '83 through '89 3.2 Carrera. This car, my '78 SCHR, is very well known as it featured in its own YouTube film called *Cruising My Religion*.

It's a car that a lot of people related to because it was what I've described as my 'budget build'. It was a former track-day car that I bought relatively inexpensively. It was a little rough around the edges, but it was a running, driving car. I simply did a six-week cosmetic makeover: essentially lowered it, swapped the rims, put the ducktail on. I removed the front half of the full cage. The seats were bought used for $150. The tartan fabric on the interior was from a roll of material we had in the Serious archive, which I also used for the RS-style door pulls. I used a sheet of ABS plastic to create a lightweight splitter. It has some black Vitaloni Sebring mirrors tucked into the body, which I got off Pelican Parts. This was a project of restraint. It wasn't a full-blown build. I wanted to build a car on a budget in less than eight weeks as an exercise in itself. It's all very well seeing cars that people have taken years building and have spent thousands and thousands on, sometimes hundreds of thousands, but a lot of Porsche fans aren't in that position. They might not have the money or the energy to do that. So the goal was to show that a cool car could be built on a tight budget.

As I said, I started with a somewhat solid running car, but it was rough around the edges, no interior and fitted with a roll bar. However, the car had been pretty well documented and respected. The point of the video was to show that these cars are affordable, they are not all high-dollar cars. I get letters all the time from people saying, 'I want to buy my first Porsche', and I always tell them there's a Porsche for every budget. You just want a Porsche, you've got five grand, go buy a Boxster. Go buy a 924. You've got twenty grand, you step up a little bit, go buy an SC or 996. And so on. The Religion car was a way of showing it can be done. Funnily enough, that car really resonates with people, and I am always being asked about it. Just recently, a pal of mine came to visit from the UK and before he left home his wife had made him promise that he wouldn't come back from California with a car that he didn't need and couldn't afford. He'd agreed and was totally intent on being well behaved when he arrived. Then, on day one of his visit, about two hours in, he saw the Religion car in the flesh, his favourite, and made me an offer on it there and then. Luckily for his marriage, it wasn't for sale.

Another interesting tale with a similar car was when I bought what seemed to be a '79 SC. Again, it was a former track car, and I had it in my garage across the road for a year and a half while I was working on other things. Originally, it was red with white wheels and a Turbo tail, and I ended up doing a two-tone gold respray on it first and then a while later I had it painted black. Anyway, long story short, my buddy Ollie really liked this car, and as he had never owned a Porsche he really wanted to know if I would sell it to him. At first I didn't really want to sell, and then one day I decided, *You know what? Fuck it, it's his first car.* It was kind of ideal for him. However, there was a sting in the tail, for me anyway! I never looked at the title in close enough detail; well, turns out this was *actually* a '76 Carrera. For some reason, it had got titled as a '79 SC, but it was in fact a '76 Carrera. By this point, I had given Ollie a price and maybe you don't know but there is a big difference between the value of a '76 Carrera and a '79 SC, but obviously I honoured the price and he's in love with the car, so that's all good.

So, as you can see, I've had my fair share of Porsches. Now my goal is to have one of every 911 model, every series, and there's seven of them. So I'm currently up to the 964, which is the last of the short-hood, iconic G-bodied style of air-cooled car. In reality, the 993 is the last air-cooled 911, but it doesn't look like that. The 964 essentially doesn't look that much different to an SC other than the big bumpers and side rockers. Without going into an in-depth history of various 911 generations here, even though the DNA and under-pinnings are vastly different on the 964, visually it's very, very similar.

Since *Urban Outlaw* and all the publicity I've had, my builds are widely anticipated and hugely scrutinized. Truth be told, you are only ever as good as your last car. Well, as I write this book, the build that in some ways is still my signature car is the '72 STR that the Ingrams bought, and we know all about that story. However, I am very proud of my most recent build, which is just starting to gain attention: a slate-grey 964.

The 964 is the follow-up to the '72 STR in the sense of it being a full-blown, big build. At the point I started the 964, I had actually barely built ten variations of outlaw cars (rather than just cosmetic makeovers). My 964 is obviously instantly recognizable as a 911, but it's the details that you've got to soak in. There's elements of a 356 in it, there's elements of the Sport Classic, there's elements of the current GT3 RS with the channelled roof and hood. This is my updated interpretation of throwing quite a few different cars into the blender and making a new creation that is better than the sum of the parts.

There are two common approaches with 964s. The first is to backdate these cars to look like a '73 RSR or an ST, which is a really popular trend. Some people building these RS lightweights in essence just take a lot of shit out and are not really changing the car. Alternatively, others create a wide-bodied conversion that looks like a monster race car and eventually doesn't resemble a 964 at all. I felt that no one was doing a narrow-bodied 964 outlaw. So I decided to build on that idea and bring in elements to update the 964 but still keep the original DNA of that model. By that I mean I didn't go mega-wide-bodied with big, flared wings, I built it unique and distinctive but still very much a 964.

We didn't pay much money for the 964; it was another former track car that had gone off the road backwards, so we had to replace the rear quarter. This beat-up race car already had a 993 motor in it, so that was never going to be returned to stock. My 964 build is all about stealth. It's all distressed leather inside because I want it to have elements of an old, aged look. I have used a classic colour combo of slate grey with a red interior, which is actually the same colour combo as my '64 911. At first glance, the 964 is a subdued car because it's just wrapped in slate grey. It's not all these different colours with boy-racer speed stripes. I decided the car was so cool that it didn't need multicolours – that would probably have taken away from the ethos of the car. However, don't be fooled. From a performance point of view, this is the most focused build I have done to date. The car weighs around 2,376 lb dry, so it's a touch under 1,100 kilos. It's got a 993 3.8 RS motor that's punching out about 340 horsepower. It's got a Brembo club race brake package all around.

There's not a square edge on that car, it's organic, there's a flow and that's ultimately what's great about it. For example, the wheel arches of 964s have a squared edge. Well, on mine we've rounded those off; that's hundreds of hours of bodywork just there. Maybe at first glance you don't notice, but the detail is there if you want to soak it in. Almost everything on the car has been tweaked. From the front bumper that has been filled in, to the channelled hood, the channelled roof, the channelled whale tail, the louvred front fenders, the stretched, more aggressive-looking flares. The only thing that's really not changed on that car are the two doors.

Look at the hood, for example. The Turbo has got a

twenty-two-inch scoop, but this one has been channelled and customized down to twelve-inch. It has a whole custom roof skin. The original car had a sunroof, but I don't like the wind in my hair and the sun on my face, plus half the time they don't work. But if this car had been a non-sunroofed car, I probably would never have done the scooped channelled hood. One of my favourite Porsches, the Sport Classic, has a channelled roof, so I took elements from that as well as the current 991 GT3 RS which has a channelled roof, too. This was more of a retro interpretation of that idea. These are all precise and very carefully thought-out details that refine the car and make it stand out as a true one-off.

Perhaps one of the most notable features on the 964 is that the fenders have louvres in them. This mimics the louvred deck lids that I am known for, but let me tell you, putting them on fenders instead is a far from straightforward process. Porsche first put louvres on the 917 back in 1970 and then, of course, the slant-nose had louvres. However, if you look at those louvres they're just flat, they aren't radius-ed, it was just an insert really. Unlike a straight deck lid, the fender is obviously curved, so when you start to insert louvres on there, every one has to be made with precision, the arch and angle of the curve has to be exact. That takes a very long time – just to do one louvre is hours and hours of work. It's something that's never been done before.

Because it had never been done before, that meant there was no precedent, no previous example to draw upon. In this case, I hooked up with Rod Emory, the legendary 356 outlaw guy, took him a fender and told him what I wanted to do. Rod is a super-talented guy; he'd never done it before, but he was up for the challenge. I had gone through a couple of people trying to find someone to make a louvred dye, but they weren't really set up to do it. It's a team effort, I'm not building these cars ōn my own, there's a lot of outsourcing, but essentially I come up with the concept and project-manage.

The work on the fender's curve is so fragile, you don't want the metal to crack or split; there is a lot that can go wrong on every single louvre. These are not eye-balled by a laser, it's all done by the human hand, real craftsmanship. If you are one sixteenth of an inch off square, they are all going to be off, the bad louvre will stick out like a sore thumb and all your work is scrapped. It's about as precise as you can get. The 964 has two louvred fenders, a dozen louvres in total, and that's exactly how many times that process had ever been done before, at that point.

The window crank and glass is from a '65 912 and it dropped right in to the existing 964 frames. The actual pressings in the doors were no different to the SC or the 3.2, which you could get with manual windows. I didn't have to modify anything, just dropped it right in. So this just goes to show how well Porsche engineered the 911 in 1964. That's why I talk about those first thirty years being interchangeable. The cars from the period I am fascinated with are so well engineered. My outlaw 964 is the perfect example of that. You couldn't take a 1965 Ferrari glass and put it in a 1990 car.

So, visually the 964 might not look as much like an outlaw 911 as other cars, but in the purest sense, it's the most intense outlaw build I've done to date. There's way more bodywork in it than anything I've built previously, and there's way more performance and suspension and upgrades in it than anything else, so if you want to pick out the definitive outlaw build that I've done to this date then, yes . . . the slate-grey 964 is that car.

That car also represents a degree of reinventing my own signature touches. If I only ever do the same thing with each build, I will get bored. I have to keep moving, keep creating. I'd like to say I think this is what separates me from most other guys. There are people out there building similarly inspired cars from similar eras, but the difference is, in my opinion, that a lot of people aren't putting as much of their own personality into their cars, or maybe they are just emulating something that the factory did. I would like to think that a lot of my builds stand out because of my personal taste, my individuality and how that comes through on the car.

Sometimes people ask me where I get my ideas from. Well, I believe that's pretty simple: the car determines the path. The 964 had a sunroof, that is why it came to have a channelled roof. Other cars need a much lighter touch, so, for example, on the first US-production Turbo ever sold, the only thing I've done is lowered it, because you are not going to modify that car. Same with the '64 911, original matching-numbers cars in original colours. These cars have become so valuable. Why would I modify them?

The cars that I leave stock tend to get less attention. I'm known as this rebel outlaw customizer, hot-rodder, whatever you want to call it. I think that's more interesting to a lot of people from a journalistic point of view. There will always be the purists that like to keep everything original and matching numbers. However, this whole 'outlaw versus stock' debate is a nonsense when you think about it. A car is only original once. As soon as you replace a tyre or nut or bolt, it's no longer original, so where do you draw the line? Actually, although I am most well known for my outlaw cars, half of the cars in the garage are original matching-numbers cars. I actually wrote an article about 'stock versus Rod' for *Total 911*.

However, to me, *all* these cars are special because they all have personality and that's why they are still here. For example, I don't know if I'm going to sell the 964 outlaw. That's not the plan. It wasn't built to be sold. It's just a way for me to put my personality on to a car, to realize a vision I had for how a 964 build could look.

There's not that many cars out there that have been sold with my true DNA. There's a handful, maybe six. Those are the ones that have really been injected with personality. In addition to that, there's about a dozen earlier restorations and cars that I owned ten or so years ago but never did much to in terms of my personal touches. Some of those cars I was just playing around with and never planning to sell, but then someone makes you an offer. I had seen some of these so-called 'ex-Magnus Walker 911' cars selling for forty grand before *Urban Outlaw* and now, after the film, they are selling for five times that. Some cars you connect with, some you don't. I don't currently have all fifty Porsches that I've owned because I didn't fully connect with most of the thirty or so that I let go. At one time, I had a bunch of the first thousand 911s, and, yes, I can quote the VIN numbers, so I had car numbers 174, 310, 342, 365, 841 and 1036. Those cars were special, but I didn't keep them all. There's only so much room, sometimes you've got to pay bills, so you let certain ones go, maybe to buy another one or, very occasionally, something else. However, certain cars are irreplaceable and will never be sold.

The prices of all air-cooled Porsches have escalated a lot in recent years, and my profile has certainly helped with my own cars because my stock value or social currency, or whatever you want to call it, has gone up. However, these numbers don't really mean much if I'm not selling them anyway; their theoretical value is kind of irrelevant. If I do finally decide to sell one of my builds, then it will feel more special than buying from someone who is putting out dozens of cars all the time. At the time of writing, the last real outlaw build I sold was over three years ago, when the Ingrams bought the STR.

With escalating prices in mind, one question I often get asked is, 'How do I go about buying my first air-cooled 911?' My advice is the same: don't expect perfection. Remember how the '75 Turbo had the only pre-purchase inspection I'd ever done? Maybe some people think that's crazy, but my motto has always been the same – expect the worst and hope for the best. Of course, don't be reckless with your money, but rust is the number-one issue with these old Porsches, and you should expect surprises with the floors, rockers and front suspension, too. But this book isn't the place for me to issue a buyer's guide! The point is, generally these cars are so in demand now, you don't have time to procrastinate. You've got to be ready to pull the trigger, bite the bullet and go for it. So I advise people to just dive right in. I have a buddy who has been searching for the perfect 911 now for three years. I'm like, 'Dude, you should have just bought one because there is no such thing as a perfect 911.' Having owned over fifty of them, I've never bought one at any price point that didn't need something doing to it, so you've just got to be prepared for that. But mostly my advice to people is just don't be too picky, get behind the seat and figure out the kinks as you go along, that's part of the thrill and the adventure.

The 911 obsession has kinda evolved for me, if I am being honest. The big goal now, once I've completed my 911 ambitions, is to have one of every Porsche sports car ever made. So that's front-engined water-cooled, which covers the 924, 928, 944, 968, and then mid-engined air- and water-cooled, so I already have two 914s and next on the list will probably be a Cayman. I like roofs, I'm not a big Boxster fan, but the Cayman will cover the water-cooled, mid-engined era. That way I get to experience everything Porsche has ever made in a sports car.

In the garage at this precise moment, there are over twenty 911s. Inevitably perhaps, people often ask me why am I compelled to buy so many cars. There are a few reasons. Firstly, I want to have completeness in my collection. As you now know, initially the idea was to collect one each of every 911 from '64 through '73. Then the Turbo idea took root. Now I'm chasing the wider goal – what I call 'air and water'. So the goal is to get a 993 and then obviously the water-cooled 996, 997 and then ultimately, possibly a 991. It's great to have that variety. You don't want to drink the same milkshake every day, do you? It would be hard for me just to have one Porsche. Each car is rewarding and challenging in a different way, and there is something in each and every 911 that I'm really drawn to. You can't always say what the individual appeal is – it's a feeling. It's hard to describe, but when you are in that car, it's the smell, it's the sound, it's a unique adventure.

It can be addictive. Chasing the car itself is a really exhilarating process, sometimes you win and sometimes you don't, but along the way you meet all sorts of fascinating people, and I love the whole process.

Another reason I have so many cars is time travel. If I go for a drive in the Irish Green, I am literally stepping back in time fifty years. If I get in the silver Turbo, then I am suddenly thrust into the mid seventies. So – next question I get – why do I want them all at the same time? Because I want to have the ability to choose the year, select the era that I want to travel back in time to. These cars don't drive the same, they don't give you the same feeling, the same sense of time, the same experience. That also allows me to compare and contrast each car. Each one is individual.

So . . . I keep more than one.

Okay, in my case, over twenty.

Occasionally, people will ask me how I would feel if I didn't have any of these cars and what would my life be like if I didn't have a 911 . . . Well, I don't actually remember what that was like.

Chapter 13

Karen

On 28 October 2015, my beautiful wife Karen passed away suddenly in the night. I hope you understand that I don't want to go into any detail about what happened, because it is private. All I want to say is that she passed away completely unexpectedly and it devastated me. It's very difficult to talk about, to be honest, but I do want to tell you all about Karen, my lil' Georgia Peach, my soulmate and the most amazing woman I have ever met. I've avoided working on this chapter because I knew it was going to be difficult, but I am going to try because I want everyone who reads this book to know just how incredible she was.

I was super-lucky the day I met Karen. She was this little 5 ft tall, 95 lb bombshell, a real southern charmer. Super-sexy, super-beautiful. As you know, we just really clicked. Absolutely inseparable. She could have had the pick of anybody, and I am so lucky that she chose me.

You know some of the back-story of how Karen and I met. Once Karen joined Serious, that was an amazing period of our lives, we were designing these amazing clothes, we had all these celebrities and rock stars wearing our gear and coming over to the warehouse, we were in love and enjoyed being with each other every minute of the day, it was just amazing. I mentioned we used to party hard but work hard, too. I'll tell you a funny story about one of our party nights . . .

Karen was a little bit of a tomboy when she was a kid, but apparently she was also a little clumsy. She used to tell this story of one time she was on a skateboard but she didn't really have great balance, so she fell off and knocked her two front teeth out. She came running home and her friend was carrying the two front teeth with her, covered in blood, and Karen's mum was obviously mortified! So as an adult, Karen always had two fake front teeth. Long story short, she had a lot of dental work done and at one point she had a little temporary tooth put in place. Anyway, one night during the mid nineties we got invited to a party that Courtney Love was throwing for the actor Ed Norton. Well, literally just twenty minutes before we were supposed to go, Karen's temporary tooth actually cracked and fell out. Now, most people probably would not have gone out to this glitzy show-biz party, but not Karen. She was like, 'Fuck it, it'll be like my party trick, this gap in my teeth!' When we arrived, the Spice Girls were there and all sorts of other celebrities. This actress came up to Karen and she said, 'You know, you should get that fixed . . .' and we just burst out laughing. That was Karen's spirit, she made the most out of all those moments, she was a real firecracker.

Karen always told great stories, I don't necessarily have the gift of the gab and the charm that she did. She used to tell people about this one time when she thought I was being really cool and laid-back. Why? Well, on this particular night we found ourselves sitting next to Pamela Anderson and Tommy Lee, who at the time were one of the most high-profile celebrity couples in the world. At one point, Pammy leaned over to me and said, 'I really like your hair,' and I was like, 'Oh, cool, thanks, that's good of you to say. I really like your coat,' and that was pretty much that. Now Karen saw this little exchange and later said that she couldn't believe how laid-back I was. I wasn't phased or even remotely star-struck by meeting Pammy, this globally famous superstar. Truth be told? I didn't realize who it was.

Everybody loved Karen. Everybody just wanted to be around Karen, she brought out the best in everyone, she was the life and soul of every party. A typical southern belle. I'm not really the party guy or the social type, that was Karen. It would always be Karen making the arrangements to go out with people, and we had a whole posse of friends; when I look back and think about that period, it was just great. One time we went back to Atlanta and visited her mum and, as I was a big *Dukes of Hazzard* fan, Karen took me to Hazzard County. I met her brother Tommy and all her friends down there, too.

We weren't married at that time, that came way later. Having both been married before, we just felt there was no need, we had ultimate trust in each other, we were never separated, ever. We had the new loft we lived in, which we fitted out with our own design ideas. I was never a cat person, but once I met Karen we'd always had one or two cats. We had our beloved dog Skynyrd, who sadly also passed away in 2015. Many of the other couples around us were always fighting, and they didn't even work together and might not see each other for eight hours a day. Although we were partying a lot, we were still getting business done. Party hard, but get shit done, always. For Serious, these were the glory years, too, when the business had gone from, let's say five hundred grand to a million bucks to two million a year – we were on fire. We were together 24/7 in a pretty stressful, demanding environment, going to all these trade shows, working on five clothing lines a year, organizing around two hundred thousand units every twelve months. We were joined at the hip, on the same page, what a team. Working together, living together, always in each other's pockets . . . and I still couldn't see enough of her.

Karen was a clever woman, too. Very clever. Serious had around ten employees and Karen would make sure the business side was always done perfectly – so intelligent. It just seemed like, fuck, this was heaven. For the next ten years, everything just clicked, you know. We opened the first Serious store that I mentioned on Melrose and then we opened the second one in '99. We were doing more business than ever, it was just easy. Everything was flowing and then Karen found Willow – I told you that whole story. As you know, after initially passing up on the property, I went back and bought the warehouse, and I still smile when I remember coming home that night and telling her I'd bought it. Amazing memories.

We finally got married on Karen's fortieth birthday, 5/1/05, a double header in Las Vegas. We didn't really tell anybody; the fact was that as we'd both been married before we didn't feel like making a big deal of the actual day, so no one was there. It was just Karen and me. We got married at the Mandalay Bay Hotel.

We travelled the world together. We went to the Far East and Europe, and Karen loved England, she completely fell in love with the country, she loved the history. She'd read all these novels from classic literature, *Jane Eyre*, *Wuthering Heights*, and so she loved when we went to places like Chatsworth. We talk about Willow being a hundred and ten years old and that's a vintage building for the US, but in England that's nothing. Karen loved how old England was in places. She loved Bakewell, for example, this sleepy little northern town with its market and all the history. I really enjoy visiting England these days, too, and I think you have a different view of Britishness when you live overseas. Some of that is real fun – like I always chuckle when I see five workmen standing around one guy digging a hole, and you'll have all five of them sipping a brew, talking. Karen loved all those cultural differences.

One time we were driving down this typical English country road, pretty narrow, bordered by these high drystone walls, and there was an old geezer on a mobile wheelchair in the middle of nowhere. That's not exactly what we were used to in LA! Another time, on a trip for my sister's wedding reception, one morning we were in this hotel and we fancied going into Bakewell to have a look around. So we spoke to this old geezer who owned the hotel, this typical English gent, you know, Prince of Wales houndstooth check tweed suit, this brigadier in his seventies. We asked him how to get to Bakewell, and he said, 'You see that big tree there at the end of the field? You walk to that and then turn left and follow the wall down, then turn right on the main road into Bakewell.' Now these are not nice, wide American roads, these are pretty narrow country lanes with these really old dry-stone walls on either side which are probably three feet tall; there is no sidewalk, so you would be kind of walking on a muddy roadside edge, taking your life into your own hands. So we start off on this walk and about half a mile down the road this Golf GTi comes whizzing by. I didn't think anything of it, but this car suddenly pulled up, turns out it's my uncle David on his way to Bakewell! That's some 'small-world' English shit right there. That wouldn't happen in LA, but it was typical England for me. So we hopped in the car; he'd never met Karen but he'd heard all about her, of course. He called her a little firecracker and off we went to Bakewell.

I'd always gone to Bakewell as a kid, so that day was real nostalgic, a proper trip down memory lane. Uncle David showed us around, and Karen loved the town. Bakewell is picturesque, the river runs through it, all that quaint stuff. We went to the local pub, this is October time, so of course it's getting dark there by four o'clock, and it was like one of these Hammer House of Horror movies where the mist rolls in and the fog descends over a picturesque little village, people scatter and all of a sudden it's kind of desolate. Of course it's raining. Obviously, we didn't want to walk four miles back to the hotel, so we had our fish and chips and a pint and then asked the bar keeper, 'Hey, can we get a cab, please?' And he says, 'You've just missed one, I can get you one tomorrow if you want.' Just missed one – a cab! We were like, 'What the fuck?!' Karen was laughing so much.

All these special places, these stately homes that my mum and dad had showed me as a kid, which I had no interest in then, all of a sudden we were like, 'Wow, let's go to Chatsworth.' Karen fell in love with that particular place. As a kid, you don't appreciate that sense of history because it is always there. So going back was a way of revisiting my past but also broadening our horizons. Truth be told, I never felt like moving back to England, though. Karen always romanticized about moving there, but for me there is just so much to keep me busy in LA.

Karen really liked visiting Sheffield, too. My mum loved her, my dad loved her, the whole family loved her, and she fell in love with my family. She talked to Mum and Dad more than I talked to them, and I always thanked her for that. She'd call my mum at least two or three times a month, and whereas I'd have like a ten-minute conversation with Mum, Karen would have an hour-long chat! When we'd be staying with my sister, I'd go to bed at midnight, but they'd be up until one or two, drinking and talking. People would tell Karen stuff they wouldn't even tell their own mum. Everyone confided in her and loved talking to her. Karen herself was from a big and very loving family, one of five kids. She was really close to her mum, and she'd call her every single day.

She also loved London, staying at the St Martin's Lane Hotel. We were making money, but we didn't live extravagantly, we just liked tasteful things. I would always buy her whatever she wanted, maybe some jewellery, or she would sometimes get facials and treatments. Even so, Karen didn't really want that much.

Karen never said 'no'; she was just always so super-supportive. Any ideas I had for Serious, she always backed me up; buying cars, super-supportive; buying Willow and getting into the film business, building the Porsche collection, taking part in *Urban Outlaw*, just always so supportive. Don't get me wrong, she certainly didn't just agree with me all the time to keep the peace. She was a very intelligent woman with fantastic creative ideas and interesting opinions. And if she didn't agree with something I was suggesting, I would know about it. That's the way it should be. She might have voiced her opinion or said what she thought, she was outspoken, she was a Taurus, so I guess, at times, she could be kind of stubborn, just like I was. However, that was only because she cared so much and wanted to look out for me and for every-thing that we had created together. So in that sense our relationship was really straightforward. Also, Karen was always a good judge of character. She would sometimes say, 'Magnus, you know that guy . . . I don't really like him', or 'I think these guys are taking advantage of you', and she would always be right. I'm more of the kinda 'grab it and run' type, but she would be that wise voice of caution, looking out for me, always.

We didn't want for anything. I remember buying Karen a Volkswagen Type 3 Karmann Ghia Notchback for her birth-day and the '67 E-Type Jag, too. That was the least I could do. If I wanted a Mustang or a Ferrari . . . Karen never, ever said no. She completely had my back, didn't take any bullshit. I'd like to think I reciprocated; I certainly tried to. I remem-ber one story before she had closed Hooch down, this local guy had a retail store and he wasn't paying her, so I went over there and basically threatened to kick the guy's ass if he didn't pay her. I'm like, 'Fuck, why are you picking on this little girl, what the fuck are you doing here, taking advantage of her? It's time to pay up.' So, you know, we had each other's backs. And you probably won't be surprised to hear that we were always faithful to each other, never deviated. We were together twenty-one years until she passed away, and she was always my rock.

Writing this book, I have naturally watched a lot of the videos and clips again. I actually watched *Urban Outlaw* for the first time in the best part of a year and hearing her voice was very sad. Someone said to me that she is immortalized in that film, which is a nice way to think of it.

One of the common threads in everything we did together was the pursuit of 'freedom', the ability to do what we wanted to do, when we wanted to do it. We weren't planning to work for ever; we were sort of working towards this goal of early semi-retirement in our mid fifties, travelling the world or maybe getting a place in New York or who knows where, but we had so much more to give each other. That particular book wasn't written. The journey wasn't over. We created so much together, we had the most amazing times together and then suddenly she was gone. All the success we had, we had together, and we couldn't have done it separately. Karen and I just brought out the best in each other. We were the spark for each other. She was my soulmate. It's hard to believe she's not here. However, she is still with me; she might not be physically by my side, but she is with me every moment of the day.

The number of people who came out for Karen's service was just incredible. We kinda winged the service, you know. It wasn't a religious service; it was a celebration of life. We did a slide show and rented this great little place that was modelled on an English chapel which I know Karen would have loved. There's a big cross on the top of the nearby hill and we had driven by it for twenty years and never gone there, but ultimately that was where her service was.

That day was just an outpouring of love for Karen; the amount of people that came and the flowers were very touching. Everyone was welcome to speak and tell stories about their life around Karen. The common theme was that everyone said, 'Karen brought out the best in everybody.' We hadn't seen some of these friends for ten years, but they all came to her service. It didn't matter whether you had known Karen for twenty years or twenty minutes. People kind of had that same reaction of, 'Wow, she's really special.'

I have a tattoo of the day that Karen passed away, 10-28-15. We had matching Skynyrd tattoos to honour our dog. I also have the Hooch logo and her signature tattooed on me, after she signed her name on me and then the tattoo guy inked over it. We also actually tattooed each other, believe it or not. I also have one that says 'Karen Forever', which was my very first tattoo.

The memories of Karen are inked on my mind just as the tattoos are on my skin. We made the most out of every moment. Now that she's not with me, it completely endorses the way we lived when she was here. Every day was cherished, every moment and every little adventure was enjoyed. When I look at photos, we are pretty much kissing in every one, and if we are not kissing then we have the biggest smiles on our faces. There was never a single day that we regretted. That's an amazing statement to be able to make, but I genuinely mean it.

She was just a beautiful blessing to everyone who knew her. Most of all me. I used to think, *Dude, you've hit the jackpot. She's sexy, she's charming, clever, supportive, kind, she is the life and soul of the party . . . everyone wants to be around her.*

There's not a day goes by that I don't miss her.

Like the tattoo says, 'Karen Forever . . .'

Chapter 14

A Steel Town and the City of Angels

At the time of writing, I have lived in America for around three-fifths of my life. It's the best part of thirty years since I lived in England. Truth be told, Sheffield and Los Angeles are worlds apart, but I am the sum of those two amazing places. That goes back to what I said before about never forgetting your roots. Take where you live now along with who you are and mix that with where you have come from – that is what makes you unique.

I say this all the time, but when I went to America, that represented ultimate freedom to me. In the simplest terms, my dad wasn't going to tell me to cut my hair and get a job any more, but there was also a wider sense of freedom, a feeling that anything was possible. LA gave me that sense of limitless opportunity, there didn't seem to be any boundaries, I could do whatever I wanted. There's an almost chameleon-like freedom to involve yourself in different ideas. I strongly believe that is why I've been able to enjoy success in three different areas with no educational background in any of them. Yes, for sure, the first few years in LA were a struggle, but at the time it didn't really feel like that. Don't get me wrong, I had my low moments and I've shared those with you, but overall I was just enjoying living in the US, making my own way, then when the clothing took off, it really did suddenly feel like I could achieve anything.

Would I have ended up with the fashion business, with the property, location shoots and all the cars if I'd stayed in Sheffield? Let's be honest, no, I wouldn't. I could have made my jeans tight and put patches on denim jackets in Sheffield, but where would the opportunity have been to sell them? I might have started a market stall there, but realistically where would that have gone? There were thrift stores, and my cousin Oliver and I used to love going to Army Surplus and buying combat boots and military M1 jackets and stuff like that, but I never saw that as a business, even with the market-trader mentality in the family. Manchester might have been a better idea. Or obviously London, but that is a big, expensive city. I had a buddy who had gone to university down there and just always seemed to struggle because London is so expensive. With LA, yes, that's a big city too, but I felt there was an underbelly, an alternative way of getting by that was much more affordable.

In my experience, there's more opportunity, or there *appears* to be more opportunity, in America. The reality is that in America I've never worked for anyone else. Okay, there were a couple of odd jobs when I first got here thirty years ago, but ever since starting the clothing on the board-walk in the late eighties, there's been no boss for me to answer to.

LA is the land of opportunity. You know, whatever you want to do, it can be done here. You want to be a pro-skateboarder, bike guy, rock star, musician, guitar manufacturer, sound engineer, screenwriter, movie star, astronaut, design cars or work in the aerospace industry? . . . It's all here. Self-starting is encouraged, it's applauded and championed. For me, it felt pretty easy to start something out of nothing on the boardwalk in Venice. Of course, it pays not to be too idealistic about this – not everyone who comes to LA makes it and achieves their dreams – but, in my opinion, the *opportunity* is there.

However, no one is going to do it for you. All of those things are here, but they are not giving those jobs out when you arrive at Union Station at 6 a.m. on a Trailways bus. There's no Willy Wonka golden ticket to fame and fortune. For me, there was a very hard bench to lie on and a kick up the ass to move on by that security guard pretty soon after. But outside the station doors, there was opportunity waiting for me.

LA itself is kind of easy living, the weather's great, and, hell, you can drive 365 days of the year. I have buddies in Europe that tell me, 'Yeah, we're putting our cars away for winter', and I can't imagine that. Half of my cars don't even have heaters that work. Some of them have no windscreen wipers because it rains so infrequently. If you want to surf in the morning, hike up mountains in the afternoon and ski in the evening, you can do it in California. I've done road trips like that in 277; it's spectacular.

I was once invited to appear in a Steve McQueen documentary, and Gary Oldman was shooting his segment when we got there. Turns out Oldman is a Porsche guy, and we kind of clicked briefly; I told him I used to go to an Indian restaurant nearby where we saw him once. I don't think I would have run into Gary Oldman at an Indian restaurant when I was a kid. But then again, I do remember seeing Phil Oakey at a chip shop in Sheffield.

California also has these spectacular world-class driving roads, generally wide and flowing. I'm used to these spirited drives. Obviously, I'm strongly associated with the 6th Street Bridge which was near to Willow and has seen some of my more fierce drives in its time. That bridge always allowed me to put pedal to the metal and get a surge of adrenaline so close to home. Sadly, the bridge has now been demolished, as it suffered from what is known as 'concrete cancer' and had become unsafe. To mark this moment, I held an outlaw gathering by way of saying farewell to the bridge, and we had over two hundred cars turn up, which was just fantastic.

Another one of my absolute favourite drives is along Angeles Crest Highway, just eighteen miles from the warehouse, partly because there is literally no one out there. When I was in the UK for the brilliant Goodwood Revival, I remember driving to Sheffield from Goodwood on a Sunday afternoon and there's all these controlled speed limits along stretches of the motorway, I'm like, *Controlled speed limit, what the fuck is that?* Then it went down to two lanes for thirty miles even though there was no work being done in the coned-off lane at all; there weren't even any workmen having a brew. Then there was a sign saying 'Speed Camera' and I'm like, *Speed cameras, what the fuck are those?* I know full well England has got some fantastic roads – the snake from Sheffield over the Pennines into Glossop is a spectacular road – but that three-hundred-mile route from Goodwood to Sheffield that day was not a good drive.

There is a real diversity of people here in LA, which I enjoy. It's a real melting pot. There's obviously a big Mexican population with all their amazing culture and flavour, there are Australians, Japanese, Malaysians, Indonesians, Brits – the list is endless. It's almost like no one in Los Angeles is actually from LA, and that's a good characteristic. I find that hugely inspiring creatively, because wherever you go there are little traces of ideas you can pick up, whether it's some street art or a museum or architecture or food or music. In LA, it doesn't matter what you look like or whether you have a strange accent. I had what a Brit would call a typically working-class upbringing. Although we didn't really travel around the UK much at all, I was aware of the divide, the separation between north and south, that whole ridiculous idea that you're a northern monkey, you must be thick if you live 'up north'. I used to think, *Well, loads of the bright people in London weren't born in London!* When I arrived in LA, there was no class divide, no preconceptions passed down over generations about what certain people can achieve, these engrained ideas of society and your place in it – that just simply didn't exist here. I still sense a Wild West spirit, and I kind of like that. Almost a feeling of reckless abandonment.

However, let me be very clear – all these comments are not me saying Sheffield is inferior to LA. Not at all. It's just *very different*. And being brought up in Sheffield in the seventies and eighties has given me a character and personality that has actually been *completely* instrumental in what I have been trying to achieve. Growing up in Sheffield might struggle compared to LA in the areas I mentioned, but – and it's a *big* but – that UK town and living in the north of England has given me so much that I am very grateful for. Being brought up in the seventies and eighties in England has given me grit and determination to work hard, that British Bulldog spirit of never give up, that tenaciousness that my mum had and that I inherited, too. People from those parts find a way to get stuff done. I think my early stamina from running has also stood me in good stead, even now, some forty years later. Coming back full circle to the days when I was a kid loving cross-country, well, in 2016 I was asked to do a public service announcement for the LA Olympic bid in 2024. Basically, they were talking to various celebrities and high-profile people about LA, what the city meant to them and how amazing it would be to host the Olympic Games. I told the story of watching Sebastian Coe win the 1,500 metres and 800 metres at the 1984 Los Angeles Olympic Games.

Brits also have a great sense of humour, as well as the gift of the gab, and that's something that's made me not afraid to talk to people. Sheffield is an innovative town with a rich history of pioneering, especially in industry. I believe that the entrepreneurial spirit in me was already there when I arrived in the States. The Sheffield boy in me has kept me grounded, made me work hard and dedicate myself to achieving my dreams and grafting non-stop.

Of course, getting back to California, LA is the perfect place to live if you enjoy driving, particularly the cars that I collect. One of my favourite parts of living in LA is when we finish a car and I always take it for a three-hundred-mile shakedown test drive. So, for example, I might drive through the Angeles Crest Highway out to Willow Springs, then through the Tehachapi and back to California City, Mojave and finally into LA. What a ride . . . only in LA!

The Downtown arts district of LA is where I've been for almost twenty-five years now, and that's where I am rooted. So all my adventures begin in this gritty, urban part of Los Angeles. However, this is not where I was born – the industrial city of Sheffield in the north of England was my hometown growing up. It is between these two very urban places that my story has unfolded. In many ways, that tale reflects how those two cities have influenced me, and as a result I am a combination of various elements of both. And despite the apparent differences between Sheffield and Los Angeles, there is a real common thread between the cities that have been my life. I'm a city guy at heart; I didn't grow up in a rural environment on a farm in the middle of nowhere. I feel most at home in an urban environment – the buildings, the architecture, the grittiness – so it's no coincidence that a lad brought up in Steel City ended up buying a hundred-and-fifteen-year-old two-storey brick building in LA that would not look out of place in Sheffield.

People often ask me why I collect vintage Porsches. I always think, *Why wouldn't you collect them?* There is so much to be attracted to. Aside from what I said about Porches excelling at everything, these older examples are so enjoyable to be around. These cars are forty to fifty years old, so they've all been tweaked and changed. They've all got patina and DNA and character and soul, but what does that mean? Well, like I said at the very start of this book, it's blood, sweat, tears, oil and gas – you know it's encrusted and engrained in the car. These are living, driving machines with personality that you are connected to and involved with. Yeah, the modern cars may be technically faster, but they are less involving; you don't have to put as much effort in. Yes, ultimately it's just a car that goes from A to B, but that's not the purpose of it, that totally misses the point. Like living in Sheffield and LA, it is all about the *experience*.

Chapter 15

Go With Your Gut Feeling

Since the release of *Urban Outlaw*, I have been presented with some incredible opportunities, many of which I have told you about in this book. One of the most enjoyable was some two years after the film came out when I was asked to give a Ted Talk. Truth be told, I literally had no idea what I was being offered, *What's a Ted Talk?* Well, I can tell you now that it's a series of talks given by a variety of high-profile individuals and luminaries, organized on a non-profit basis, where the idea is to encourage debate and an open forum for new ideas that may be hugely beneficial to society and the wider population. So some of these talks are about poverty in the developing world, famine, global warming, pandemic health challenges, economics and everything in between. Needless to say, the list of names who have given Ted Talks is pretty impressive, including Stephen Hawking, Bill Gates, Bill Clinton, people from the entertainment world such as

Bono and J. J. Abrams, leading scientists, politicians, charity workers – it's really an amazing selection.

What happened was the people organizing a Ted Talk at UCLA contacted me and asked if I would be interested. Like I said, my initial reaction was, 'What's a Ted Talk?' They sent me a couple of samples, but I didn't say yes straight away because I've never spoken in public. As you know, I stuttered as a kid and, although it was one of those things that I got over, the experience made me kinda nervous about standing up in front of a crowd. So the idea of a talk wasn't exactly something that I was naturally drawn to. By now, I'd probably done about thirty TV shows or website interviews on camera, so I was a little more comfortable, but it was still not what I would call a natural experience for me. I might sound fluent and coherent in *Urban Outlaw*, but that's because Tamir was super-talented and was able to edit my rambling and just get the great soundbites. But in all honesty, I wasn't quite confident that I could do that myself.

I watched these sample videos and to be fair it's not all intellectual stuff about molecular biology and stem-cell research. I could see that some of these talks were super-positive and mostly informative and inspirational. So I said, 'You know what? Fuck it, I'll do it. How bad can it be?'

A couple of days before my talk was scheduled, they said that I should really go in and rehearse, and I initially said, 'No thanks, I know what I want to say,' but the point they were making was that you only have eighteen minutes to give your talk, and they are really strict about you going over time. So I go down there on a Friday around two o'clock in the afternoon for a run-through, I get up on stage and I just start telling my 'eighteen-minute' story.

Well, I just ramble on and eventually, about forty-five minutes later, they go, 'Hey, Magnus, you're really going to have to edit this down!' I also had a hundred slides ready to show people, but they said, 'You need to edit those down to six slides.' This was a bit daunting, so I went back to see Karen and we started writing all this stuff down, trying to edit the story. The problem was, the more I wrote down, the more forced and contrived it felt. When I was rehearsing the script, I was stumbling over the words. At about six o'clock that night, I just said, 'Do you know what? I'm just gonna wing it.'

So that's what I did.

I knew if I didn't get to the Porsche part of my story by ten minutes I was kinda fucked. That was my plan. As always, on the actual day I got there early, then sat through everyone else's talks, which was kinda nerve-wracking. Then it came to my turn, so I took to the stage with no cards, no notes and just ten slides. One of my opening lines of the talk is 'Eight weeks ago I didn't know what a Ted Talk was and, to be honest, I'm not quite sure why I'm here today.'

For the first minute, I was a little bit nervous because you look across this big room, it's a very unfamiliar environment, there's maybe five hundred people in an auditorium, I'm on stage, everyone's looking at me, I'm the only sort of car-related, rock 'n' roll guy there. In some of the talks before mine . . . I gotta be honest here and say I was a little bored, I was actually dozing off during one, so I was very conscious of not being another one of those. At one point early on, I stumbled a little, then I cracked a joke and the audience laughed and I just broke into a more natural calmness. I slowed my speech down and started to enjoy myself.

Up to that point, every interview or on-camera piece that I'd done was in my own environment. Also, I could stop the camera at any moment and do a retake. This was live. However, I just kept reminding myself that I was comfortable with what I was talking about – leaving school at sixteen, no education, no direction and what happened next – everything I've told you in this book. They had a little laptop in front of me that was counting down the time, so occasionally I had to look over and then speed up my story, but I got there in the end and only went a minute over, which was no big deal. When I'd finished, people cheered their support – it was unbelievable. Of course I breathed a sigh of relief, but I had actually quite enjoyed it.

Afterwards, everyone came out to meet me by 277, which I had driven there that day. I would say 95 per cent of these UCLA students had no idea who I was; they were not car people, but they seemed to relate to my story, which I'd summed up in the title of my talk: 'Go with your gut feeling'. A lot of people were coming up to me with similar stories, very different backgrounds but similar ideas. Quite a few were telling me their parents wanted them to be doctors or lawyers but that they were miserable, they weren't enjoying themselves or their courses. For me it was a super-positive and uplifting experience to see that I had had some influence on people thinking about changing their career and actually doing something they wanted to do in life.

The Ted Talk has gone on to be perhaps the most-viewed

thing that I have done online, with over three and a half million views at the time of writing. It might have even topped *Urban Outlaw*. People shoot me emails all the time, and a lot of them are from people who have watched the Ted Talk. That day at UCLA has been a very positive experience and in turn it taught me a few things: one was self-editing, the idea of 'less is more'; it also encouraged me to learn to become more comfortable and enjoy being in front of a live audience rather than freaking out. I get asked to do motivational talks all the time now, by big corporations and often in front of a lot of people. That's a new challenge for me, but I really enjoy those talks and especially enjoy meeting people and making a connection with them.

At times, I still feel like, *What words of wisdom do I have? I'm just a geezer that left school with two O levels at sixteen, what do I know?* Sometimes people say to me, 'Maybe you got lucky, Magnus?' Well, maybe I did . . . but I don't think I got lucky three times. I can see now that people relate to my story on a number of levels. That is really rewarding, and I feel humbled that what I have tried to achieve in my life has in some small way maybe inspired or at least influenced others. I am delighted when magazines suggest their readers can be motivated and get ideas from what I have done. In 2014, the *Smith Journal* called me 'the most interesting man in Los Angeles', and that same year *LA Weekly* did a feature on 'The People of 2014' and very kindly put me in there. So it is a real thrill when other people give me credits like that.

I'm not claiming to be some management guru or inspirational speaker, far from it. Long story short – and let's face it, you know the story by now – it's about *what you actually do*, not how you talk about what you do. However, if you asked me to condense my half-century of life into a few pieces of advice, then it's pretty simple stuff.

First, crucially, *go with your gut feeling*, as the guy with the beard and tattoos said at the Ted Talk. If something feels right and your gut is telling you that this is the best course of action, then go for it. When we bought the warehouse Downtown, it felt right; when we opened the first clothing store, it felt right; and, yes, it felt right when we wound Serious down. We didn't necessarily know what was coming next, but we still trusted our instincts. Most obviously, I went with my gut instinct when I got an unsolicited email from a guy called Tamir about his idea to film a short five-minute YouTube clip. You can trace it right back to my teenage years, when I was a kid in Thatcher's Britain struggling to find a focus. I went with my gut instinct and got on that plane to America. That felt right. I wasn't sure why at the time, but it felt right. It also felt right buying those old Levi's and putting patches on them on Venice Boardwalk. Reselling those pants on Melrose that I'd bought up the road for ten bucks, that was just a flash of inspiration, that felt right. I certainly hadn't planned to sell them, it had never even occurred to me, but inspiration sometimes comes along when you least expect it. I didn't set out to run a fashion business, a film-location business, or gather a huge collection of Porsches and become known around the world for my modifications. My life has been a series of decisions based on gut instinct that have led me to where I am today. This sometimes means not over-thinking things – don't take months to make a decision that only really needs a few days or even maybe a few hours.

Does it feel right? What is your gut instinct telling you?

Of course, at times you will need to be brave and take risks, depending on what your gut instinct is saying. You might need to take a deep breath and seize an opportunity. In my opinion, it is a reality that if you want to succeed, then you have to take risks. By this, I don't mean be reckless with yourself, your career or your money. That's not risk-taking. A risk is me leaving that City & Guilds course in Sports Management, Leisure and Recreation at nineteen to come to America and then find myself scrabbling around for loose change just to survive; let me tell you, that didn't exactly feel like a good risk at the time. But at least I'd had a go. At least I was trying to do something instead of staying back in Sheffield on the dole or on the construction site, playing it safe. I didn't know anybody that had come to America. It wasn't like I had a friend that went there the year before and told me how great it was. I came to America really with no preconceived plan, I didn't know what I was coming into. That was my first leap of faith and, truth be told, if I'd never come to America I don't think I would ever have done half the things that I have. I was only a kid, but I took a risk.

Back then my attitude was, *How bad can it be? What's the worst that can happen, right?* As you know, that has been a central idea in my entire life. When that production company phoned me at the Willow warehouse and asked if could they film a music video there, I didn't take a month to decide. Instead, I thought, *Yeah, why not?* If we hadn't said yes to filming, we probably wouldn't be here today. Before that, if we hadn't taken the chance on buying the building, we definitely wouldn't have been here. If we had bought a house in West Hollywood, none of this would ever have happened. In a sense, it was also a risk to do the Ted Talk. I had no background, no training, no idea of what that entailed, but I was happy to take the risk.

To take risks, you need self-belief. I've owned over fifty 911s, but I've only ever done a pre-purchase inspection on one of them, the car in Australia. Too often, people second-guess and doubt themselves, ask for too many other opinions, get confused, derailed or sidetracked. They don't have enough self-belief, so they ask a friend, but then the pal goes, 'Oh, that's never going to work', and so a good idea gets shelved. We never asked anyone's opinion. Karen and I were on the same page where we knew we could make it work. So many people thought we were crazy when we bought the building in Willow because it needed so much work. Self-belief and willpower can overcome any obstacle. Maybe that's naïveté on my part, I don't know, but for us we always knew that we'd find a way to make it work. Although my instinct tells me *How bad can it be?*, what I'm actually looking for is the best-case scenario.

I have been quoted as saying, 'If it feels slightly fearful and, *Wow, I don't know if I can do this*, then you should probably do it.' Everyone has goals and dreams. Not everyone does something about them. It's like I said earlier about when you are a kid and you walk to the top of the high diving board, you either jump or you don't jump. Be the one that jumps.

At times, if you are taking risks, then you are also doing things unconventionally. They go hand in hand. What separated Serious from a lot of our fellow competitors and peers was that we'd use non-fashion-related material in our clothing. For example, one season we had this car-seat fabric, it was thick, heavy nylon webbing mesh in bright colours. It was in some funky car, I can't remember which one, in all these garish colours such as pink, raspberry, yellow, it was kind of a very Mod/sixties look. Another time we used this upholstery fabric called swirl velvet that had never been used in fashion, but we washed it down and made it soft. So we did things that were a little bit different. You meet some people and you can tell that they don't want to step outside that box. My whole adult life has been spent outside of the box.

That brings me to my next point: whatever you choose to do, make sure it has your style. If you look at all three of the businesses I have been involved in, they all started from and were based on my own individual style, whether it be in clothing, interiors or cars, which people then bought into and appreciated. That is the common thread, the mutual connection between them. I keep saying that all the time – whatever you do, the style has to be a reflection of your personality. The materials we used at Serious were literally woven with our personality, they were clothes that we would wear ourselves and, in fact, we very often did wear them out and about. People picked up on that, they could see that what we were creating had our personality stamped on there – same with Willow and same with the Porsches. Your own unique style is exactly that – unique – no one else has that, so this has to be your strength. You really do have to stand out from the crowd, and I have been able to do that in three completely different fields, with my own slightly different twist. So at all times add your own personality and do that with flair. Don't try to emulate someone else or copy a trend. Ultimately, you have to add your own style, your own personality and *don't wait, do that straightaway*.

Tied into this idea is the absolute need to do something you are *passionate* about. If you don't, then people will sniff you out, plus – perhaps more importantly – you won't enjoy yourself. Nowadays, I get approached by huge multinational corporations to go and do talks to their staff about passion, and that's because these big companies realize that passion isn't something that you can create on a marketing plan or figure out with a spreadsheet. It is essentially very simple: I am passionate about what I do. That has been another common thread between the clothing, the property and the cars – I have such passion for all of it. This has the double benefit of making your work more unique and also making it more energetic, because your passion will shine through. If you don't have passion for what you are doing, then something needs to change . . . why are you doing it?

Associated to this idea of personality and passion is the need to never forget your roots. I always say it doesn't matter where you end up so long as you remember where you came from. There's a tattoo on my right arm that says, 'Made in Sheffield'. It's there for a reason – I love Sheffield and my background. Yes, I moved to America and that has opened doors that would not have been available to me back in the UK. However, Sheffield gave me that British Bulldog spirit, that northern, cross-country runner mentality, the self-belief to go it alone and to last the distance. Also the entrepreneurial spirit that was on my grandad's side of the family is what got me into being a bit of a wheeler-dealer, a market trader, a grafter. On the other side, my dad's mechanical engineering background and interest in cars and motor sports has, on reflection, had a massive impact. It's very easy when you move away from your roots to lose your way, get distracted and lose focus. Never forget where you came from, because that is absolutely at the core of your personality.

Now, if you use your personality and are passionate about what you are doing, that is fantastic, but you also need to have what I just touched on – a tenacious, relentless spirit, the idea that you never, ever give up. *Ever.* Personally, I think I get that from my mum, truth be told. Her tenaciousness, dedication and single-mindedness to keep plugging away is where my gritty streak came from. We moved a lot as a family, as you know, but she would never give up, she always made it work. Even now, she is talking about selling a flat and buying this old, abandoned coach house in Sheffield. She is always getting shit done.

My background wasn't necessarily great, I certainly wasn't born with a silver spoon in my mouth, but I have been able to achieve ideas that I dreamt of. I'm a goal-orientated guy. Fight for what you believe in and never give up on it. Sometimes you'll need patience. That's just a fact of life. I didn't build my Porsche collection overnight. I never thought I'd find a '64 911, but I never gave up looking and in the end I paid next to nothing for it. When we bought that land by the Fourth Street Bridge, the legal side of the process was a complete nightmare, but I just kept going, Karen too. We were relentless, and in the end we got the deal done. Without doubt, at times you will encounter difficulties and this will be stressful, that is natural, especially if you are trying to do something that is considered 'different'. However, you have to just keep on keeping on, right? There's always a way out of it. Move forward, move forward, move forward, positive, positive, positive. You have got to get good at the hustle and *never* give up.

Remember, I've been down in LA with next to nothing, almost the 'last dollar' mentality, and pulled back from that and turned it around. There have been points in the past where I've had to sell a car to keep another project moving forward. If you are motivated enough, you make shit happen. I believe things will always work out . . . I never give up. Like I said, maybe it came from the cross-country running – keep on pushing and don't give up. As you've seen, 2015 was the worst year of my life. Karen passed away, as well as my dog that I'd had for thirteen years. However, I have to keep going, keep trying to move forward. The instinct to survive is just naturally there.

Another piece of advice I like to offer is very simple – be nice to other people. What goes around comes around, you know. I've never slagged off other people online, especially about their builds. I never comment on other people's cars or projects in a negative way. I do get criticism – some people don't like my spirited driving on public roads and others take a potshot at my profile. There are always going to be haters and naysayers slagging me off, but I'm like, *Fuck, you guys are doing all the talking for me. I don't have to do anything!* They seem to have all the time in the world to critique the way I look and talk, but I never get involved in these online battles; I just let people say what they want to say. A lot of it is from guys who wish they could have done the same but didn't have the balls to go for it.

I'm not a religious man, but I do believe in karma. That happened to me when I found the '64 911. It's happened to me three times when those motors found me. Just be nice to people; even if you don't think you've had any payback, the motivation to be nice and the good feelings that generates should be payment enough.

Now for the fairly mundane part: you can listen to your gut instinct, you can seize an opportunity, be passionate and individual about what you do and never give up . . . BUT you can only do that all together with *hard work*. Good old-fashioned hard work goes a long, long, long way. I think that people looking in on someone who's been successful – in any walk of life – often severely underestimate the amount of sheer hard graft that the individual has put in. I'm talking about firing on all cylinders, year after year. Karen and I worked some unbelievably long hours for a very long time. This was never a 9-to-5, Monday-to-Friday job or lifestyle. At some points, we didn't have any time off for months. You can't expect that if you have a vision and want to deliver on that and make it work. Be your own one-man army.

Take the Serious retail stores. That was so much hard work. Likewise renovating and fitting out Willow – we spent a year building that out. Right from when they started sand-blasting the decades of old paint off the walls, it was a long, hard process. Hours and hours, weeks and weeks, for months on end. The entrepreneurial, do-it-yourself route is not an easy path, be under no illusions about that.

How can you help yourself be prepared for what lies ahead? Well, when Serious was really cooking, we'd often get phone calls from people saying, 'My kid is a huge fan of your work, she's thinking of going to fashion school, she wants to be a designer, what should she do?' Well, you can go to fashion school, but that doesn't teach you how to have an idea. That route can teach you the basics of marketing and how to sell and set up a team, but in my opinion you either have the idea or you don't. You can't go to school and learn how to have a good idea. You go to school to learn about fashion – what came before, the history, the theory – but that doesn't necessarily make you creative. Karen and I never went to fashion school. You don't need a formal education to have an idea.

I fell into the fashion industry. It wasn't planned. I bought a building, but we didn't know we were going to fall into the film business. I wasn't taught any of that in school. I was taught shit that, truth be told, was useless to me. Pythagoras's Theorem . . . I mean, what the fuck is that useful for, right? Or the fact that Pi is 3.142. I can quote that number all these years later, but it doesn't mean anything to me. Let's put it this way, the two O levels that I gained at school haven't really helped me much. I left school at sixteen, didn't have any background in fashion but built a successful clothing business that was eventually doing several million dollars' worth of business a year. I didn't go to university, get an MBA in business or entrepreneurial management or whatever the fuck it is people do. I've no idea what they do, to be honest. It sounds a little blunt, but sometimes when people say they are doing business studies I think, *What the fuck do you need that for?* You're either street-smart or you're book-smart. If you do it all yourself, no one is really going to stop you. You are either going to sink or you are going to swim. You don't have to have a PhD or take business management courses; they all help, don't get me wrong, and I am not going to be an advocate for dropping out of education. However, if you haven't got an MBA from a top college or university, you need to know that this doesn't for one second mean you can't still make a success of yourself.

In all these years, I have never done a business plan. Sometimes Karen and I would go to a bar and get inspired. When we were fitting out Willow, we might get a little napkin and maybe draw an idea out and then come back to the ware-house and meet with the contractor, then lay it all out with blue tape on the floor. All drawn up on the back of the napkin. It still worked.

This ties into what I was saying about being unconventional. Not having any specific background in what I have chosen to pursue means I didn't know where the boundaries were. That way you are able to do whatever you want to do. You are not restricted by the accepted limitations. Just because no one has ever made miniskirts out of car-seat fabric doesn't mean it can't be done. I think that goes back to being an adaptive swimmer, where you can drop into an environment and kind of make your way through it. You don't need to feel inferior if you don't have a huge file of qualifications; if you have street-smarts, self-belief, a unique idea and a passion to work very hard, then that is as good as any degree in the world.

So, like I said, those are just a few suggestions to take away with you from reading my tale. Hopefully you don't need to love cars, fashion or property to find something of value in these ideas. I don't know how much of this will be useful to you, I don't even know if you will agree with all or any of it.

I am just trying to offer a few ideas that I have learnt from what has been, for me, the most incredible and enjoyable journey. It's been a long run since those days training around the woods near my parents' home in Sheffield, but it's been worth every step . . . and I'm still running. It's an open road out there, and I am excited to see what comes next.

What I do know is that, back in the seventies, if you'd told the story in this book to that stuttering kid timidly putting his hand up during the school register each morning when they shouted out 'Magnus' . . . well, I think he'd be pretty pleased. Wow. Dream come true, right?

You see, in many ways it's real simple: listen to your gut instinct, take risks and seize opportunities, inject your personality into everything you do and make sure you stay passionate about your work, remember where you came from, never give up on the goal, never give up on the dream, stay motivated, stay dedicated, work hard, don't be restricted by convention and tradition, never settle and always, always, *always* keep moving forward. How bad can it be, right?

And never, ever let dirt slow you down.

Acknowledgements

Many thanks to: my mum, Linda Walker; my sister and her husband, Naomi and Alex McGregor, and the bin lids, Naimh, Jessica and James; our kid St. John and Nicky Walker; Martin Roach; Liam Howlett; Joost Hermes; Erik Kouwenhoven; Henry Vines.

Stateside: Tamir Moscovici; Helmut Wahl; Ray Campbell; Justin Bell; Karina 'the Latina' Macias; the Caid family down in Georgia; Sergio Contreras; Matt J. Bown; Jon White; Phil Slate; Frank Turner; Chalmers Niemeyer.

Larry Chen; Sean Klingelhoefer; Andrew Ritter; Maurice Van den Tillaard; Eli Kogan; Brad Beardow; Matt Crooke; Dorian Valenzuela.

Index

Abrams, J. J. 232
Ace Cafe 174
Action Retailer, on Serious Clothing 80
Albuquerque, '75 Turbo roller 194–6
Alternative Press, interview 80
America *see* United States
American TV 28
Anderson, Pamela 34, 213
Andretti, Mario 178–9
Angeles Crest Highway, LA xi, 226
Angelo, Robert, and *Jay Leno's Garage* 160
Arendt, Anthony 148
Atlanta Pussy Posse (Karen & friends) 74
Atlanta visit 213
Austin 7s 11
Australia, 911-930 '75 Turbo 192–4
Auto Trader 128
autographs and fans 172–3
Autohaus Hamilton, Sydney 193
Axcess, Serious Clothing on cover 80

Bakewell 7
  visiting with Karen 215–17
BBC heavy metal documentary 114–15
Beckham, Victoria, at Willow warehouse 115–16
Bennett, Bib and Joe (Walker's grandparents) 6
  market traders 6–7, 48–62, 240–1
  Renault 5 63
Bentley 172
Bentley Boys 125

Bill Haley and His Comets 5
Billion Dollar Babies 90
Black Crowes 70, 80
Black Sabbath 21, 114–15
Block, Ken 177, 180
Blomqvist, Stig 12
Bob Smith Porsche 189, 191
Bodecker, Sandy 152–3
Bond Esprit 120
Bono 232
boys and cars, 1970s 1–4
Bridlington 9
British sense of humour 228
Broomhill Infants School 23
Brumos Porsche
  911 '65 video 189
  stripes 139, 141
Burbank, Jay Leno's garage 160–4
Burning Man counterculture 55–6
Butler, Geezer 114–15

Cadillac, 60s, Karen's 75
Cadwell Park 12
California, driving in 225, 226, 228–9
California Speedway 125
Camp America
  Lake Michigan 26, 27, 28–33, 41–2
  New Jersey 40, 41–2
Canada 32
Captain America 52, 98
Car and Driver 152
car-related American TV and movies 28
Cash, Johnny 80

Cat House (club) 43
'Cat in the Hat' hats 54, 56
Century City 48
Chapman, Colin 120
Château de Grandson car Museum 10
Chatsworth, visiting with Karen 215, 217
Cherry, club 79
Chevy Corvette 169
Chris (Karen's friend) 74
Cisneros, Henrique, Momo wheels 178–9
Clark, Roger 12
Clinton, Bill 231
clothes
  re-making/selling 53–62
    production/sales costs 58
  second-hand, at Venice Beach 48–62, 236
  clothing catalogue, first 56
  see also Serious Clothing; Venetian Paradise
Cobain, Kurt 74
Coe, Sebastian 14, 15
  wins at 1984 LA Olympics 228
Cooper, Alice
  reference from 85
  tour with 89
  wears Serious Clothing 80, 88–90
Costa Mesa, Karen at 74–6
Craigslist 128
Cram, Steve 14
cross-country running 14–16, 19, 242, 246
Cruising My Religion (Youtube video) 198–200
Culver City rented house 69

Daimlers 10
David, Uncle
  and cars 11
  and Lotus Type 47 122
  at Bakewell 216
De La Soul, wears Venetian Paradise 70
Dean, James 134
decisions, gut instinct 236–40
Detroit 32
  Motor City Outlaw 33
Dibnah, Fred 163
Digital Underground, wears Venetian Paradise 70
Disneyland theme parks
  first order 57
  reference from 85
Doc Martens 59
Dodge '69 Super Bees 80, 119, 121–2
Donington 12

Downe, Taime (Faster Pussycat) 36–7, 43
  and Pretty Ugly Club 79
  works at Serious Clothing store 81–2
Downtown LA see under Los Angeles
DP (after-market tuner) 67
Dukes of Hazzard 52, 120, 121, 182, 213

Earls Court Motor Show 2–4, 66
Early S Registry 130
East LA, former Masons Lodge bought 107
Echo & the Bunnymen 20
El Coyote 44
Emory, Rod 182
  and 964 fenders 203–4
  Emory Motorsports 134
entrepreneurs, and schools 243–5
Evel Knievel 28, 52, 58, 98, 139

Facebook 151
Fairbanks, Douglas Jr 75
family holidays 9–11
fans and autographs 172–3
fashion trade fairs 172–3
  first success 56–7
Fast N' Loud 181
Faster Pussycat (band) 36–7, 43
Fédération Internationale de l'Automobile 198
Ferraris 3, 10–11, 120
  308 GTB 3, 11
  '79 308 GTB 119, 122–3
  512 Berlinetta Boxer 2
Ferrari, Dino 11
Ferrari, Enzo, on E-Type 120
fifteen52 Urban Outlaw signature wheel 177–8, 194
Fisherman's Wharf SF 38
Flavor Flav, wears Venetian Paradise 70
Ford Cortinas 11
Ford Mustang 169–70
Foster, Brendan 14
Fourth Street Bridge, buying land under 107–8, 241
Frankfurt Auto Show 1963 169
Fuchs wheel 177–8

Gap seconds, hawking 49–50
garage (MW's) 59–60, 183–4
Gates, Bill 231
Gemballa, after-market tuner 67
Germany, cross-country 15
Glamour magazine, reference from 85
Gmünd Coupe 175
Gold's Gym 68

Goldberg, Bill, muscle-car collection 182
Gooding & Company, auction Porsche STR 174–5
Goodwood Festival 168
Goodwood Revival 168–9, 226
Greektown, Detroit 32
Griffith Observatory 76
grunge replacing rave 70
Guatemalan hats 54–5
guitar incident 18
Gulf War 1990, and patriotism 57
Guns and Roses 28
gut feeling, going with xv, 81, 150, 231–2, 234, 236–40
  and business 111
  Camp America opportunity 28
  Melrose pants sale 37
  New York trade show 56
  Urban Outlaw 147
  Willow warehouse 92, 93

Hagar, Sammy 113–14
Hallamshire Harriers 15, 60
Hanoi Rocks look 36, 43
Happy Mondays (band) 55
hard work 7, 49–50, 59, 182, 243
  Serious Clothing 71, 73, 83, 243
hats, floppy, making/selling 54–62
Hatter, Tony (Porsche designer) 168
Hawking, Stephen, Ted Talk 231
Hazzard County 213
Hermès, Joost
  and Rotterdam outlaw run 171, 188
  at London Raindance 155, 188
  finds '64 911 185–6, 188
Heywood, Hurley 139
Hillsborough park 15
Hollywood
  Century City 48
  first visit 34–8
  sign 76
Hollywood Boulevard 35–8, 44–5
Hollywood Hills, rented house 104–5
Honda of Hollywood 64
Hooch clothing company 73, 77, 218–19
Hoosier tyres 141
Hot Topic, sales to 71, 77, 83, 96
Hot Wheels cars, MW's models 179
house painting 49–50
Howlett, Liam
  and Porsche 68R 131–2, 149–50
    Schuco 1:43 scale model 179
  at London Raindance 155–6
Hunt, James 12

IKEA 98
individual style, forming 78
Ingrams
  buy Porsche STR 175–7
  Porsche Unexpected: Discoveries in Collecting 177, 201
Inspiral Carpets (band) 55
interior design offers 105
International Jeanswear Show, Miami 73–4
Isaak, Chris
  reference from 85
  wears Serious Clothing 80

Jaguars 120
  E-Type 11
    Series 1 119, 120–1, 123, 124
    '67 E-Type 218
  XJ6 121
Jalopnik 152, 165
Javits Center, trade show success 56–7
Jay Leno's Garage
  appearances 160–4
  debuts Porsche STR02 171
Jay Z, at Willow warehouse 116
Jennings, Shooter 182
Jennings, Waylon 182
Johnny (MW's friend) 64
Johnny Outrageous (band) 42–4
Jose (car painter) 129
Just Seventeen, Serious Clothing on cover 80

karma 243
  Porsche 194–8
Kerrang! 20
Kouwenhoven, Erik 133–5, 171
Kremer, after-market tuner 67

LA Weekly 235
Laguna Seca 125, 127, 133
Lake Michigan Camp America
  journey 29–30
  culture shock 30–3
Lamborghinis 3, 123
  Countach 2
Lancia Stratos 2
Landenberger, Dieter (Porsche curator) 166, 190
Las Vegas
  SEMA car show 159–60
  Speedway 125, 127
  wedding 214–15
Leadmill (club) 20
Lee, Tommy 213
Lemmy (Motörhead) 114–15

Leno, Jay
  Jay Leno's Garage 160–4
  restoration projects 163
  steam cars 161, 163–4
Let It Rock (clothes shop) 36
Levi jeans, patching, selling 51–5, 236
Lip Service 80
Liz (Karen's friend) 74
London
  Borough Market 107–8
  first visit 2–4
  Raindance Film Festival, *Urban
    Outlaw* screening 155–6
  visiting with Karen 217
Los Angeles (LA) 28
  clubs 43, 44
  diversity 227
  Downtown LA ix–xi, 57, 76, 121–2,
    165, 179, 229
    gentrification 99–100, 108–9
    Gladys warehouse, move to 71–2, 78
    rundown in 1990s 92–3
    Willow warehouse 91–107, 236
  driving in 228–9
  first visit, from Detroit 33–4, 38–9
  Fourth Street Bridge, buying land
    under 107–8, 241
  Olympics bid, speaking for 228
  Olympics 1984 228
  represents limitless opportunity
    223–30
  second visit
    happy times 42–8
    living off friends 47–8
  sightseeing tour, MW's 75–6
  Sixth Street Bridge 226
  Union Station 34
Los Angeles Auto Show 167
Los Angeles Times, 'Explorers of the
  Lost City' 99–100
Lotus cars 120
  Europa '73 119, 122
  Type 47 11, 122
Love, Courtney 212
Lynyrd Skynyrd 52

Mad Hatter hat 56
Mad Max-inspired clothing 89
'Madchester' scene UK 55
Madonna
  and Willow warehouse 94
  costumes 90
magnuswalker911 blog 151
Mallory Park 12
Mandalay Bay Hotel, Las Vegas 215
Manson, Marilyn, wears Serious
  Clothing 80

market trader spirit 240–1
  at Venice Beach 48–62
Marty, and 911-930 '76 Turbo 190–1
Mauer, Michael 168
McLarens 161
McQueen, Chad 182
McQueen, Steve 28
  documentary 226
Melrose 43
  Serious Clothing store 81–3, 214
  shops, selling to 54, 236
Memphis 33
Miami, International Jeanswear Show
  74
Miami Vice 66
Michael Schenker Group (MSG) 21
Mick, Uncle, E-Type Jag 11
Mobil 1, SEMA 2014 172–3
Momo signature steering wheel 178–9
Monroe, Marilyn, style, Karen and 73,
  74
Monsters of Rock Festival 20
Monterey Historics, Porsche STR
  auction 174–7
Morocco, holiday 29
Morohoshi-san 180
Moscovici, Tamir
  Between the Walls 147
  Urban Outlaw 145–82, 232
    trailer 151–3
  YouTube documentary proposal 147,
    236
motivation 60–1, 168, 235–40
Mötley Crüe 28, 30
Motor City Outlaw 33
Motor Link 8–9
Motörhead
  'Ace of Spades' 19
  at Willow warehouse 114–15
moving forward 241–2
MTV, reference from 85
Mustang '65 GT350R replica 119–20,
  123

Nakai-san 180
NaNa stores 59
Nashville Pussy 80
National Trust houses 97
Need for Speed video game, MW speed
  icon in 179–80
New Jersey, Camp America 41–2
New Mexico, thrift-store shopping 89
New York
  1988 stopover 29
  first trade show success 56–7
  visiting from NJ 41–2
New York boutique show 72–3

Newman, Paul 28
Niemeyer, Chalmers, sends Porsche
    shield 166–7
Nike Action Sports Division, Willow
    summit 152–3
Nine Inch Nails, wears Serious Clothing
    80
NME 20
No Doubt, wears Serious Clothing 80
Norton, Ed 212

Oakey, Phil 226
Oakley 172
Oldman, Gary 226
Oliver, cousin 10
    first LA visit 33–6, 38
    dresses mod 36
Ollie, and Porsche 911 '76 Carrera 200
Omega watches 180
Oulton Park 12
outlaw Porsches 130–5, 200–6
Outlaw Fever 194
overthinking, avoiding 236–40
Ovett, Steve 14

parent pressure 234
passion
    in business 96, 106, 110–11, 130–2,
        240–1, 243–6
    for Porsche 131–2, 137, 148–50,
        153–6, 165, 167, 170, 184
Pebble Beach, Monterey Historics
    174–5
Peet, Amanda 104
Pelican Parts 129–30, 131, 147, 151,
    185, 199
Penrhyn Road house 18
people, being nice to 129, 172–3, 242–3
performers, and Serious Clothing 80
Perry, Fred, mod clothes 36
Perry, Matthew 104
Peter Max bedspread 51–2
Phil (car restorer) 131
Phoenix Speedway 125, 127
phone calling cards 39
Pickford, Mary 75
Pirelli 172
Platen, Detlev von 167
Police, and MW in Super Bee 121–2
Pomona Swap Meet 66, 137, 183
Porno for Pyros, wears Serious Clothing
    80
Porsche Cars (company)
    answers MW letter 4, 63, 165, 169
    in 2013 169–80
    invites MW to Stuttgart factory
        165–6

Porsche Canada, debut Panamera at
    Willow 167
Porsche GB 168
Special Wishes programme 67
work with 168
Porsche cars
    collecting x–xv, 119, 123–4, 229–30,
        236, 239
    buying/selling 127–35
    'Porsche Collection – Out of
        Control Hobby' 129–30
    restoring/upgrading 66–9, 107, 117,
        128–35
    builds, publicity 145
    documenting 129–35
    engines, why swapped 196–7
    outlaw 130–5
    signature touches 130–5
Porsche cars, specific
    Porsche 356 154
        outlaw 134
    Porsche 911s xii, 120, 125
        air-cooled, buying 193, 207–8, 238
        50th anniversary 168, 169–80
        '64, matching-numbers
            as holy grail 184–5, 205
            finding 185–8
        '65 188–9
            no. 365, engine found 198
            no. 1036, engine found 197–8
        '66 Irish Green x, 157, 188, 209
            in *Urban Outlaw* 149
        '67 172–3, 192
        68R 131–2
            in *Urban Outlaw* 149–50
        '73 RS Carrera 138, 185
        '74 Carrera, restoring 128
        '76 Carrera 200
        Cayman 208
        Martini Turbo 3, 66
        '78 SC x, 3
        '78 SCHR, 'budget build' 198–200
        slant-nose 1974, MW's first 65–9,
            119, 183
        Sport Classic 168, 203
        STR 131, 132
            auction at Monterey Historics
                174–7, 201
        STR02 170–1
        911-930 Turbo 1, 3
            generation car 189
            European Minerva blue 194
            Turbo Fever video 191
            '75 Turbo
                search for 191–4
                left-hand drive 194
                right-hand drive 192–4

roller 194–6
  original engine 195–6
'76 Turbo 166
  prototypes, documented 190
  silver 189–91, 209
'77 Turbo, ice-green metallic
  194
911T '69, restoring 128, 189
911T '71 '277' x–xiv, 168, 234
  at Road to Rennsport 2015 179
  at SEMA 2014 172–3
  in Jay Leno's Garage 160, 162
  in Need for Speed video game 180
  in Urban Outlaw 150
  Schuco 1:43 scale model 179
  'street-able track car' 139–44
  crash 143–4
  customizing 137–44
  seats 142–3
912s 129
918 supercar, dreadlocks stuck in
  door 173
924s 3, 11
964 outlaw 200–6
993 200, 208
991 208
991-911 277-liveried, prospective
  168–8
996 water-cooled 208
997 208
Porsche Owners Club 124–7, 131
  MW instructor 126
  numbers 139–40
  racing 124–7
  safety requirements 138–9
  year-end review book 2004 125–6
Porsche people 63–9, 87–8, 123,
  184–203
  and London Raindance 154–5
  heritage event Laguna Seca 133
  karma 194–8
  online forums 128–9
  passion 131–2, 137, 148–50, 153–6,
    165, 167, 170, 184–209
  Porsche as language 167
  runs 174
  videos 168–9
Power Tools club 43
Pretty Ugly Club 79
Prince, and Willow warehouse 115
Prodigy (band) 131–2, 149–50, 155–6
property (real estate) buying 69, 91,
  107–9, 214, 224, 240
publicity 145

rappers, wear Venetian Paradise
  clothing 70–1

rave culture 55–6
reality shows, Willow warehouse 105
Recycler, The 66
Redford, Robert 28
  911-930 '76 Turbo rumour 190–1
'Religion car' Porsche 911 SCHR '78,
  'budget build' 198–9
Rennsport Reunion 143
Retail Slut (clothes shop) 36–8
risk-taking 56, 81, 237–40
Risky Devil drift crew 180
Rizzo, Chuck
  '64 911 185–8, 243
  and MW's Irish Green '66 188
Road & Track 152, 171
Road to Rennsport Porsche event 179
Rockford, Jim, Firebird 120
Rolling Stone magazine 47
  Serious Clothing on cover 80, 85
roots, remembering 223–30, 240
Rose, Axl 34, 43
Rotterdam, outlaw run 171, 188
Roxie, Ryan, wears Serious Clothing 88
Roy, Alex 182
Royal Oak, Detroit 32
  Incognito (store) 58–9
RS Porsche magazine 133
  Porsche Fest 171
RUF, after-market tuner 67
'Runner's Almanac' 15
running, cross-country 14–16, 19, 242,
  246

S Registry 151
Saab 119
  Turbo SPG 65, 68, 75
San Francisco, first visit 38
Santa Monica
  Boulevard, clubs 79
  DMV, MW passes driving test 64
  Mountains, road to xi–xiv
Saxon (band) 19, 21
Scarborough 9
Scargill, Arthur 25
schools and entrepreneurs 243–5
Schuco 1:43 scale models, MW's cars
  179
Schwarzenegger, Arnold 68
Scream (club) 43
Scuderia Filipinetti 10
Seinfeld, Jerry, and STR 176
SEMA 2014 191
Sergio (car mechanic) 128, 189
Serious Clothing 71–3, 167, 172, 173–4
  and non-fashion-related material
    238–9
  at Willow warehouse 96–7, 99

Serious Clothing (*cont.*)
  custom clothes 88–90
  expansion 81–3
  individual style forming 78
  Karen improves women's line 78
  Melrose store 81–3, 214
  moves to Gladys warehouse 71–2
  popularity 80
  publicity 80, 145
  staff 71
  starts to wind down 107, 109–10
    closed 110–11
  sewing contractor, first 57, 58
Sheene, Barry 12
Sheffield 'Steel City', life in
  and Los Angeles 223–30, 240–2
  character-building 228, 240–1
  childhood xiv, 1–16
  entrepreneurial spirit 228, 240–1
  Karen in 217
  mining industry collapse 25
    unemployment 24–5
  night life 19–20
  opportunities missing 224
  returning from Hollywood 39–41
  Sheaf market 6
  teens 17–26
  Wigfull Road, Walker home 8
Sheffield Schoolboys Championship 15
Sheffield Wednesday 15
Sherman, Ben, mod clothes 36
Silverdale School 21–2
skateboard incident 18
Skegness 9
Skynyrd (MW's dog) 104, 214
  passed away 242
  tattoos 220
Smith Journal 235
smog cut-off 1976 139
So-Cal bike scene 133
Social Distortion, wears Serious
  Clothing 80
Soho House, Hollywood 153
Sparco and Recaro 142
Speed cameras, UK 226–7
Speed Hunters 165
Spice Girls 212
Sports Car Trader 65–6, 122
St Martins Lane Hotel 156, 217
Stabbing Westward, wears Serious
  Clothing 80
Stanley and White steam cars 163–4
Stannington College 25
Staples Center 155
Starck, Philippe, sink 98
Stars & Stripes-inspired jeans 57–8
steam cars 10, 161, 163–4

Stefani, Gwen 80
Stewart, Jackie 178, 179
Stone Temple Pilots, wears Serious
  Clothing 80
'Street-able track cars' 131–35
Stringfellow, Peter, Sheffield club 19
style/personality, individual,
  maintaining 239–40
sunglasses, not endorsed 180–1
Supplemental (production company)
  148
Switzerland
  family holidays 9–10, 27
  Porsche run 174

TAG Heuer 158, 180
tattoos 220, 240
Techno Classica Essen 168
Ted Talks 231–5
Tennessee 33
Thatcher, Margaret, and mines 25
Thornburg, Barbara, *L.A. Lofts*, on
  Willow warehouse 99
Thunderhill 125, 127
Todt, Jean 197–8
Todt, Nicolas, buys Porsche 911 no.
  1036 197–8
Tommy (Karen's brother) 213
Top Gear, and *Urban Outlaw* trailer
  151–2
Top of the Pops 19
Top Trumps 2
Total 911 (magazine) 133–5
  at London Raindance 156
  MW guest edits 171
Toyota Corolla 2TC 1977 64–5, 119
trade shows 70, 73
Trailways bus to Detroit 29–30
Trappers Alley, Detroit 32
Trip clothing 80
Turbo Fever video 191
TV show 181–2
Twiggy 80
277 *see* Porsche 911T '71 '277'

UCLA, MW's Ted Talk 232–5
UK visits 86–7, 155–7, 215–18
  driving in 226–7
Uncle Sam Stars & Stripes hat 58
underground, Venice Beach 55–6
United Artists 75–6
United States
  F1 Grand Prix 2014 197
  first visits 26, 27, 28–33, 40, 41–2,
    237
  representing freedom/opportunity
    223–30

Universal Studios, MTV awards party
42
Urban Outlaw documentary 145–82
and Porsche 911 50th anniversary
169–80
filming 148–50
trailer 151–3
release 157, 158–60
rough cut screening 153
finished 153–5
impact 159–82, 201, 206, 231, 232
Karen's part in 218, 219
London Raindance screening 155–6
magazine coverage 164–5
on Momo Prototipo wheel 178
Urban Outlaw fifteen52 wheel 177–8
Urban Outlaw nickname, *Total 911*
article 134–5, 147
Urban Outlaw retail store 158
USA Today interview 62

van den Tillard, Maurice, article
133–4, 171
Van Halen, Eddie, promo video 113–14
Venetian Paradise, first company
59–62, 236
challenges to 69–70
hats, knock-offs 69–70
media coverage 62
original clothing 70–1
publicity 145
becomes Serious Clothing 71
Venice Beach 47, 48–62
boardwalk 48–62, 236
market trader spirit 48–62
Vitaloni Sebring mirrors 199
Vogue, Serious Clothing on cover 80,
85
Volkswagen Type 3 Karmann Ghia
Notchback 218
Volvo 172

Walker family 5–12
and Karen 217
Oliver, cousin 10, 33–6, 38
holidays 9–11
in London 155–7
Uncle David 11, 122, 216
Uncle Mick 11
visits to LA 84
sightseeing tour 75–6
Walker, Grandpa
antiques 6, 8, 9
Moskvitch sales rep 6
RAF mechanic 5
Walker, Karen (MW's wife) 6
and MW

first meetings 72–6, 211–12
moves to LA 74
at Costa Mesa 74–6
as couple 76, 77–9, 91–3
being with 211–21
'lil' Georgia Peach' 211
marries MW, Las Vegas 214–15
in England 87, 155–7, 215–19
and MW's family 217
passed away 211, 242
celebration of life service 220
and business 214
and property 109
Fourth Street Bridge land 107–8,
241
Hooch clothing company 73, 77,
218–19
Serious Clothing 80–4, 109–11,
145, 172–3, 212, 214, 217
improves women's line 78
and *Urban Outlaw* 147–9, 151,
155–7, 218, 219
TV show, proposed 181
Willow warehouse 91–3, 95, 97,
103–4, 214–17, 218, 236,
237–9
and cars 119, 121–2
60s Cadillac 75
Volkswagen Type 3 Karmann Ghia
Notchback 218
Jaguar E-Type '67 218
and MW's Porsche collection
127–8, 160–1, 163–4, 187,
218
and Willow Springs track 124, 126
mother & family 213, 217
motivation 217–19
and MW's Ted Talk 233–5
going with gut feeling 81, 92, 93,
111
judge of character 218
pursuit of freedom 219
style 211–14
and cats 214
changes hair 79
front teeth story 212
Marilyn Monroe style 73, 74
stories 212
Walker, Linda (MW's mum) 5
as breadwinner 23
Broomhill Infants School job, 23
tenaciousness 241
postcards to 39, 49–50, 53, 57,
61–2
Walker, Linda (MW's first wife) 69–72
at Venice Beach 48–62
divorce/ buyout from 72

Walker, Magnus Lucian Titus 13
 early life
  childhood xiv, 1–16
   and cars 10–12
   and Porsche 3–4
   Magnus as name, and bullying
    13–14
   not mechanical 3–4
  teens 17–26
   clothes customizing 20–1
   girlfriends, first 22, 24
   unemployed post-school 22
   construction labouring job 23–4
   non-political 25
  cross-country running 14–16, 19,
    242, 246
  school 13–15
   lifeguard certification 26
   returns to education 25–6
   secondary school failure 21–2
   Sports C&G study 25–6, 237
  Sheffield life see Sheffield
 America, visits
  Camp America as 'camp counsellor'
    26, 27, 28–33, 40, 41–2
   as 'adaptive swimmer' 31–2, 38
   West Coast, first visits 33–9
   goes home to Sheffield 39–41
  alligator pants, tailors & goes
    shopping 35–8
   Retail Slut buys 37–8
  glam-punk look 24, 30, 33–4, 35,
    49
  hair 22–4, 79
 America, living
  green card application, references
    85–6
  emergency green card 87
  cars
   first car 64–5
   first Porsche 65–9
   driving tests 63–4
    avoiding videos 145
  motivation 60–1, 168, 235–40
   Ted Talk 231–5
  Porsche collecting/working on see
    Porsche headings
  property (real estate) buying 69,
    91, 107–9, 214, 224, 240, 241
  Serious Clothing see Serious
    Clothing
  Urban Outlaw see Urban Outlaw
  Venice Beach 47, 48–62
  Venetian Paradise see Venetian
    Paradise

  Willow warehouse see Willow
    warehouse
  with Karen see Walker, Karen
Walker, Miguel (Mig, MW's dad) 5
 and cars/motorsport 11, 12–13, 241
  company car 63
  Earls Court Motor Show 2–4, 66
  Motor Link 8–9
 and precision clocks and watches 8
 in sales 8–9
 mechanical engineering 5–6, 241
  on turbo function 3
 personality 17–18, 22
 unemployed 22–3
 passed away 157
Walker, St. John (MW's brother) 13
Ward, Bill 114–15
Whisky A Go Go, club 79
White Zombie, wears Serious Clothing
  80
Whole Ten Yards, The, filming at
  Willow warehouse 104, 112–13
wholesaling 56–62
Williamson, John 'Otto', Porsche
  dealership 68, 124
Willis, Bruce 104, 112–13, 148
Willow Springs track 124, 125, 138
Willow warehouse ix–xi, 91–107, 215,
  218
 business issues 105–6
 Serious Clothing at 96–7, 99
 filming at 113–17
  first music video 101–3
  location filming 100–7, 112–13,
    130, 236, 237
  reality shows 105
  Urban Outlaw 148–50
 living space, eclectic decor 97–9
 Los Angeles Times spread 99–100
 nearby loft as home 105
 Porsche Cars Canada debut Panamera
   167
 publicity 145
 renovation 94–100, 243
 website 104
World of Sport (TV) 12–13
Wythenshawe College 8

Youngs, John, on Venetian Paradise hats
  62

Zeros (band) 43
Zombie, Rob 174
Zuffenhausen factory, Porsche videos
  168